NOT YOUR FATHER'S UNION MOVEMENT

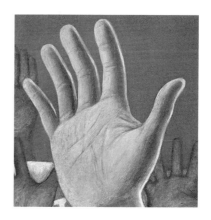

NOT YOUR FATHER'S UNION MOVEMENT

Inside the AFL-CIO

EDITED BY *jo-ann mort*

First published by Verso 1998
© the contributors 1998
All rights reserved
Paper edition reprinted 1999

VERSO
UK: 6 Meard Street, London W1V 3HR
USA: 180 Varick Street, New York, NY 10014-4606

Verso is the imprint of New Left Books

Design by POLLEN

ISBN 1-85984-286-0 (paper)
ISBN 1-85984-889-3 (cloth)

British Library Cataloguing in Publication Data
A catalog record for this book is available from the British Library

Library of Congress Cataloging-in-Publication Data
A catalog record for this book is available from the Library of Congress

CONTENTS

ACKNOWLEDGMENTS

Many thanks to those who assisted in preparing this book, including the staff of the UNITE communications department, especially Carrie Kim, Opal Mita, and Cara Metz; Denise Mitchell and her entire AFL-CIO public affairs staff—especially Angie Morris & Lane Windham—for fact checking, photo gathering, and for assistance in making sure that the articles got written; to staff in the political, international affairs, organizing, women's, and public policy departments at the AFL-CIO; to all the communications staff at various unions who assisted in information and photo gathering, to my editor, Colin Robinson, for having the idea; to Harold Meyerson and Guy Molyneux for brainstorming sessions and decades of friendship and activism; and in memory of two who would love to be here to see how it all turns out: Irving Howe and Michael Harrington.

In October 1995, an historic election took place and a new leadership took charge at American Federation of Labor-Congress of Industrial Organizations (AFL-CIO) head-quarters on Washington, DC's 16th Street. Led by John Sweeney, a coalition of unions forced the first democratic election of top officers in the history of the AFL-CIO. The new team, including Sweeney as President, Rich Trumka as Secretary-Treasurer, and Linda Chavez-Thompson as Executive Vice President, came to power promising changes from within the AFL-CIO. With the new leadership came a virtually complete reorganization of the federation—to meet the needs of working families in a changing economy and to rebuild the most critical link in fighting for a more progressive and egalitarian America.

This collection begins to tell the story of why and how the change took place, and what's happened since that important election. These articles are written, for the most part, by the practitioners—who are implementing change in today's labor movement. Journalists who observed the changes contributed several chapters, too.

This book is not another collection of speculative arguments or proposals for a progressive agenda. It's a practical guide. The new AFL-CIO is giving working people a fighting chance, putting to the test—every single day— practical ways to curb corporate power and to strengthen the hand of working people.

This volume should also serve as a good introduction to a new generation of activists: workers, union members, and future organizers.

Even with all the positive press the new AFL-CIO has received in the last few years, there have been some rough spots. It's not easy to challenge corporate power; nor is it simple to rebuild, in an American context, a labor movement that has been on the decline for several decades. It won't be easy for the labor movement to regain its rightful place in American society, but, as you'll read in these chapters, the commitment of the activists in the movement is stronger than ever.

In compiling this collection, it became clear immediately that one volume would not suffice to include everything—every new program and plan— that the AFL-CIO and affiliated unions are pursuing. An attempt was made to document as many unions as possible, but lack of space negated inclusion of many more topics.

Here, we emphasize the AFL-CIO's focus on the fight to raise working and living standards, the organization of the new workforce, and political action. Special attention is paid to the workforce of immigrants, women, and low-wage workers, all of whom Sweeney has made it his mandate to organize. As journalist Harold Meyerson writes in his overview piece, the renaissance of American unions can reverse the trend toward declining living standards and put a different face—a human face—on the global economy.

Union Density by State

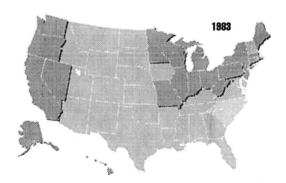

1983

▓ 0% to 8%   ■ 10 to 20%   ■ 21% and Over

1996

Source: The Union Membership Databook; Compilation for Current Population Survey, Census.

Richard Bensinger, who led the AFL-CIO Organizing Department from 1995 to 1998, describes the kind of organizing in which the unions are involved, and the obstacles faced by workers trying to unionize in an anti-worker climate. He also sets the stage for later chapters in the book regarding unionizing the new, immigrant workforce.

In my own piece, I discuss the internal and external changes that the AFL-CIO instituted to improve the public face of labor.

With the new AFL-CIO came a new Women's Department. Veteran feminist Karen Nussbaum discusses the department and its program in her chapter. In a companion piece, the AFL-CIO's pollsters, Peter D. Hart Research Associates, present the results of a poll they conducted in early 1998. They were released at a women's organizing conference in March, 1998, regarding women, the economy, and unions.

Hector Figueroa, a researcher at Service Employees' International Union (SEIU), one of the largest of the AFL-CIO affiliated unions, discusses the newfound activism of low-wage immigrant workers, including Hispanic and Asian workers.

Steve Rosenthal, the director of the Political Department, gives an overview of some of the political successes the unions have enjoyed thus far, and shares some plans for the future. Guy Molyneux and Geoff Garin, pollsters with Hart Associates, offer their "Ten Rules for Union Political Action," which have become indispensable to the unions' political activity. Kelly Candaele tells the story from a personal perspective—how he and Gil Cedillo, two trade unionists, ran for political office and won in Los Angeles.

Marc Baldwin, of the revamped AFL-CIO Policy Department, gives the intellectual underpinnings of many of the projects put forward by the AFL-CIO since 1995.

Barbara Shailor, head of the new International Department, presents an overview of the new international perspective at the AFL-CIO. She and Clayola Brown, a vice president of Union of Needletrades, Industrial & Textile Employees (UNITE), take us on a trip to Indonesia to inspect the conditions in garment factories, and illustrates how the AFL-CIO is tackling the global economy.

The AFL-CIO has made great strides toward revitalizing local labor councils. In her chapter, Amy Dean, head of the San Jose labor council and of the Union Cities AFL-CIO task force, describes that process.

David Kusnet, former Clinton speechwriter and author, chronicles the successful "America Needs a Raise" campaign, begun after Sweeney was elected and continuing to this day. This signature campaign of the Sweeney regime aims to raise the living standards of all American workers.

Matt Witt and Rand Wilson discuss the successful United Parcel Service strike run by the Teamsters in the summer of 1997. At the time of this writing, the leadership of the

Teamsters' Union was in flux, but that strike still serves as a model for a union campaign.

In "Fast Track Derailed," journalist and labor observer David Glenn tells the story behind the defeat of fast-track trade legislation—a story which was never told by the media.

Veteran labor journalist David Moberg writes about the new efforts labor is employing to challenge capital.

Noel Beasley, a midwest-based vice president of UNITE, describes what it's like on the front lines for him and other union leaders—Dave Foster of the Steelworkers, Bob King of the UAW, and Monica Russo of UNITE—in today's climate.

Finally, New York journalist Juan Gonzalez interviews John Sweeney, who offers his thoughts about how far labor has come and how far it must go.

Personally, I have spent more than a decade in the trade union movement, having the privilege of spending my days serving the workers of my union, UNITE. It has always been fulfilling and challenging work, but there is no more exciting time to be a trade unionist than today, and probably no more exciting place in which to be fighting than in the American union movement. No matter how small the U.S. labor movement is compared to other industrialized nations, the very fact that we are the labor movement of the world's last superpower makes us the vital link in the global fight over economic control. Sometimes, our underdog status makes us scrappier and bolder. Certainly, there is no more dedicated group of people than the workers active in their unions and those of us who join in the fight to make the U.S. and today's global arena more just.

Indeed, no movement in America is so multidimensional in its inclusion of every race, ethnic group, gender, generation, and lifestyle. Finally, the movement of American workers is the only movement that can re-ignite a progressive vision for the country, because it promotes a pragmatic program. If these chapters provide a roadmap to a different future for America as we approach the next century, a century that could be "conscious and truly democratic," in the words of the late socialist leader Michael Harrington, they will have done their job. For the most simple description of the word "union" is people joining together to seize control of their own lives, and the simplest outcome is a sharing of the world's riches and the lessening of economic, intellectual, and spiritual poverty for all.

NOT YOUR FATHER'S UNION MOVEMENT

A SECOND CHANCE

The New AFL-CIO and the Prospective Revival of American Labor

harold meyerson

SHADES OF 1958

Probably the clearest tribute to John Sweeney's achievements in rebuilding the power of American labor may be that, just two years after he took the helm of the AFL-CIO, he has already returned unions to their historic place atop the Republicans' hit list. By early 1998, the GOP's assault on labor had become a central theme of its campaign year. In four states, conservative operatives had placed initiatives on the ballot that sought to restrict unions' abilities to devote their resources to politics. In thirty other states, such measures were being introduced into legislatures. No such sustained and coordinated attack on union power had been seen since 1958, when Republicans sought to enact right-to-work legislation in half a dozen northern and western states.

And 1998 may have been the first year since 1958 in which American labor won truly major victories at the ballot box. Four decades ago, when union membership still comprised over thirty percent of the American work force, labor repulsed the right-to-work campaigns in five of the six states where they were waged. But if labor was too strong to defeat in 1958, it soon became too weak to plausibly campaign against. In 1994, the Republicans retook Congress without really bothering to go after unions in their advertising or campaign materials. Who, in the early 1990s, could plausibly campaign against the specter of union power? What power would that be? Had anyone under forty ever seen it in action?

Now, a scant four years later, union power is suddenly back, and the Right's attack on union political action campaigns has emerged as a centerpiece of its electoral strategies. In 1998, as in 1958, it was in California that labor turned back the brunt of the right's attack—defeating in the June primary an initiative designed to cripple its political action programs, just as it defeated the right-to-work initiative forty years earlier. The Republicans' assault is the direct consequence of the successes the new AFL-CIO has had in the political arena: stopping the president's fast-track trade proposal in the fall of 1997, pushing a minimum-wage hike through the Republican congress in the summer of 1996, and waging such a massive and aggressive campaign in the Congressional elections of 1996 that the Republicans returned to the Hill thoroughly chastened in their desire to enact any further right-wing reforms.

The revitalization of labor's political program was just one part of the broader renaissance of American unions that John Sweeney, Richard Trumka, and Linda Chavez-Thompson promised when their insurgent campaign for AFL-CIO leadership prevailed at the Federation's biennial convention in New York in October of 1995. The primary commitment of their "New Voice" campaign was to organize—to turn around a forty-year decline in membership that had seen the unionized percentage of the workforce slip from 35 percent in 1955, the year that the American Federation of Labor and the Congress of Industrial Organizations had merged, to a sickening 15 percent, and just 10 percent in the private sector, by the mid–1990s. Sweeney pledged to devote one-third of the Federation's budget to expand the Organizing Institute's training programs, and to convert the Federation's far-flung staff, whether in the venerable International Affairs Department or in the new Corporate Affairs Department, into a force that abetted unions' efforts to grow.

But politics was the only part of the Sweeney program where labor could realize a quick return on its investment. Reinventing the lost culture of organizing would be the work of many years. To be sure, one-third of the Federation's budget did get redirected into organizing; the AFL-CIO initiated several joint organizing campaigns, and a number of major internationals greatly increased their organizing budgets. The Federation's staff did go through a vast and innovative restructuring. The revitalized movement was the subject of more media coverage than the Federation had seen in decades, and on college campuses, going to work for a union became a more compelling career choice than it had been since the 1940s. More workers (385,000) were organized in 1997 than had been organized in years.

With the unionized sectors of the workforce in continuing decline, however, all this activity was still not enough to arrest the movement's numerical descent to 14.1 percent of the work force in 1997 (according to Department of Labor statistics). More ambitious organizing drives were on the drawing boards, but they would take time and a vast commitment of resources.

"Does a movement ever get a second chance?" critic Irving Howe once asked of socialism after Stalin—a question that can surely be applied to the union movement in the time of John Sweeney. For forty years, labor had watched—at first, with arrogant indifference, later, with stunned helplessness—as economic and political changes eroded its ability to secure middle-class living standards for American workers. For the first twenty years after the AFL-CIO's 1955 merger, its attitude toward its strength had best been expressed by Federation president George Meany's airy assertion, when asked if he was worried about the growing number of unorganized workers, that "the organized fellow is the fellow who counts." Over the subsequent twenty years, labor—at least, everyone but Meany's successor as Federation president, Lane Kirkland—slowly came to realize that it was growing relentlessly smaller as a percentage of the workforce, and was unable to provide the kind of income and benefits to its members that it had offered in its heyday. Labor lamented its weakness in the face of a dysfunctional labor law and implacably hostile employers.

The question of whether labor can come back bears on more than the future of American unions. The waning of American labor is a prime factor in the rising levels of income polarization in the United States over the past quarter-century; in the relative stagnation of wages in the midst of soaring profits; in the attack on both government- and employer-provided health and retirement benefits and the rise of for-profit health-maintenance organizations; and in the growth of temporary, part-time and contingent jobs. The renaissance of American unions could alter these trends. It could also create an important new force for regulating the global economy to ensure a more equitable distribution of wealth—much as the union movement of the 1930s and 1940s played a key role in regulating the national economy to the same end. These are all causes that the

AFL-CIO under Sweeney's leadership has taken up—already, in some instances, to considerable effect. But they are causes in which Sweeney and Co. know they cannot ultimately prevail unless and until union membership takes a quantum leap upwards.

If the Sweeney regime has delivered in many particulars, it has yet to increase labor's numbers. As a result, Republicans have sharpened their attacks, before the pendulum swings too far.

THE MAKING OF THE PRESIDENT, 1995

It was, appropriately enough, the dismal performance of the Federation's political program in the 1994 elections that led to the insurgency against the *ancién regime* at the AFL-CIO— the first such insurgency in the 109-year history of the organization and its predecessors.

For, even as the rate of unionization had toppled and wages had stagnated while profits soared, there remained as labor's last line of defense the Democratic-controlled House of Representatives. So long as the Democrats held the House, pro-union committee chairmen would bottle up whatever union-busting brainstorms and bludgeoning of the welfare state bubbled forth from Newt Gingrich and other Hill Republicans. In November of 1994, though, forty years of Democratic rule in the House came to an abrupt end. In a little under a year, forty years of old-guard rule in labor's house met a similar fate.

The presidents of two of the Federation's four million-member unions, Gerald McEntee of the American Federation of State, County & Municipal Employees (AFSCME) and John J. Sweeney of the Service Employees International Union (SEIU), began the revolt. Historically, AFSCME and SEIU were among the relative handful of Federation unions with large-scale and highly effective political action programs of their own: as public sector unions (AFSCME almost entirely so, SEIU about half), they had a more direct stake than other Federation members in the outcomes of elections. And historically, like other politically active internationals, they had grown accustomed to bypassing the Federation's own political programs when necessary. The problem wasn't simply that the Federation's programs were too modest and too top-down to make a difference. For decades, the Federation had also tended to steer clear of campaign alliances with community, civil rights and feminist groups, while unions like AFSCME and SEIU characteristically viewed such constituencies as natural allies on matters of ideology and indispensable partners in assembling effective coalitions.

It wasn't just a critique of past Federation programs that set McEntee and Sweeney into action, however; it was also a presentiment that the current leadership would be unable to impede the Gingrich juggernaut. Shortly after the election, AFSCME and SEIU set up a multi-union coalition with a range of non-labor progressive organizations to plot strategies and to coordinate resources over the next two years. It was a direct challenge to the AFL-CIO hierarchy at 16th Street. "We don't trust you to mount the right kind of program," Sweeney and McEntee seemed to be telling Lane Kirkland and his operatives.

By the first few weeks of 1995, the challenge had proceeded further. McEntee in particular had begun talking to his fellow international presidents about replacing Kirkland as AFL-CIO president, and shortly thereafter he went public with his challenge.

To say that McEntee and Sweeney had strayed onto terra incognita would be to understate. No one had ever campaigned against a sitting president of the AFL-CIO. By all statistical measures, in fact, it seemed the single safest job in America. Since the American Federation of Labor had been founded by Samuel Gompers in 1886, the AFL and then the merged AFL-CIO had had just five presidents in its 109–year history— four, if you don't count the guy who held the office for one year during the middle of

Gomper's thirty-seven-year tenure. During this time, there were twenty presidents of the United States and nine popes. The House of Labor was not to be rushed to judgment.

AFL-CIO presidents are elected by the presidents of all member AFL-CIO unions, each casting a ballot weighted to the size of his or her international (the president of the Teamsters casts 1.4 million votes, and so on down the line). Thus the Federation president was also protected by a most exquisite expression of working-class solidarity: an injury to one union president is an injury to all union presidents. Deposing Lane Kirkland meant he would have to be bumped by his peers, at the Federation's upcoming convention slated for October in New York.

Not that his peers didn't have a litany of discontents, which reached well back into the tenure of Kirkland's predecessor, George Meany. Kirkland's critics invariably voiced some or all of the following grievances:

Over the past four decades, the Federation had gone from viewing organizing as unnecessary to viewing organizing as impossible. The Federation was gripped by a Brezhnevian torpor, and that attitude permeated the entire movement. The one comprehensive research project that sought to deduce just what percentage of union resources were devoted to organizing measured all union activity in California in the mid-1980s, and concluded it was roughly 2 percent. Despite the unions' decline, Kirkland bewilderingly insisted that the union movement was still the powerhouse of yore, and that the cries of alarm rising from unionists and their friends amounted to unjustified hand-wringing that only served to give aid and comfort to labor's enemies (or "labor's afflicters," as Kirkland put it).

While not directly responsible for labor's neglect of organizing, the Federation had a clear responsibility for marshaling labor's political forces, and here, it had failed dismally as well. Mobilizing any sizable number of union members to pressure Congress or to swing elections was plainly beyond its capacities. Politics had come to consist of donating money to Democratic pols, who often waged campaigns devoid of issues of concern to unions. Even when it came to lobbying Capitol Hill, lobbyists for internationals complained that the Federation had failed to build a consensus for a clear legislative program in the 1993–1994 session, which proved a factor in the chaos that dissolved the session.

Once communism and the Soviet bloc collapsed in the early 1990s, a number of Federation foreign policy operatives had trouble defining their mission, while Kirkland himself, a cold war intellectual above all else, seemed to lose focus. One widely voiced complaint was that he was out of the country for the five weeks leading up to a vote on a striker replacement bill that was devastating for labor.

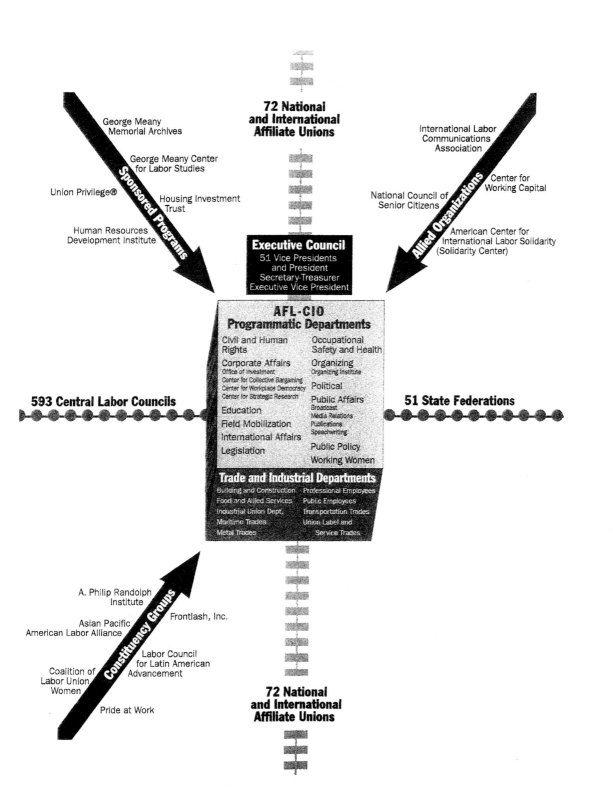

72 National and International Affiliate Unions

George Meany Memorial Archives

George Meany Center for Labor Studies

Union Privilege®

Housing Investment Trust

Human Resources Development Institute

Sponsored Programs

International Labor Communications Association

Center for Working Capital

National Council of Senior Citizens

American Center for International Labor Solidarity (Solidarity Center)

Allied Organizations

Executive Council
51 Vice Presidents and President
Secretary-Treasurer
Executive Vice President

AFL-CIO Programmatic Departments

Civil and Human Rights

Corporate Affairs
Office of Investment
Center for Collective Bargaining
Center for Workplace Democracy
Center for Strategic Research

Education

Field Mobilization

International Affairs

Legislation

Occupational Safety and Health

Organizing
Organizing Institute

Political

Public Affairs
Broadcast
Media Relations
Publications
Speechwriting

Public Policy

Working Women

Trade and Industrial Departments

Building and Construction
Food and Allied Services
Industrial Union Dept.
Maritime Trades
Metal Trades

Professional Employees
Public Employees
Transportation Trades
Union Label and
Service Trades

593 Central Labor Councils

51 State Federations

A. Philip Randolph Institute

Asian Pacific American Labor Alliance

Frontlash, Inc.

Labor Council for Latin American Advancement

Coalition of Labor Union Women

Pride at Work

Constituency Groups

72 National and International Affiliate Unions

Above all, the Federation under Kirkland was accused of having no public presence, no private planning capacity, and no energy whatever. Labor leaders were distressed that Kirkland had let Ross Perot, the eccentric nationalist billionaire, become the leading voice against the North American Free Trade Agreement (NAFTA). "They're convinced we can't organize and they've devoted no resources to figuring out what we can do," one senior official for a leading international said in the week that the revolt broke out into the open. "The Right has a number of well-funded think tanks. We have the Economic Policy Institute, and that's all." Nor did labor fare any better with mass opinion than it did in shaping elite opinion. One 1994 poll conducted by the Peter Hart firm for the AFL-CIO showed that while the public said it would favor workers over management in disputes by a 52 to 17 percent margin, it would favor unions over management by a mere 38 to 30 percent margin. The word that most commonly arose in discussing unions in the focus groups was "dinosaur."

Finally, there was the enigmatic figure of Kirkland himself. A onetime foreign policy expert who had been a speechwriter for Adlai Stevenson during the 1952 campaign, he had succeeded the eighty-five-year-old George Meany as Federation president just six weeks before Meany's death in 1979 (after serving as the Federation's secretary-treasurer). In an increasingly media-driven age, Kirkland had a profound aversion to talk shows or interviews, as well as an unconcealed contempt for the press. His speeches and press conferences were marked by a stilted, almost nineteenth-century style reminiscent of the Southern courthouse rhetoric of his childhood. (Kirkland grew up in South Carolina.) In the midst of the AFL-CIO's 1995 executive council meeting, when the revolt against him broke wide open, he conducted two press conferences, remarkable for the level of antagonism he displayed to questioners—"I'll try to conform my answers to your short attention spans," he said—and his quaint answers. Asked about the Republican's Contract with America, he responded by extolling the Depression-era achievements of the Civilian Conservation Corps and recalling how the Rural Electrification Agency eliminated the kerosene lamp.

Discontent with the permanent government at 16th Street had long been a feature of intra-labor politics, but for years it had been confined to a distinct wing of the labor movement. In the late 1970s, opposition on the AFL-CIO executive council (comprised chiefly of the presidents of the larger AFL-CIO internationals) to Meany's and then Kirkland's policies was largely confined to three presidents: Doug Fraser of the United Auto Workers (UAW), Jerry Wurf (AFSCME), and William Winpisinger of the International Association of Machinists and Aerospace Workers (IAM). Each set up his own liberal alliances to circumvent more conservative Federation policies (Fraser established the Progressive Alliance, Wurf the Coalition of American Public Employees, Winpisinger the Citizen-Labor Energy Coalition). Each reached out to social movements that had arisen in the 1960s, an effort both to rebuild American liberalism after the rifts of the Vietnam War and to bring new blood to the unions themselves. Each lined up in intra-Democratic Party battles with their new coalition partners against more traditional cold war, Southern, and anti-reformer coalitions anchored by the AFL-CIO. All were influenced by Michael Harrington, the democratic socialist leader who sought to be a bridge between the insurgents of the 1960s and the institutions of the 1930s, and who was in turn viewed as an apostate by the more right-wing social democrats who staffed key Federation positions under both Meany and Kirkland.

During the 1970s and 1980s, other internationals that were not part of this well-defined AFL-CIO opposition caucus nonetheless began to deviate from Federation practice, if not yet from theory. The Amalgamated Clothing & Textile Workers, the Communications Workers, and the SEIU were among the few unions that persisted in organizing campaigns, and thus in hiring younger activists sympathetic to newer social movements. In the early 1990s, under the leadership of the dynamic young Richard Trumka, the United Mineworkers waged one of the very few successful strikes of the Reagan-Bush years at the Pittston, Virginia mines, from which Trumka emerged as a tribune for those union activists critical of the Federation's lethargy and timidity.

At some of these unions, a culture devoted to more militant organizing and more aggressive political action had emerged by the 1990s. Occasionally, officials of these internationals were able to persuade the Federation to embrace one of their programs, most notably the Organizing Institute, an in-house academy that trained students and rank-and-filers in the ABCs of organizing. But no clear opposition bloc developed until after the electoral debacle of 1994.

By the time the AFL-CIO executive council repaired to its winter meeting in Bal Harbour, Florida, in February, 1995, there were already three key groups of insurgent unions. The first consisted of the manufacturing unions, many of which had the most long-standing arguments with the Federation old guard: these included the UAW, the IAM, the Steelworkers, and the Mine Workers. The second comprised the two million-member public sector unions, AFSCME, and SEIU. The third was the new-model Teamsters. There, in 1991, a federally-mandated, and supervised election had elevated veteran dissident leader Ron Carey to the Teamster presidency. Carey had moved aggressively against the corrupt old guard within his union, and surrounded himself with a number of left-leaning reform activists. All three of these groups were thor-

oughly discontented with Kirkland's entire regime, and together they constituted over forty percent of the Federation's membership.

Yet this insurgency was not ideologically based. The revolt would not have broken out even among the most diehard anti-Kirkland unions had the Democrats maintained their hold on Congress. Nor would the revolt have succeeded without the backing of a number of historically centrist unions, from the building trades and elsewhere, whose leaders simply saw no future for American labor without a complete shift in direction at the top. The original sin of Kirklandism, finally, wasn't ideology; it was narcolepsy. While unions had declined, the Federation slept. McEntee and Sweeney had sounded a wake-up call.

No one on the executive council could remember the procedure for reviewing the performance of the Federation's president because there was no procedure. So when the council met at Bal Harbour in February of 1995, the members finally decided to close the doors and proceed around the table, letting every member have his say. By several accounts, it took five increasingly bitter hours to get around the table. When it was done, not just the three anti-Kirkland clusters were on record wishing Kirkland to go, but also some key building trades internationals: the Carpenters, Operating Engineers, Laborers, Painters, and Sheet Metal Workers. The president of the last of the Federation's four million-member internationals to be heard from, the United Food & Commercial Workers, expressed major misgivings about Kirkland's tenure. Unions whose strength amounted to nearly half the Federation members were clearly in the "Lane-Must-Go" camp, while Kirkland's defenders accounted for little more than a quarter of Federation membership. The rest of the unions perched uneasily on the fence. The insurgents were leaving Bal Harbour with a near-majority of support. And without a candidate.

There was, to be sure, a candidate who had broad support within the coalition and among the fence-sitters—only he didn't want to run against Kirkland. The reluctant candidate was Tom Donahue, the then-sixty-seven-year-old Federation secretary-treasurer who was widely acknowledged as one of the most articulate and talented leaders in the movement. Donahue had gone to work for New York's building service local in the 1950s and become one of the Federation's brightest lights under Meany—so bright that Kirkland had elevated him to the position of secretary-treasurer when he became president in 1979.

Over the years, without really rocking the Federation boat, Donahue had worked diligently to undo the groundless complacency that Kirkland seemed determined to perpetuate in every Federation policy. Donahue convened and chaired committees that issued bleak reports about labor's future. After McEntee and Sweeney and other member presidents had begun the Organizing Institute, Donahue brought the institute under the Federation's wing fighting the hide-bound and threatened Federation functionaries who sought to have it killed. And, though it was not widely realized even within labor's topmost circles, relations between Kirkland and Donahue had been chilly for years.

But Donahue would not run against the man who sponsored his rise. And there, with its candidate flatly unavailable, the insurgency paused. But it did not founder.

For McEntee, Sweeney, and their associates had realized that victory was in their grasp, and that they could now do something that was unthinkable even two months earlier: run a public campaign for control of the AFL-CIO that raised all the questions about strategy and vision that union activists had been discussing privately for years. The insurgents began drawing up a platform and settling on a slate.

McEntee had been to that point the most visible leader of the revolt, but much of what made McEntee so implacable a foe of Kirkland—his indifference to peer group pressure, his abrasiveness, his arrogance—also made him unelectable among his fellow presidents. Mineworker President Richard Trumka was supported by some progressives as a canny strategist and dynamic speaker, but at forty-six he was widely thought to be too young and too militant to win the kind of support it would take to defeat Kirkland. Inevitably, then, the insurgents turned to Sweeney.

At first glance, John J. Sweeney seemed the most improbable of revolutionists. Portly, bald, placid in demeanor, with a voice off the sidewalks of New York, the then-sixty-one-year-old Sweeney looked like one of the Fifth-Avenue doormen he had represented at SEIU's building service local in New York. But Sweeney, in fact, had had a brilliant career as a union leader. In his fifteen year tenure at the helm of SEIU, it had grown from 625,000 to 1.1 million members—partly through mergers, but also through innovative organizing drives among public employees, health care workers, and big-city janitors. SEIU's Justice for Janitors campaign had succeeded in organizing workers whom conventional wisdom said were unorganizable—service sector workers, many of them immigrants, spread out over many worksites and different shifts, employed by contractors often based in other cities. Building coalitions with a range of community and religious organizations and re-introducing such militant tactics as sit-downs and bridge-blocking into the arsenal of organizing, the SEIU managed to organize tens of thousands of janitors around the country. At the same time, Sweeney presided over the difficult transformation of SEIU's leadership from the typical assemblage of middle-aged white men to a much more racially and sexually diverse corps of leaders.

What stood out above all else, though, was the near-doubling of SEIU's size during Sweeney's presidency. And the fact that, while most unions were spending virtually nothing on organizing and had no notion of how to grow, the SEIU under Sweeney was spending a third of its budget on getting new members and had a strategic plan for expansion.

By mid-spring, the insurgents had settled on a slate of Sweeney-for-President and Trumka-for-Secretary-Treasurer. In no small part to dramatize their commitment to racial and gender diversity (particularly since polling showed non-whites and women far more favorably disposed to unions than their white male counterparts), they rounded out the slate with Linda Chavez-Thompson as candidate for the new position of Executive Vice-President, which the upcoming convention would have to create. Chavez-Thompson, a Mexican-American born to cotton sharecropper parents in Lubbock, Texas, had been active in organizing public sector workers in right-to-work Texas, as an AFSCME vice president.

And yet, just as Donahue had a Kirkland problem, Sweeney had a Donahue problem. The two were old friends, both Bronx-born veterans of the same SEIU local, New York's 32B-32J. The announcement of the slate was delayed for a few weeks while Sweeney asked Donahue to make the run. Not until June did the insurgents announce their slate and proclaim their platform, at an outdoor Washington rally designed to convey the unmistakable impression that this would be a real campaign.

Like all campaigns, the "New Voice" insurgency came complete with a slogan— "America Needs a Raise"—and a program. The slogan itself defined the campaign as something novel in labor politics: it clearly suggested a strategic mission for the labor movement, tapped into pre-existing public concern about rising inequality and working-class poverty, indicated a target population for union organizing, and sought to recapture a moral clarity that the movement had been lacking for decades. The slogan was accompanied by a program that called for devoting a third of the Federation's resources to organizing, for establishing an organizing department within the AFL-CIO

that would help unions coordinate and target their efforts, for creating an independent political action program based on mobilizing members, and for a host of other reforms. Both the slogan and the program were designed to excite broad public interest and the intense interest of union activists, which they certainly did.

In the weeks immediately preceding the announcement of the slate, Kirkland realized that he could not prevail at October's convention. Belatedly, he informed Donahue of his decision, and Donahue tried at the last moment to forestall Sweeney's announcement—only to find that a solid coalition of unions had already settled on its candidates and its program. Kirkland announced his resignation shortly after the "New Voice" challenge was unveiled in June, and Donahue became interim president of the Federation, elevating CWA official Barbara Easterling to the position of secretary-treasurer. Donahue also became the candidate of the unions, such as the American Federation of Teachers, that had up until to that point stuck with Kirkland, as well as of other unions, like the UFCW, that had been critical of Kirkland but unwilling to align themselves with the "New Voice" forces.

In short, Donahue was in an extremely difficult position. Like Sweeney, he promised wholesale change and a quantum leap in organizing; unlike Sweeney, he presided over the ancient regime and needed its backing to hold onto his office. "He should be firing one hundred people here, and he knows who they are," said one disgruntled Federation official during the brief summer of Donahue's presidency. "But he won't—he's not a confrontational kind of guy." At most, Donahue promised a remixing of old guard and new, while the unions in the New Voice coalition were already envisioning a labor movement moving in directions the old guard wouldn't abide. Trapped between regimes, Donahue became the Kerensky of labor's quasi-revolution.

During summer and early autumn, both the Sweeney and Donahue campaigns hit the road, with the two principles debating in a number of major cities their strategies and visions for the labor movement and their bona fides for leading it. One point of contention, up until their final debate at the New York convention, was the use of disruptive tactics like sit-downs and bridge occupations during organizing drives. In Washington, Sweeney's SEIU had closed down one of the bridges spanning the Potomac during such a campaign; Donahue charged this measure epitomized a kind of reckless confrontationalism that would only estrange public opinion. Sweeney responded that he normally sought to build bridges but recognized that there were certain conditions which more than justified blocking them. This dispute was largely symbolic: Donahue, at the prodding of his old guard supporters, used the issue to imply that Sweeney would sweep the confrontationalists of the 1960s into power with him; Sweeney used the issue to excite the most committed reformers in his ranks while counting on his reputation as pragmatic unionist to allay the apprehensions of his more centrist supporters.

By the time of the AFL-CIO convention in late October, Donahue's only hope was to pry away Sweeney's supporters in the building trades and other more traditional unions. He had one success—Doug McCarron, the new president of the Carpenters, did switch his union to Donahue's column, a shift chiefly prompted by the Byzantine politics of the building trades. The other unions held to their commitments, and Sweeney and Trumka were elected by a 56 to 44 percent margin over Donahue and Easterling. Donahue's supporters then agreed to elect Chavez-Thompson by acclamation, and both sides agreed on a common slate for an expanded executive council, which grew from thirty-five to fifty-four members. The new council was nearly 30 percent female and minority, and included such leaders as Bill Lucy, AFSCME's secretary-treasurer and the longtime president of the Coalition of Black Trade Unionists, whom Kirkland had kept from executive council membership, and Arturo Rodriguez, president of the United Farm Workers, whose founder, the late Cesar Chavez, had also been kept off the council.

"YOU HAVE TO ROW": ORGANIZING IN THE SWEENEY ERA

Once in office, Sweeney, Trumka, and Chavez-Thompson maintained the same kind of travel schedules they had kept while campaigning. During their tenure, the Federation has held scores of regional conferences on organizing, political action, constituency groups activities, and the like, which the three constitutional officers frequently attend. All three also travelled to the sites of notable organizing drives and strikes.

Sweeney's travels are a marked departure from the more placid schedules of Meany and Kirkland (though Kirkland did travel extensively in Europe, his chief field of interest), and reflect a different conception of his office. Meany and Kirkland saw themselves primarily as bureaucratic leaders, behind-the-scenes operators for a movement that didn't require their public encouragement. Sweeney conducts his share of closed-door negotiations, too, but he also sees himself as a movement leader, whose presence symbolizes a commitment that can encourage and materially help organizers and workers embroiled in a conflict, students pondering a commitment to labor, and liberals trying to reconstruct a progressive coalition.

At the AFL-CIO's 1997 convention in Pittsburgh, Sweeney was preceded to the podium by a parade of one hundred activists from organizing drives around the country, a number of which Sweeney had visited. The display, which would have been unimaginable at any previous AFL-CIO convention, was a testament to how much labor had changed in the first two years of the Sweeney presidency—and how far it still had to ensure its survival. Clearly, there was more organizing going on than in decades. But many of the workers onstage came from drives that had yet to succeed, like the Farmworkers' campaign to organize strawberry workers in Watsonville. Most of the organizing was still confined to about a dozen unions—and even if all this organizing were successful, it would be barely sufficient to arrest the decline in the unionized share of the workforce.

The Federation had begun shifting resources to organizing almost immediately after Sweeney took office. The Organizing Institute (OI) was greatly expanded. An Organizing Department was established, under the leadership of former OI Director Richard Bensinger, who became a roving apostle of organizing to internationals and central labor councils. Unions were given assistance in how to shift resources and personnel from servicing their current members to organizing new ones. Under Bensinger's leadership, the Organizing Department also identified a small number of promising campaigns to which it would provide its own staffers and funds—among them, the Farmworkers drive in Watsonville and the joint campaign of fifteen building trades unions to organize construction workers in Las Vegas.

Other departments of the Federation were also enlisted in the campaign to rebuild organizing. The International Affairs Department coordinated pressure on foreign multi-nationals that were the targets of U.S.-based organizing drives; the Corporate Affairs Department began to plan long-term organizing campaigns for entire sectors of the American economy. The number of unions committed to large-scale joint organizing drives remained small, however, and Sweeney's more ambitious plan to help foster the consolidation of the Federation's seventy-two member unions into a more sectorally-log-ical and organizing-efficient fifteen unions was shot down by the unions themselves.

But it is at the level of the individual internationals that organizing is still either undertaken or sloughed off. A number of unions have increased their organizing bud-gets and staffs over the past two years, and some have won notable victories: the Teamsters at Continental Airlines, the CWA at US Air, the Laborers among New York asbestos workers, the Farmworkers in the San Joaquin Valley. The Hotel and Restaurant Employees have continued their success in organizing Las Vegas hotel workers, 45,000 of whom now work under contract in Vegas hotels. But precious few major corporations have gone union during Sweeney's tenure.

The union that is setting the pace in converting to an organizing structure is Sweeney's own Service Employees. Under the leadership of Andy Stern, formerly the union's organizing director who succeeded Sweeney as president in 1996, SEIU is currently putting 47 percent of its resources into organizing. By 1998, more than one hundred of SEIU's locals, including virtually all the major ones, will be spending at least 20 percent of their budgets on organizing, too. In the winter of 1998, the inter-national had over 200 organizers on staff, while another 200 organizers worked for various SEIU locals.

This transformation has been anything but easy. In order to hire so many organiz-ers, seven of SEIU's headquarter departments had to be closed down. At the local level, the shift of staff into organizing requires that the elected and volunteer member leaders, the shop stewards, handle the grievance processing and other member services that tra-ditionally have been performed by staff. Elected leaders of some locals have been called upon to help other locals draft contracts. The international devotes considerable resources to helping their member locals make these kinds of transitions. "We don't know the best way to shift resources," Stern admits. "We don't know the best way to rebuild the steward system. But we have to get people in motion. You have to row before you can steer."

Nor has finding so many organizers been a simple chore. With community organizing in decline, the union has hired many off-campus organizers. It has also encountered what Stern calls the "missing generation" problem: with so few veteran organizers in the labor movement, the number of people with the experience to head a local's organizing program is woefully small. Yet for all its problems, SEIU organized 58,000 new members in 1997, and has major organizing drives among hospital, nursing home, and home health care workers underway today—often involving an entire chain, not simply one facility.

While Sweeney's emphasis on organizing is roundly applauded, the organizing programs themselves are not without their critics. The Organizing Institute's emphasis on recruiting students, which is now also common practice at SEIU and other internationals, has been questioned by other organizers who favor recruiting from within the union membership (though a number of these organizers themselves entered the movement as students). Even the critics concede, though, that by emphasizing unions' role in securing social justice and by targeting campuses with programs like Union Summer, the Federation has tapped into a new generation of activists who might otherwise never have considered working for unions.

Other critics complain, though quietly, that under Sweeney, the Federation has disproportionately prioritized low-wage workers and is relying too heavily on the rhetoric and symbols of the left in their organizing drives. Defenders of the Sweeney approach argue that polling shows that non-white and female workers—disproportionately to be found in low-wage jobs, and often connected to communities where the legacy of the civil rights movement still persists—are far more receptive to unionization than their white and male counterparts.

In June of 1998, Sweeney discharged Bensinger, whose outspoken criticism of the anemic organizing programs of many internationals had won him few friends on the Federation's executive council. As his successor, Sweeney appointed Kirk Adams, a widely respected veteran SEIU organizer who in recent years had been working as Southeastern Regional director for the AFL-CIO's field mobilization programs. Adams' appointment was not viewed as signaling a de-emphasis in the importance the Federation placed on organizing, or a shift in the Federation's organizing strategy.

For now at least, Sweeney's critics are not willing to make a major issue of their criticisms of that strategy. "During Kirkland's presidency, we were intellectually convinced—because of the law, because of the economy—that organizing was impossible," one staffer close to Kirkland said. "The people around Sweeney believe they can organize. And because of that, they just may."

FROM NAFTA TO FAST TRACK TO 226: POLITICS AT THE AFL-CIO

Sweeney's commitment to transform the Federation's political program was second only to his commitment to rebuild organizing. The "New Voice" campaign called for a shift in emphasis away from donating money to candidates and toward waging labor-run campaigns on behalf of candidates and causes the movement prioritized. It called for cultivating thousands of labor candidates and tens of thousands of labor volunteers. In 1996 only a fledgling effort to field such a campaign was made, but it impressed the Republicans to the extent that they have spent much of 1998 trying to keep it from happening again.

For his new political director, Sweeney appointed Steve Rosenthal, a longtime CWA activist, former deputy to legendary Democratic Party strategist Paul Tully, and lieutenant to Labor Secretary Robert Reich. Shortly after Sweeney took office, the executive council voted to allot $35 million for an AFL-CIO independent campaign connected to the 1996 congressional elections. Of that, just over $20 million went to a media campaign that took on Republican members of Congress for their opposition to a minimum wage hike and their desire to scale back Medicare and Social Security. The remaining $14 million funded an ambitious field campaign, which ended up employing 135 full-time staffers in selected congressional districts around the country.

Even before the Federation's new program was in place, Sweeney and McEntee played a key role in convincing Clinton—with the help of AFL-CIO-commissioned polls—that he could successfully stand up to Republican demands to cut universal entitlement programs. Along with pollster Stan Greenberg, Sweeney and McEntee helped persuade the president that there were politically popular progressive alternatives to Dick Morris's policy of accommodation of the Republicans on the budget.

The old model of politics—check-writing to Democratic candidates—was not abandoned in 1996: unions made $37 million in PAC donations during the 1995–1996 political cycle. Still, with the total of all donations during this period at $2.2 billion, the ability of unions to impact races financially was quite limited. What was novel were the special campaigns they waged, on the air and on the ground, in key congressional districts, and the extensive candidate- and campaign-manager-training sessions they held for union members. When all the trainings and all the campaigning were done, they had not put the House back in Democratic hands. They had, however, increased the share of union households among all voters from a dismal 14 percent in 1994's turnout to 23 percent in 1996's.

Union political action campaigns were most successful in those places where the perestroika of American labor reached down to the local level. Just a few months after

Sweeney became AFL-CIO president, for instance, a new generation of more activist leaders took control of both the California and Los Angeles labor Federations; and California, at least, saw a near-total transformation of its political programs in the 1996 vote. Within clusters of congressional and legislative districts targeted by national, state, and local federations, thousands of volunteers flooded the districts in the campaign's closing weeks. On election day, Democrats carried a range of California districts they had not won in decades, returning the Legislature to Democratic control. In all of these districts, labor made the difference.

These were also disproportionately districts with large immigrant and/or Latino populations—the district that Loretta Sanchez took from Bob Dornan among them. In California and throughout the nation, Latinos have been moving both to the polls and to the Democrats in angry response to the Republicans' support for anti-immigrant provisions in the federal welfare bill and California's Proposition 187. By and large, it has been

labor—through its naturalization and get-out-the-vote programs—that has translated that anger into clout at the polls. Much as CIO organizers reached out to the second wave of immigrants in the industrial Midwest during the 1936 elections, the new union organizers—many of them involved in organizing immigrants at their worksites—are bringing the third wave of immigrants to the polls today in cities across America.

While labor did not succeed in restoring the House to Democratic control, it did indeed succeed in helping derail the Republican agenda and disorient the Republican delegation. But a clearer index of labor's new clout came in the fall of 1997, when the administration's fast-track proposal failed to pass the House. It's instructive to compare the Federation's success at stopping fast track to its failure, under far more propitious conditions, to stop NAFTA in 1993. NAFTA came before a Democratic Congress in a time of high unemployment and economic anxiety, and labor was joined in its efforts to stop it by such right-wing nationalist leaders as Ross Perot and Pat Buchanan. Despite that, labor was only able to command the support of 60 percent of House Democrats, and NAFTA squeaked through.

In 1997, fast track went up to Congress at a time of low unemployment and relatively high economic contentment. Labor's nationalist allies were nowhere to be found, and labor had to somehow win over a much higher percentage of Democratic members than it did in 1993, since the Republicans were now in the majority. Labor succeeded, securing the votes of 80 percent of House Democrats, leaving the president with a scant 20 percent support from his own party.

The AFL-CIO's political program made all the difference. Labor had shown itself in 1996 to be the indispensable force in Democratic House races. In many districts, its 1996 campaign coordinators were still in place, organizing against fast track. Individual internationals had become more active, too. One hundred seventy thousand members of the Steelworkers sent off letters to their congressional representatives. "We couldn't have done this," one steelworker official commented, "when we were at the height of our power forty years ago."

The AFL-CIO's plans for the 1998 elections are in some ways even more ambitious than those for 1996. After imposing a special dollar-a-member assessment on member unions to try to fend off ballot measures that would defund unions' political programs, the Federation's financial commitment for independent campaigns in 1998 has risen to $29 million. And with more lead time to hold training sessions, the number of Federation political coordinators in the field will rise from 135 to 300 this year.

Many of those organizers were sent to California in the spring of 1998 to coordinate what many experts viewed as campaign doomed to defeat: the effort to turn back

Proposition 226, the initiative that required unions to obtain the annual signed permission from members in order to spend dues money for political purposes. The measure would have had a chilling effect on union political programs: in Washington, the one state where an analogous measure has been enacted, union political spending has been more than halved, and the legislature and congressional delegation has gone from Scoop Jackson-Democrat to Christian right-Republican. With Democratic fortunes in California district elections heavily dependent on unions' ability to contribute money and volunteer time, an even greater political shift was forecast if, as expected, 226 passed. Indeed, 226's sponsors, most especially Grover Norquist, director of Americans for Tax Reform and a key lieutenant of Newt Gingrich, backed the measure chiefly because they felt it would enable Republicans to retake the state legislature and to hold the statehouse—thereby producing a GOP-friendly congressional reapportionment after the year 2000 census. In short, the paychecks that this so-called "paycheck-protection" measure were most intended to protect were those of the Republican majority staffers on Capitol Hill.

On its face, the initiative sounded all but unarguable: who would oppose getting members' consent for spending their money? In fact, unions seldom engaged the individual-rights argument—though when they did, they pointed out that under the Supreme Court's Beck decision, members already had the right to withhold dues, and that the turnover rate among local union leadership was high enough to suggest that discontent with union leadership does not go unregistered. Instead, unions chiefly focused on the aggregate effect that 226 would have, and on the agendas of its backers. The measure, they argued, mandated a shift in class power in California, for it was only unions that were required to obtain such permission; corporations, for instance, did not have to obtain shareholder permission to make political donations.

While Norquist and his allies have complained that the unions ducked a discussion of the issues that 226 raised, in fact labor's campaign, which addressed the effects of erasing unions from California's political landscape, was entirely on point. Union-sponsored advertising highlighted such issues as the increased privatization of education, the continued export of jobs, and the reduction in the pressure for HMO reform—all predictable consequences of 226's enactment. The advertisements were just one part of a massive campaign the AFL-CIO threw together in a few short months. Under the direction of political director Rosenthal, roughly $20 million was allotted for field campaigns. Nearly sixty union staffers coordinated an effort which saw tens of thousands of AFL-CIO members walk more than 5,000 precincts, phone 650,000 union households, and hold meetings in more than 18,000 worksites. It was the most massive political mobilization the movement had mounted since 1958. And, confounding the predictions of virtually every pundit, it succeeded: a measure that had over 70 percent support in February polling went down to defeat in June by a 46 to 54 percent margin.

The unions' efforts among their own members were particularly critical. In the February polling, 67 percent of union household voters supported the measure. On election day, 64 percent of union household voters opposed it, as did 71 percent of AFL-CIO union members, and 81 percent of AFL-CIO members familiar with their union's position. Perhaps most impressive—indeed, astonishing—was the finding of one exit poll that fully 35 percent of primary voters came from union households. In a state where the rate of unionization is just 17 percent, labor's mobilization of its own members was key to the measurer's defeat. Perhaps just as impressive, Latinos opposed 226 by a 75 to 25 percent margin—a reflection of unions' increased focus on Latino workers, and a confirmation of an overall organizing strategy that increasingly targets heavily Latino workforces.

By forcing labor to spend so much time and energy on defeating 226, Norquist and Co. did succeed in delaying labor from imposing its agenda on the broader 1998 campaign: such themes as opposing the privatization of Social Security or demanding HMO reform were still largely unvoiced at summer's outset. Despite that, the campaign against 226 had raised the level of mobilization among union members to a forty-year high, and union leaders were hopeful that they could maintain that activism for the fall campaign. The "No-on-226" campaign may have produced a defensive victory, but it was nonetheless labor's greatest victory not just of the Sweeney years but of the several preceding decades.

There is one other striking departure from past practice in labor's political program: the new *sine qua non* for supporting a candidate is that candidate's support for union organizing efforts. The most dramatic effect this has had on Democratic candidates has come at the level of presidential politics. Both Vice-President Albert Gore and Democratic House leader Richard Gephardt—the leading contestants for the party's presidential nomination in the year 2000—now routinely appear with workers involved in organizing campaigns, condemn employers who have violated labor law in order to thwart those campaigns, and call for strengthening the employer sanctions in the nation's labor laws. Like every other program at the AFL-CIO, the goal of politics is to support organizing.

THE TEAMSTER PROBLEM AND ITS SPILLOVER

By late 1997, the Sweeney regime encountered a problem that threatened to undo much of its work to rebuild labor's good name—ironically, as the result of its interactions with a member international that also had produced labor's greatest recent success.

The problem came from the Teamsters, which, in the summer of 1997, had conducted the most successful national strike any union had waged in decades. The 180,000 Teamsters at United Parcel Service struck in late summer over several issues, above all, the lower pay and benefits accorded to part-time workers, many of whom actually worked at or near full-time. Under the leadership of president Ron Carey, the Teamsters managed to keep the vast majority of its members from crossing the line, and to build what the polls showed as two-to-one support for the strikers among a public clearly concerned about the emergence of a two-tier workforce.

But the Teamsters' success at UPS was followed one week later by a series of guilty pleas from three figures involved in Carey's 1996 re-election campaign. The irony was that Carey had always been something of poster-child for union reform. Elected in a federally-supervised mail ballot of members in 1991, he had distinguished himself in his five-year term by attacking all the practices that had made the Teamsters a notorious union for decades. The salaries and perks of topmost leaders were slashed; the practice of officials pulling down multiple paychecks curtailed. Seventy teamster locals, some of them clearly mobbed-up, were placed in trusteeship.

In 1996, though, Carey faced a strong re-election challenge from attorney James Hoffa, Jr., son of Teamsters' legend Jimmy. He scraped through by a 52 to 48 percent margin, but shortly after the election, the federally-appointed official supervising the vote reported that Teamster funds going to the liberal organization Citizen Action for its work in the 1996 federal elections had been routed to a campaign-service vendor whose wife then made a sizable contribution to an organization backing Carey's re-election. A subsequent investigation by a federal prosecutor yielded guilty pleas from Carey's campaign manager, consultant, and the vendor. Carey, under investigation from his union's independent review board, stepped down from the Teamster presidency.

Carey's campaign had been a *cause célèbre* for the reform wing of the labor movement, and a number of its leaders were implicated in the charges. Yet another investigation from a federally-appointed attorney contained allegations that prominent figures in the Sweeney regime—chiefly, AFSCME's Gerald McEntee—had raised funds for Carey's re-election in violation of the court order which governed the terms of the Teamster contest. It also alleged that AFL-CIO Secretary-Treasurer Trumka had enabled the Teamsters to contribute funds to the Federation that the Federation would give to Citizen Action, and which would return to finance Carey's campaign. Trumka flatly denied the allegations, as did McEntee.

Nonetheless, the charges led to a brief series of attacks on Sweeney's stewardship from some defenders of labor's *ancién regime*, most of them unnamed, in the press. It also stoked the fires of congressional Republicans eager to diminish labor's political clout, though their chief vehicle for making those attacks, the hearings chaired by Michigan Congressman Peter Hoekstra, failed to yield any new information about the charges.

REINVENTING LIBERALISM

What may be the greatest, albeit unheralded, success of John Sweeney's AFL-CIO is a new direction for contemporary liberalism. At a time when liberalism was largely stalled in the cul-de-sac of identity politics, and when support for other long-standing liberal causes was clearly collapsing, Sweeney's emphasis on issues of wage and income equity placed economic inequality at the center of modern progressivism.

Sweeney's insistence that "America needs a raise" did more than just place a new emphasis on low-wage workers whom labor would seek to organize. It also tapped into a vast public uneasiness at the Dickensian polarities of the new American economy. Even as welfare and affirmative action programs were being repealed, labor-liberal coalitions won a string of victories in campaigns to raise the minimum wage, to establish "living wage" guarantees for municipal workers, to support low-wage part-timers at UPS, and to defeat fast-track trade authority.

Labor's much-maligned position on trade, in fact, also tapped into Americans' anxiety about the long-term consequences of globalization, and offered liberals a nuanced and politically sustainable approach to this increasingly critical issue. Though attacked by both Republicans and New Democrats for espousing "protectionist" trade policies, Sweeney actually advanced a vision of a global mixed economy or social democracy. "If this global economy cannot be made to work for working people," Sweeney warned the annual gathering of megacapitalists at Davos, Switzerland, in 1997, "it will reap a reaction that may make the twentieth century seem tranquil by comparison."

Ironically, the fact that U.S. workers have been vulnerable for at least two decades to the kinds of corporate flight that their European counterparts are only now experiencing has meant that the American labor movement has taken the point in pushing for minimum labor and human rights standards on the global level. At the Singapore conference that established the World Trade Organization, the AFL-CIO was the leading advocate for enforceable standards. On an ongoing basis, the Federation's international department meets with unions from other nations toward the goal of formulating realistic social charters.

Freed from the strictures of a cold war foreign policy that saw the Federation align itself with every union that claimed an anti-communist pedigree, the AFL-CIO is now reaching out to a range of independent unions, "to develop cross-border organizing and bargaining strategies," as Sweeney said in a 1997 Mexico City address. Newly independent unions in Mexico have received Federation support for their struggles to organize in the maquiladoras. And in the 1997 bargaining by a dozen U.S.-based unions (coordinated by Trumka) with that most global of corporations, General Electric, the U.S. unions brought representatives from Brazil and elsewhere with GE contracts of their own to join them at the bargaining table.

The Federation's newly redirected global activism comes at a time when governments and unions throughout the world have yet to evolve a minimally effective response to the transnationalization of both corporations and investment. European workers retain the kind of wages and benefits that American workers have given up over the past two decades, though their hold grows steadily weaker as Europe-based corporations increasingly invest abroad. America, of course, has little trouble creating jobs, though many pay low wages and most offer fewer benefits than was the norm a generation ago. Europe has a growing unemployment problem, but it is Americans who place bars on their windows and gates around their homes. Neither model can be judged a success from the standpoint of working people; the Federation has recognized that a supranational model is required to address these problems, though the particulars of that model will take many years to develop.

While it is plainly too early to pass judgment on the efforts of the new AFL-CIO to rebuild the American labor movement, there can be little doubt that labor does not have an abundance of time. In 1997, the rate of private sector unionization slipped into single digits for the first time since before the New Deal. How long a de-unionized private sector workforce will be willing to support a unionized public sector workforce is a question that the movement would rather not confront, but it will have to unless the private sector organizing now getting underway results in significant victories.

What the new AFL-CIO has imparted to that movement is a new sense of urgency— and possibility. "John Sweeney has forced unions to confront whether they'll just be grave-diggers, or have a role in the new millennium," one senior official of a leading international commented in early 1998. "We're still wrestling with moving resources into organizing, and it's not easy. Still, I see people struggling with the right questions— and that's something labor hasn't seen in decades."

WHEN WE TRY MORE, WE WIN MORE

Organizing The New Workforce

richard bensinger

When the Ark Restaurants Corp. in Las Vegas fired eight union activists who were leading a thousand co-workers in an organizing campaign, the labor movement fought back. The union didn't strike, however, and didn't picket. They didn't rely solely on labor law either, because it is antiquated and virtually worthless. Instead, HERE (Hotel Employees & Restaurant Employees) mobilized their tens of thousands of members in Las Vegas to act. Hundreds of union members participated in a "sip-in" at the restaurant, where they took up every seat in the restaurant, only ordering water for three hours before tipping the servers and leaving. Soon after, ten thousand unionists and community supporters, including local religious leaders, marched on the hotel to expose the company's actions and to demand union recognition for these workers, 85 percent of whom had signed union cards.

The Ark's response to employee organizing is typical of decades-old management tactics: scare them, fire them, turn them against one another, stop the union. In some cases, employers even call for a union vote, knowing full well that they've terrorized their workers into voting no. HERE's coordinated response, however, is indicative of labor's new approach. What labor has embarked on in the last few years is nothing short of a radical, fundamental cultural transformation in our approach to organizing. In some ways, we are rediscovering our organizing roots, and in some ways we are reinventing ourselves.

For years, our ability to organize has been strangled by forces from outside and from within our own ranks. On the one hand, we are faced with labor laws which are virtually useless and have actually prevented millions of workers from organizing each year. While these laws were once meant to help workers organize for change in their workplace, now the laws are actually routinely used against workers trying to win a union vote. As strange as it sounds, it is now the employer's decision whether to have a union in the workplace, rather than the decision of the workers.

On the other hand, real challenge lies within. For decades, the labor movement has neglected its organizing potential. When John Sweeney was elected the new president of the AFL-CIO, 97 percent of locals had no existing organizing programs and no membership involvement in organizing. At best, less than 5 percent of our total resources went to new-member organizing, and unions operated in almost complete isolation of the community. Many of our own leaders and members understood neither the need to organize, nor the kind of employer opposition workers face in campaigns.

The truth is that I'm no better than most union leaders on this issue. In the 1980s, after my local union in Colorado had some big organizing wins, I shifted all the organizing staff to servicing in order to defend our base. This response is understandable, though not justifiable. It's true that workers and union staff are battling for survival every day against plant closings and attempts

by management to get unions out of plants. Increasingly workers are fighting to keep their jobs from being filled by temporary staffers, and live knowing that one week's missed paycheck could do them in. In this context, organizing new workers often seems like a good idea, but not important enough to outweigh the immediate crisis.

The fact is, however, that the labor movement is in crisis precisely because we haven't been organizing. The result of this neglect has been a shrinkage in our ranks that, if unchecked, will continue until labor vanishes from the picture of power in America altogether. Meanwhile, working families stand to lose the very institutions, unions, which were created to ensure economic justice and a sense of balance in society. Although everyone seems to be talking about how we're living in a time of great economic disparity, very few are pointing to organizing unions as the answer. The media has made much of the fact that corporate CEOs' paychecks have doubled in the last five years, while young workers today make 25 percent less in real dollars than their parents did at the same age. Yet analysts continue to turn to stopgap measures like increases in the minimum wage which, though important, are no substitute for democratic institutions that give workers the legal right to negotiate, year after year, no matter who is in Congress or in the White House.

In response to the overwhelming need to shift our focus to expand organizing capacity, the AFL-CIO has proposed a fundamental, even radical, urgent institutional shift, inspired by courageous local unions who are organizing to change. Our goal is to organize millions of people in the next decade, but this won't be easy. We need to organize 350,000 workers a year just to keep membership levels even, and we need to organize 1.2 million workers a year just to grow by 1 percent.

We've developed an agenda that offers a vision of how we can organize at the pace and scale necessary to meet this challenge. Our program has three major components. First, we must increase our capacity to organize by leading a cultural transformation of our institutions and by increasing resources devoted to organizing. Second, we need an offensive plan to establish the right to organize through community outreach and member mobilization. Finally, we must increase our effectiveness by organizing strategically both on a larger scale than ever before and through cooperative efforts that cross union lines and use our members to build real power. Our agenda goes beyond the theoretical and is, in fact, campaign-driven. In conjunction with AFL-CIO union affiliates, we work on real, ongoing organizing campaigns across the country to implement this three-point plan.

INCREASE CAPACITY TO ORGANIZE

Until recently, unions simply no longer had the capacity to organize. We had created a culture in which organizing was not a part of our internal discussions. For years, we debated politics and arbitrations. We argued mostly about contract language and grievances. The AFL-CIO's new organizing program attempts to change the terms of labor's internal debate, making organizing an issue, and to begin a process of institutional redefinition. We aim to build labor's capacity to organize through increased resources, more trained organizers, increased membership involvement, and a renewed will to make organizing a success.

The AFL-CIO has attempted to make itself a living example of the organizing model by working to shift 30 percent of our own resources to organizing, and then asking all affiliates to do the same by the year 2000. We're expanding the Organizing Institute in order to attract and to train more organizers to meet the increased demand from unions who are newly organizing. We're building an organizing program in partnership with affiliate unions.

Last year the AFL-CIO held fourteen regional meetings on organizing involving thousands of rank-and-file activists and leaders. Union members and local leaders discussed how difficult it is to devote time and energy to organizing new members when their unions are under constant attack from corporations. Yet they also agreed to hold themselves responsible for the need to organize because they know that for unions to gain more power for themselves, as well as for all working Americans, unions must grow. The dilemma we discussed at these conferences was how to make that happen.

Our regional conferences were inspirational, implementing a vision of hope through actions to support organizing drives in each of the conference cities. In Miami, for instance, the 800 conference attendees and AFL-CIO President Sweeney were slated to visit Hebrew Home nursing home, where the workers had won their union election but were battling for a contract. The nursing home owner called the union on the morning of the march, and finally agreed to a first contract. Instead of holding a rally, we celebrated that day in front of the nursing home, clearly marking a victory clinched by a newly-invigorated labor movement.

Organizing conferences, however, are only the starting point for actually running an effective, movement-wide organizing program. "Money, after all, is the only true measure of rhetoric when it comes to organizing," argues Tom Woodruff, organizing director of the Service Employees International Union (SEIU). Good organizing certainly needs lots of resources—resources that often must be shifted from other areas of the organization, and unions are beginning to show this kind of real commitment. A little more than a year ago, only fifteen local unions would qualify for the AFL-CIO's Changing to Organize program, but today at

least 150 local unions put 10 to 20 percent of their resources into organizing, and are moving toward meeting the challenge to put in 30 percent.

Even more unions are gearing up to follow suit. In a series of AFL-CIO sponsored Elected Leaders Task Force retreats, union leaders have peer-driven conversations on how to change to organize. They emphasize internal obstacles to change, rather than dismissing organizing as "impossible" due to the law or other external obstacles. The discussions are candid. "We need to hold the mirror up to our face," said Steve Fantauzo, head of the American Federation of State, County & Municipal Employees (AFSCME) Indiana District Council. "This is a leadership problem, not a membership problem."

Gerald McEntee, President of AFSCME, often talks about how we have to change the psychology of unions in order to make way for organizing. The culture of many unions is such that for years organizing has been viewed as the role of the international—and not that of the local. Seventy-five percent of the unions' resources, however, are at the local level. In order to have any impact in organizing, local leaders will have to follow in the footsteps of leaders like Henry Bayer of the AFSCME Illinois District Council, who jump-started his brand-new organizing program by hiring seventeen organizers.

Cultural change and adequate resources are keys to increasing our capacity to organize, but we also need a new generation of organizers. The Organizing Institute (OI), which recruits and trains organizers, is expanding under the new AFL-CIO organizing program. The OI has graduated 800 organizers since its inception, and 300 of them in the last two years.

OI participants go through a rigorous selection and training process run by a collective of people drawn from many organizing unions. A three-day training staffed by organizers, many who are in the middle of actual campaigns, provides the ABCs of house calling, running meetings and listening to workers' concerns. Participants are then grouped for a three-week internship working on an affiliate union's campaign. Past internships have included organizing poultry workers in Louisiana, nursing home workers in Pennsylvania, and textile workers in North Carolina. Finally, a number of applicants go on to do three-month apprenticeships, learning the intricacies of organizing first-hand from experienced organizers.

The Organizing Institute graduates are a diverse crowd. Sixty-five percent are rank-and-file members of affiliate unions, and many of the rest are recent college graduates. The OI has put special emphasis on recruiting women and people of color to organizing, in order to best represent the communities that are unionizing. Women workers have joined unions at a faster rate than men in the last five years, and people of color have been organizing even faster, in part because these workers find that unions provide a way to win equal pay and fair treatment at work. Groups such as the Asian Pacific American Labor Alliance (APALA) have worked in conjunction with the OI to recruit organizers from various ethnic communities.

In addition, the OI has a new one-day member-organizing training program. The number of workers who are out knocking on other workers' doors, often in their own communities, has risen sharply in the last two years. The AFL-CIO's Education Department has started the MEMO (Member Education) program based on a similar building trades program. MEMO helps to change labor's culture by inspiring rank-and-file workers to learn about and to discuss the organizing imperative.

Finally, the AFL-CIO launched Union Summer in 1996, which brought more than a thousand workers and college students out into organizing campaigns for three-week programs. Participants helped organize workers such as janitors and hotels workers in more than twenty cities. The program received widespread media attention, including articles such as "It's Hip to Be Union" in *Newsweek* magazine. Senior Summer was then launched in 1997 to involve retirees in much the same way.

UnionSummer is really our investment in the next generation, and the next generation's investment in us, and it's a strategy that seems to be working. At a recent meet-

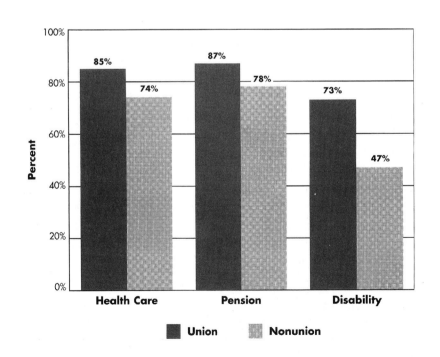

UNION WORKERS ARE MORE LIKELY TO HAVE
HEALTH AND PENSION BENEFITS, 1995

Percent

- Health Care: Union 85%, Nonunion 74%
- Pension: Union 87%, Nonunion 78%
- Disability: Union 73%, Nonunion 47%

■ Union   ▨ Nonunion

ing at United Farm Workers headquarters in La Paz, California, twelve young people discussed why they wanted to volunteer a year of their time to work with the UFW's strawberry workers' campaign. Eleven of the twelve were union summer graduates.

RIGHT TO ORGANIZE

Polling shows that 44 percent of non-union workers who aren't managers want to be members of a union, which works out to about 48 million Americans. Yet far fewer people than that are actually joining unions. The root of this discrepancy lies in employers'

campaigns of terror against unionizing workers. Regardless of what the laws on the books say, American workers are harassed, intimidated, and threatened to such a degree by employers that the legal right to organize has been stolen from them. When there is no such employer opposition to unionization, the majority of workers choose a union. For instance, about 60 percent of public sector workers belong to unions.

American workers do not have a real right to organize unions. First, the workers sign union cards, then they have to go through a ten-week election period in which the employer, aided by a half-billion dollar a year union-busting industry, declares open season on its workforce. The union doesn't have a legal right to talk to the workers in the captive audience meetings. They can only pass out leaflets outside the plant gate, and invite workers to meetings after work or in their homes. This is not democracy. This is like running a presidential election in which the President has total access to the American people, and forces them to come to his daily meetings to keep their jobs. Meanwhile, his opponent must stand at the Canadian or Mexican border handing out leaflets as people drive into the U.S.

In 98 percent of the contested elections, employers break the law to such an extent that the union is forced to file unfair labor practice charges with the federal government. Many management firms actually advise their clients to go ahead and break the law. After all, they know that American labor law is so weak that there are no significant monetary fines when employers deprive workers of their right to organize. Our society imposes fines for polluting the environment, and even for mistreating animals. Yet the worst thing that can happen to employers for violating workers' rights is having to post a blue and white sign which says they broke the law, and then perhaps paying fired workers back-pay—a minimal amount that is often less than the workers would have taken home in their paychecks. While we still have plans to work toward enacting decent labor law, this is a long-term goal and does little to help the millions of workers who need a union now.

We need to build an offensive strategy and use it movement-wide, based on educating and mobilizing the community on workers' right to organize and thus lessening employer opposition to organizing. By making visible the kinds of injustices suffered by organizing workers, we can at least begin to level the playing field.

In our society, the right to organize for better pay and benefits through a union is not just a labor issue, it's a civil rights issue as well. For example, at the Atlanta organizing conference, a thousand unionists marched on the county commissioner's office to support sanitation workers who were organizing with the Georgia State Employees Union. The commissioner had backed out on her pledge to support the workers, the majority of whom are people of color. "Thirty years ago Martin Luther King, Jr. marched with sanitation workers in Memphis for the exact same right—the right to organize a union," pointed out Stewart Acuff, President of the Atlanta Labor Council, "and here we are again today. Together, we can win this fight."

There is a real silence in our society about economic inequality. Much of the public is waiting for someone to step in as a moral authority, and to point out the fact that workers' paychecks are shrinking, their families don't have insurance, and their futures are unstable, at best. Unions can be this force, and can lead the way for the rest of the community by educating people about the need for unions and then mobilizing them around the right to organize. We can engage community leaders in challenging anti-union behavior through local Workers' Rights Boards and similar vehicles. We can seek pledges to support the right-to-organize from candidates seeking the votes of working families. The right to organize campaign goes beyond simply winning card check, or bypassing the National Labor Relations Board. It is about focusing public attention on the injustices suffered by workers, and shaming employers into at least lessening their opposition to workers who want to form unions.

STRATEGIC ORGANIZING

Along with building our capacity and ensuring the right to organize, we also must have a tactical plan to increase our effectiveness in organizing. Strategic organizing demands first looking at where the economy is going and then comparing that to where we have density in our membership base and where we can build on our existing bargaining relationships to support organizing. Then, we must organize at a scale and pace that we haven't done in generations.

Only by organizing entire corporations, geographic regions, industries, and economic sectors are we going to build real power. Take, for example, the victory by asbestos workers in New York who organized more than two thousand asbestos workers and now represent 85 percent of their industry. Two years ago, Local 78 of the Laborers' International Union (LIUNA) only had 113 members. They faced a formidable organizing challenge with 200 non-union asbestos abatement firms in their area, forty of which were large companies. Under new leadership, the local put 50 percent of their resources into organizing. Two AFL-CIO Organizing Institute staffers and one organizer trained forty rank-and-file members on how to talk to fellow asbestos workers about unionizing. The group made an astounding 1,600 home visits in a three-week period.

In addition, Local 78 launched a true right-to-organize campaign. With a workforce that was half Latino and half Polish, they garnered support from the community, and made their issue a civil rights' cause in the city. Within two and a half months, the local had leveraged union recognitions for 85 percent of the asbestos workers in New York City. Their success meant real, immediate change in these working families' lives. The workers' wages increased by 33 percent in the first contract, and they won an additional four dollar an hour increase in benefits.

Many unions are becoming more savvy about using their existing membership base to support organizing. The Steelworkers, for instance, have established SWOC II (Steelworkers Organizing Committee). SWOC II exposes the hypocrisy of companies who have relatively congenial bargaining relationships with their members, but then launch all-out wars against workers in the same company attempting to organize.

Other unions are successfully targeting bigger strategic units. The Communications Workers of America (CWA) recently organized 10,000 USAirways workers in the biggest private-sector organizing victory in a decade. This campaign was exemplary in that, despite its size, it was truly worker-driven. An organizing committee of several hundred made sure the company never got the chance to portray the union as an outsider. The committee members became the face of the union by taking advantage of their free-flying benefit, and meetings with workers nationwide, often one-on-one. The International union, meanwhile, played a coordinating role. This campaign took huge resources on the part of CWA, but it is indicative of the kind of campaigns that labor needs to run in order to organize on a mass scale.

In addition to using their own bases to run big campaigns, all elements of the labor movement must join forces across international unions. For years we've been able to see how cooperating in politics was to our collective benefit. Now it's time to do the same for organizing. The AFL-CIO has two initiatives that seek to bring unions together on the organizing front. One is supporting multi-union campaigns that target whole industries, sectors of the economy, or geographic

BUILDING TRADES ORGANIZING PROJECT • LAS VEGAS

ORGANIZE TO SURVIVE

702/878-3885

areas. The other is to help mobilize workers from a range of affiliates to support organizing efforts through marches and demonstrations, key elements of our Street Heat and Union Cities programs.

Cooperative efforts sometimes mean that unions who are organizing in the same geographic area simply share infrastructure, such as training, offices, mobilizations, and public relations. Other unions, however, cooperate by sharing targets. The organizing project in New Orleans, targeting 9,500 hotel workers, is an example of both these approaches. The Operating Engineers, HERE, and SEIU have formed a council to organize these mostly African-American workers in a city with the lowest per-capita income in the country. They plan to sign up a majority of workers, and then launch a right-to-organize fight that will involve the community and will attempt to shame the hotels into curtailing their fight. The workers are meeting with religious leaders and elected political officials, calling on them to support the workers' struggle for rights and dignity at work. Dozens of community leaders have already joined the struggle.

Finally, the labor movement is turning out the troops to support one another's organizing drive, first contract campaigns, and strikes. There are dramatic examples, such as the ten thousand person marches in Las Vegas, but communities all across the country are being shaken up by union members who are taking their fight to the streets. The results are often striking and swift. In Minneapolis, through an AFL-CIO Street Heat action, a thousand people joined a boisterous rally to support several hundred workers organizing at a nursing home with SEIU. When the crowd neared the hospital's quiet zone, they held a silent vigil, and AFL-CIO President Sweeney delivered several bouquets of flowers to the head of the administration. Three days later, the company recognized the union.

Time after time, we've found that members are overwhelmingly enthusiastic about mobilizing to support organizing once they get a taste of it. People really want to respond to crises, whether that means fighting cancer or fighting corporate cancer. Our challenge is to tap into that kind of energy, and channel it into new member organizing.

BUILDING ON OUR ORGANIZING WINS

A three-point plan built on increasing our capacity to organize, defending the right to organize, and planning strategically is a viable one as demonstrated by the success of HERE Local 226 in Las Vegas, which organized an astonishing 9,000 workers last year. HERE underwent a radical internal change a decade ago when they saw that hotel after hotel was opening non-union in Vegas. Ten years ago they only spent 2 percent of their budget on organizing where today they spend an exemplary 55 percent. Of the local's ninety person staff, forty-two people are organizers. The local has learned to mobilize its membership base and the community to defend workers' right to organize, such as during the "sip-in" at the Ark Restaurants Corp. Finally, they have a strategic plan to take back their industry, which has resulted in their successfully organizing virtually the entire Las Vegas strip.

HERE's commitment to organizing has, in fact, strengthened the entire local's program. The recent Frontier Hotel strike, in which workers and their union fought for six years and won in a spectacular show of solidarity, demonstrates the tenacity and perseverance that are the root of this local's organizing success. Thousands of HERE members, including many members who only became unionized after the strike had already begun, walked the daily picket lines outside the Frontier.

The labor movement has a long way to go before it reaches the Las Vegas scale of organizing nationwide, but the numbers are promising. Just about every International union marked its best year ever for organizing last year. We organized more than 400,000 workers last year, when for decades we have averaged about 200,000 a year. SEIU organized 81,000 workers last year after two-thirds of its locals shifted at least 20 percent of their resources to organizing. The American Federation of Teachers organized 22,000 workers, including a single unit of 9,500 in Dallas—the largest single group of teachers to choose a union in twenty years. The Teamsters organized 33,000 workers last year, up from a 13,000 average in previous years. The Amalgamated Transit Union held forty-five elections last year, up from thirteen in 1996, and organized four times as many workers as previously.

Organizing successes are based on membership involvement, but they also require strong leadership. It's not surprising that when leaders such as Maria Elena Dorazo, of HERE in Los Angeles, dedicate 50 percent of resources to organizing, the whole union and its contracts grow stronger. It's not surprising that when a leader such as Bruce Raynor, Secretary-Treasurer of UNITE, organizes 25,000 workers in the anti-union South over a decade, the success is a result of tough decision making and risk taking. It's not surprising that strong leadership, such as that of Tom Woodruff of SEIU, can lead an 800-member Midwest local to grow to 13,000 members in a little over ten years.

There are no quick fixes to organizing workers. It takes enormous dedication and courage on the part of workers and their unions in order to win just small campaigns, let alone industry-wide ones. But we do know that when we try more, we win more. That doesn't mean that we should just throw out more fishing lines and hope that a winning election will bite. We need to think strategically about where our strength lies, and how we can expand the resources available to us, such as in recruiting community allies. We also have to look within our ranks to our members, both to help organize and to mobilize, in order to defend the right to organize.

This is truly a a time of great opportunity for the labor movement. On the one hand, we have the crisis in society in which workers are struggling more and more just to get by, while corporate profits soar. On the other hand, unions are changing our approach to organizing, along with our whole relationship to union membership, resulting in a kind of rebirth of unions as they were originally meant to be—real workers' organizations.

There is no guarantee that we will succeed. History, however, has proven that the impossible can be achieved. In his letter from Birmingham Jail, Martin Luther King, Jr. explained his decision to use civil disobedience by writing that "Progress never rolls in on the wheels of inevitability." Change, after all, only happens when we make it happen, and what we're seeing here is a beginning—but only a beginning—of change.

For the last two years the television show *Wheel of Fortune* has featured union members and union made prizes during Labor Day week.

FINDING A VOICE

The AFL-CIO Communicates

jo-ann mort

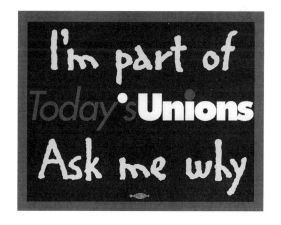

Before John Sweeney's "New Voice" coalition swept into power at the AFL-CIO, the public relations department was called "The Department of Information," reminiscent of a war bureau, or a propaganda machine. True to its name, it gave out information upon request, but the public relations professionals who worked there didn't search out news coverage, nor was there a coherent strategy to combine the activities of the Federation with a media outreach strategy. In fact, under Lane Kirkland's presidency, the perceived mistrust of the media was so great that reporters were often made to feel unwelcome even at open press conferences. Indeed, it was the lack of an inviting public face that helped propel a new leadership into place at the AFL-CIO.

CNN commentator Bill Schneider tells a story of having been invited to speak before a group of political staff at the last AFL-CIO executive council that Kirkland headed. Schneider made innocent comments that opened a wound exposing the tensions, or growing pains, within the AFL-CIO. Answering a question about how the image of labor could be improved, Schneider, himself a professor and writer who has honed his TV skills, said that "You need someone who is good on TV." He had no idea that he was flying into the wind of the controversy surrounding the future of the AFL-CIO, and was taken aback when, at a press conference in a Bal Harbour, Florida hotel, Kirkland made a pointed, disparaging remark about "those guests invited to the house of labor" who seek to castigate the labor movement.

Indeed, the winter meetings of the Executive Council in Bal Harbour, Florida were the one time of the year when the handful of reporters who followed organized labor descended in a pack to cover labor, but what they ended up covering was a set of meetings and fancy receptions—rather than the people who are active union members. Union media professionals lived in yearly fear of the TV crew that ventured poolside to capture labor's winter retreat. If form followed function, the concern that public relations personnel had regarding coverage of the February meetings spoke most clearly to the need for a new image, a new form, and a new program for the AFL-CIO.

One of the first things Sweeney did as head of the AFL-CIO was to discontinue the February meetings and substitute them with a winter meeting to be held in a different city each year, to highlight labor activism in various sites. The first city was Los Angeles, where immigrant workers are being organized; the second, Las Vegas, where there are massive organizing campaigns ongoing among hotel, restaurant, health care, building trades workers, and others.

Even before the Sweeney revolution, under the leadership of former AFL-CIO president Tom Donahue, there was a sense that things had to change. Donahue commissioned a study prepared for the AFL-CIO by the public relations firm Greer, Margolis, Mitchell and Burns to examine ways to improve internal and external public relations capacity for the labor movement. The report recommended a range of measures from "core positioning and message discipline" familiar to political campaigns to linking communications to substantive actions and goals. With that report as a building block, the new AFL-CIO leadership proceeded to restructure the communications component of the Federation. Indeed, many of the recommendations made in that report have become gospel today, including talking points and messages fashioned around the economic concerns of all working families, highlighting the particular concerns of union members, not of labor as an institution.

From the moment Sweeney was elected, the communications operation at the AFL-CIO became transformed, linked intimately to the frenetic activity in the reviving labor federation. According to Denise Mitchell, Assistant to the President for Public Affairs and someone who worked with Sweeney at SEIU, after the election of Sweeney, Trumka and Chavez-Thompson, "We needed to hit the ground running. A campaign mode was important."

Mitchell assembled a working group of public relations directors (myself included) from various unions to suggest a new communications structure to the AFL-CIO Executive Council. This working group mirrored other groups set up by Sweeney immediately after taking office to propose ways to implement new AFL-CIO initiatives in organizing, political action, strategic campaigns, and union education and training.

America @work

Ideas, Info and Ammo for AFL-CIO Leaders and Activists   OCTOBER 1996

The **AFL-CIO News** will retire as new publication debuts.
See story, **Page 8.**

AFL-CIO NEWS

VOLUME 41, NUMBER 17   **OCTOBER 14, 1996**

Campaign foils anti-worker Congress

Allen Zak Photography

Jean Fightmaster of AFSCME is interviewed by the local television station in Columbus, Ohio, as unions and their allies took Working Women Vote Week coast to coast. **See story, Page 4.**

FedEx special favor is disappointment

By Mike Hall

The 104th Congress that roared like a dangerous lion when it came to Washington last year armed with a "Contract on America" left town meekly after passing an omnibus spending bill that left worker programs with funds and anti-worker riders on the shelf.

"This was a major victory," said AFL-CIO Legislative Director Peggy Taylor, who credited the federation's persistent, high-profile grass-roots campaign that kept the pressure on members of Congress in their home districts throughout the year.

Workers not only beat back assaults on programs important to working families and insidious attacks on unions, but they came away with a minimum wage increase that no one thought this Congress would pass.

Still, workers at Federal Express suffered a setback in their organizing attempts when the Senate passed an FAA measure that contained language, slipped into the bill at FedEx's behest, that the company could use to argue that its workers come under the auspices of the Rail Labor Act instead of the National Labor Relations Act.

The spending bill, with Labor/HHS appropriations and five other unfinished spending measures for fiscal 1997 wrapped into it, sailed through as the budget cutters kept their knives in check.

House Republicans earlier had passed a Labor/HHS bill that cut funding for the Occupational Safety and Health Administration, the National Labor Relations Board, education and training and wage enforcement services, as well as several anti-worker riders.

One of those provisions banned use of "official time" — the time union reps spend on labor-management programs and other representational activities — at the Social Security Administration and the Health Care Financing Administration. Another would have allowed prisoners to be paid less than the minimum wage to make products that compete with privately manufactured ones, thus undercutting the private sector.

House and Senate Democrats and the Clinton administration vowed to restore cuts in vital spending programs and fight the anti-worker provisions.

With campaigns beckoning, the end of the fiscal year approaching and still scarred from their government shutdowns when they refused to compromise on fiscal 1996 spending, GOP leaders backed down and dealt.

Continued on Page 4

Voter turnout efforts take hold

Electronic voter guides punctuate Labor '96 drive

By Michael Byrne

More than 10,000 new union activists are busy in congressional districts across the country, explaining the issues to their union brothers and sisters and urging them to get out and vote this Nov. 5.

Labor '96 has moved into the all-important get-out-the-vote (GOTV) phase, as AFL-CIO and affiliated union staff have dispersed to help coordinators mobilize union workers around issues important to working families.

At the same time, the federation was airing new television and radio voter guides providing information to voters on where candidates stand on the issues.

"The electronic voter guides are one more step in the AFL-CIO's continuing effort to raise the issues that are central to the lives of working Americans and to shine a light on Congress's and candidates' records with respect to those issues," said AFL-CIO President John J. Sweeney.

"We plan to continue to lobby officeholders and would-be officeholders to adopt positions on issues like education, health care and retirement security that are good for working people," he said.

This year, working women were being engaged in the political discussion as never before, with a full week of outreach cosponsored by the AFL-CIO Working Women's Department and 9to5, the National Association of Working Women. **(See story, Page 4.)**

The AFL-CIO's issues-based campaign continued to draw fire from the Republican Party leadership, which filed suit to force the Federal Election Commission to act on its numerous complaints. The suit amounts to "another publicity stunt," said AFL-CIO General Counsel Jon Hiatt, who said it was filed "to distract public attention from the real issue in this

Continued on Page 4

Seven-year battle yields card-check win at SF Marriott

By Muriel H. Cooper

Workers at the Marriott Hotel in San Francisco won an historic, hard-fought victory for representation by the Hotel Employees and Restaurant Employees Local 2.

The Marriott — the largest nonunion hotel in the city — agreed to recognize the local through a card-check agreement. The union is hoping to start contract negotiations by the end of the year.

"This is an historical breakthrough that is directly related to the local restructuring and its emphasis on organizing," said AFL-CIO Organizing Director Richard Bensinger in a ceremony attended by workers and San Francisco Mayor Willie Brown, who applauded the recognition.

Marriott traditionally has resisted unions rather forcefully. "We look forward to a period of mutual respect between Marriott and the employees of their company here in San Francisco," said Bensinger.

Marriott had entered into a card-check agreement with the local years before it opened its doors in 1989. But then the hotel rejected moves by the union to implement the card check.

"Their definition was different than ours," said Michael Casey, the local's president. "We had a different interpretation of what the agreement was."

A legal battle and boycott ensued until 1995, when the parties agreed to mediation to settle the lawsuit short of a trial. Last month, Special Master John Kagel certified that a majority of the workers had signed cards authorizing the local to represent them.

The commitment of financial and human resources made this win happen, Casey said.

"We told our members that this fight is critical for us to continue to set standards for all working families," he said. "We realigned our resources and took $200,000 out of the strike fund and put it into organizing. Then the members agreed to use $2 a month in dues money for organizing.

"We had a strong in-house committee of about 60 workers who got cards signed in about a week," Casey said. "We also had many community allies who helped."

There is a valuable lesson in the San Francisco experience, Bensinger said. "The futility of going through the labor board process is so great that the AFL-CIO is less and less choosing that route.

Continued on Page 3

The key tenets of this working group's report to the AFL-CIO became the guiding precepts of how the AFL-CIO is conducting communications. "Unless we change the public face of the labor movement, we will fail to organize, bargain good contracts or win political and legislative gains for working people," the report begins. We require a "strategic plan, a common message and new images."

MEDIA OUTREACH

No longer does the Department of Information founder with one beleaguered staffer devoted to answering press queries. Today, the AFL-CIO has a handful of media outreach professionals, whose job is to pitch stories to a press increasingly interested in news related both to the labor movement and to working families. Sweeney often travels with a press person, who is available to set up press conferences or simply answer media requests.

When critical campaigns—either organizing, political action, or legislative—arise, media training for union leadership is on the agenda. For instance, as part of the unions' fight against the assault on their new activism by the Republicans' union dues initiatives (Republican state and federal legislation to limit the use of union dues for political education and issues advocacy, deviously called the "Paycheck Protection Act"), the AFL-CIO called a weekend meeting of leadership and staff from affiliates, state and local federations not simply to plan a retaliatory strategy, but to coach each participant in how to conduct him or herself in a TV interview, applying a message crafted by the AFL-CIO, in consultation with both union and non-union workers.

INTERNAL COMMUNICATIONS

One of the first things to change internally at the AFL-CIO was the weekly publication, the *AFL-CIO News*, a newspaper that read too often like a collection of press releases from the leadership. As Denise Mitchell recalls, someone asked the question: "What job does the *AFL-CIO News* do for us and is that the priority job? It was a medium of record, but it wasn't movement building." Today, the AFL-CIO publishes a monthly magazine called *America@Work*, a magazine fashioned to look like a cross between *Rolling Stone* and *Newsweek* magazine's Periscope front section, filled with pithy news items, ideas for activists, and features like profiles of organizers, primers on the usefulness of affirmative action, suggestions on how to fight for health and safety on the job, and economics for working people. The magazine has a letters to the editor section and asks for feedback, either through mail or e-mail. It includes clip-out charts on the economy for use in local newsletters or local union meetings. *America@Work* presently reaches between 60,000 and 75,000 top and secondary leaders, local union presidents, shop stewards, and activists.

Replacing the timeliness of the *AFL-CIO News* came *Work in Progress*, a weekly fax sheet that goes out to several thousand union leaders, modeled on a weekly news fax used by several international unions to connect staff and members who live and work around the country, listing everything from organizing to political mobilizations, coalitional campaigns, visits by AFL-CIO officers to particular regions of the country, legislative victories, elections, deaths, and other items of interest. To bring home a point, *WIP* always puts organizing wins first. Both publications are sent out to the media, providing a resource for future stories.

Additionally, the AFL-CIO now has a broadcast division, where professionals create videos for use in union campaigns and mobilizations. One of the first produced was the "Change to Organize" video to support the AFL-CIO's stated goals to step up organizing. "Rather than media as an end in itself," Mitchell explains, the video staff produces "rapid response tools" and "tools for activists." (Before the broadcast division, the AFL-CIO maintained a department known as LIPA [the Labor Institute for Public Affairs] established in the 1980s to create cutting edge video, which it did, but without any relation to the activities and mobilization of union campaigns).

The AFL-CIO website has been given a face lift, but more importantly, it now contains specialized sites devoted to specific campaigns. For instance, there was a page on the site for the fast track legislative campaign, with information on how to get active and how to contact legislators. From the site, someone can download flyers, send e-mail, and obtain fact sheets. A page called "Executive Pay Watch" made headlines when it was first put up. It includes the salaries of some of America's richest and speaks to the new populist tone of the AFL-CIO.

There is also ongoing discussion about how best to integrate the efforts of the affiliate unions' publications with the ongoing work of the Federation. Every union has some sort of national publication that reaches most of its members. Additionally, individual unions produce videos, websites, educational publications, weekly faxes, and more for their own membership. Many unions on the regional and local levels have internal communications mechanisms. Honing in on a unified message for key campaigns, sharing graphics, and inter-linking websites are all being looked at as ways to strengthen the overall voice of American workers.

FORM FOLLOWS FUNCTION

Almost immediately after taking office, Sweeney, Trumka, and Chavez-Thompson fanned out around the country, joining local union leadership in "America Needs a Raise" Town Hall Meetings in twenty-four cities, coinciding with the 1996 congressional fight on raising the minimum wage. Each meeting brought a slew of press coverage as workers got up and testified about their workplace, family, and broad economic concerns. The meetings were augmented by a paid TV and radio ad campaign highlighting the debate and grassroots action to assist union members in voicing their concerns to Congress. In the end, the unexpected—even unbelievable—happened. The minimum wage went up under a Republican-majority Congress.

But an important ingredient of the AFL-CIO-led fight to raise the minimum wage was that the fight was perceived—rightly so—as a fight for all workers, in fact, largely for non-union workers—since most unionized workers already either earn above the minimum wage or have the benefit of a union contract by which to fight for their wage increases. Unlike past union struggles around more parochial issues like legislation to protect striking workers, this fight was waged on behalf of America. In fact, when "America Needs a Raise" was first conceived, it was intended to highlight America's wage gap. The coincidence of the minimum wage legislation worked quite well.

The "America Needs A Raise" slogan resonated because it was unparochial and it reflected the concerns—both economical and moral—many workers feel today about a broad range of declining economic and workplace standards. In an America that needs to raise the standards by which it treats its workers, the animated voice of the AFL-CIO is being heard.

Much of the organizing and activism of the labor movement presently is focused on a more sympathetic workforce. The fight to organize farmworkers, who have long been considered the soul of the labor movement, the fight to eradicate sweatshops, and the fight to give a voice to immigrant workers in hotels and restaurants—all illuminate the need for coalition building, for building "new bridges to other parts of the social justice world by doing it around goals we all share," according to Mitchell. We are banding together in struggles that organized labor should be waging regardless—on behalf of low-wage workers in an economy where the low-wage sector is expanding.

Trade unions can't grow without expanding the pool of coalition allies, and the only way to win an economic agenda that addresses the concerns of American workers is by building a majority. In another successful legislative battle once seen as quixotic—to

British singer/songwriter Billy Bragg performing at an anti-sweatshop rally in New York City.

defeat fast track trade authority in 1997—the AFL-CIO embraced the environmental community's message of concern regarding clean water and unregulated pesticides sprayed on food coming from Mexico, even airing TV ads about food safety, rather than a more expected message about job retention. Food safety issues helped sway votes by expanding support for labor's position. Were the ads solely about job loss, or even about the more expansive concern of workers' rights at home and abroad, it's unlikely that the congressional vote pool needed to defeat fast track would have been expanded. In effect, the AFL-CIO was talking about the global economy in a new and resonant manner to a new audience.

A column by Sweeney in *America@Work* titled "Building Community Ties" lists recent issues where coalition work aided workers' struggles: the UPS strike, job safety at the Avondale naval shipyard outside New Orleans where religious leaders joined workers in forcing an employer to sit with the union after severe job injuries and a long organizing campaign, fighting sweatshops and child labor, and a contract campaign at a nursing home in Alabama where workers were joined by patients' families, among others. The cross-fertilization at work here both bolsters and is bolstered by labor's changing image.

REPOSITIONING CAMPAIGN

"You Have A Voice; Make It Heard; Today's Unions," now the tag line for the AFL-CIO, was emblazoned on a large backdrop on a concert stage in downtown Pittsburgh, where the final night of the 1997 AFL-CIO Convention ended with a concert featuring British rocker Billy Bragg and American folk musicians Tish Hinajosa and Toshi Reagan. The AFL-CIO sent their top leadership with a message to the twenty-something college crowd. Before the music began, Sweeney and Chavez-Thompson stood to the right of the stage and offered a message about the future of the economy that embraced the audience.

Earlier that day, Bragg had performed a solo guitar version of "There is Power in a Union," one of his signature songs, to an audience of top union leadership, many of whom, up till that point, had no idea who Bragg was. Bragg, delighted to be attending the AFL-CIO convention as an "honored guest," reciprocated after the Pittsburgh meeting by volunteering to perform at an anti-sweatshop

The Bones of Contention

rally in New York City's Herald Square hours before he was scheduled for a club performance. Labor is becoming hip. For the first time ever, polling conducted by Hart Research has shown that the twenty-something generation is open to a union message that speaks to the insecurity in today's economy.

The repositioning campaign launched by the AFL-CIO began in 1997, with ads and slogans airing in five test markets. But a repositioning campaign for labor has to be about more than creative advertising. The repositioning TV campaign is part of the ongoing field mobilization activity of the Federation. In each community where the ads appear, community outreach programs are planned, along with local union meetings to build on local campaigns. Cities are chosen after consulting with the local union leadership to once again ensure media and grassroots coverage. TV alone does not a movement make. Yet in the TV age, seeing positive, even inviting images of union members, lends a needed legitimacy to the AFL-CIO's efforts especially to young people. Part of repositioning after all is literally re-positioning, that is, reaching out to new groups of people, like American youth.

Immediately after the AFL-CIO election in 1995, two labor historians, Steve Fraser and Nelson Lichtenstein, authored a letter of support from a long list of intellectuals and academics to the new leadership. The letter, which was published in the *New York Review of Books* and as an op-ed in the *Washington Post*, spawned a standing-room only crowd at a teach-in at Columbia University, which was backed by the AFL-CIO. The point of the teach-in was to link "nitty-gritty" workplace issues related to graduate students, faculty or working personnel to the broader issues of all workers and to build support for the new AFL-CIO and to strategies of workers trying to organize. After Columbia, the steering group of academics, writers, and trade union staff helped organize nine other teach-ins, from elite schools to community colleges. Building on this effort, others organized on their own, culminating in over thirty teach-ins so far, at colleges in every region of the country. Fraser said that once the Columbia teach-in was perceived as a success—with news coverage in the *New York Times,* the *Los Angeles Times ,* the *Chicago Tribune,* many journals and magazines, and an airing on C-span—the other teach-ins were organized, "partly because the AFL-CIO took a direct role and a great many were spontaneous."

The payoff of re-igniting the intellectual-union alliance is just beginning to surface. "Before the teach-ins," Fraser told me, "the image of labor on most college campuses was probably invisible or irrelevant. The impact of the teach-ins has been to establish a presence that says to the university community—you ought to take notice or care about labor." Fraser said that the teach-ins highlighted the question, "How do we as intellectuals understand our identity as working people and what is our connection to all working people?"

Indeed, in addition to recruiting the next generation of workers to union membership and union activism, the teach-ins spotlighted increasing labor disputes within the universities as institutions, where the growth of the service and white-collar sector is felt acutely. In fact, a long and bitter struggle for a fair contract by Barnard College's clerical workers (represented by the UAW) ended just before the teach-in. The victorious workers shared the stage with Columbia's President Rupp who, himself, settled a dispute with his own university's support workers months after the teach-in, clearly influenced by the positive association forged between the AFL-CIO and the university at the Columbia teach-in. The teach-ins have spawned a new academic-intellectual labor-support group, Scholars, Artists, & Writers for Social Justice (SAWSJ), with which the AFL-CIO continues to work.

But just as important as using the university as a recruitment mechanism, the end of the schism between labor and the intellectual class is an historic and useful resolution to a split that occurred in the early 1960s. The corporatist, conservative agenda needs to be challenged both by a mobilized movement of workers and by new ideas forged in the academy, and more importantly, presented in the op-ed pages, on the air waves, and in cyberspace. Workers need an echo chamber to reinforce their own voices, demands, and concerns. In the shouting match that has become the stage and screen for American media and punditry, anti-corporate voices and ideas need to be multiplied ten-fold.

As someone who has worked in labor communications for over a decade, I have long bemoaned the lack of coverage given to working Americans and, by extension, to the AFL-CIO. I can no longer make that complaint. For example, on February 5, 1998, the *New York Times* had four stories about the labor movement in one day, something virtually unheard of just a few years ago. On the national page, an article chronicled the triumphant resolution to the longest strike in the U.S. in almost four decades, by workers at Las Vegas' Frontier Hotel and Casino who walked off the job in September, 1991. The front page of the Metropolitan section carried a story about the successful end of a bitter four-year strike of restaurant workers at a high-end New York City restaurant. Though both of these strikes began way before labor's overhaul, the newfound strength and image of organized labor were factors in their triumphal resolutions, and certainly in the prominent press coverage. Meanwhile, a well-placed article in the business section ran with the headline "Rare Bird in Davos: Labor Chief Makes His Points," as the story offered an account of John Sweeney's visit to the Davos World Economic Forum, hardly the typical stop for union leaders. (In fact, Sweeney was the first U.S. union official ever to attend, though 1998 was his second visit, having also attended the previous year.) His actions—speaking out to the global corporate elite about the impact of the global economy on working people—made news while making a point. The final article, also in the Metro section, dealt with a local union official accused of financial improprieties in the running of his union. Yet, where once an article like that would have been the only news seen fit to print, put in the context of today's labor movement, readers can view it with the proper perspective as a bad seed in an otherwise fertile and exuberant field.

As a movement, we have come a long way in a short time, though we are not yet where we need to be. We are still fragile enough that any negative publicity appears to threaten the very essence of the trade union movement. Increasing power for American workers, through more union organizing and more successful anti-corporate campaigns, will strengthen labor's hand by placing workers at the core of the fight for how America enters the next century. The ultimate public relations challenge is for the union movement in today's America to take its rightful and incontestable place in the fabric of American civil society, the place unions hold in Europe, and increasingly in other industrialized nations of the world like South Africa and Korea—a place we once held. The threads by which we regain our hold on American society are the intertwining threads of form and function.

WOMEN IN LABOR

Always the Bridesmaid?

karen nussbaum

When I was 23, I had my astrological chart read. The astrologer had much to say; it took her a good five hours to get through it all. I quickly forgot most of what she said, but one thing stayed with me because I couldn't make head or tail of it. She prophesied that there would be many men in my life—old, heavy-set, bald men with pinky rings. I didn't get it. Who were these guys? Why were they in my future? The only person I could think of who fit the description was my grandfather, Papa Phil, who had passed away years before.

A few years later, the prophecy came true. In 1975, I entered the labor movement, and there they were—pinky rings and all. But now it was my turn to make a prophecy. I looked at the labor movement and I saw big changes in the offing. The biggest sector of the workforce was composed of women office workers, some 20 million strong. In them I saw the seeds of a great transformation. It wouldn't be long, I predicted, before women workers, led by secretaries, file clerks, and bank tellers, would expand the women's movement out of the middle class and into the workplace. The voice of working women would transform the labor movement. A great wave of organizing would sweep the country, bringing women into unions by the millions.

It didn't happen exactly the way I foresaw, but I got quite a few things right. Around the time of my astrological reading, a small group of friends and I started 9 to 5, Boston's organization for office workers. We went on to create our own union affiliated with the Service Employees International Union (SEIU). When we first joined up with SEIU, there weren't many women leaders. It wasn't until 1980 that this majority-female union had a woman vice-president. When I joined the Executive Board in 1984, only eighteen percent of us were women.

I was a little off about which sector of the workforce would take the lead. While clerical organizing has been important in the last few decades, it is women workers in health care, food service, and light manufacturing who have really taken off. And everything took a bit longer than I expected—what I thought would be a five-year timetable turned into 25 years. It was years before women were to be included in the leadership of unions, years before women were to be accepted as serious organizers, years before women's issues were to be understood as workers' issues and union issues. We were at the party, but had no one to dance with. Year

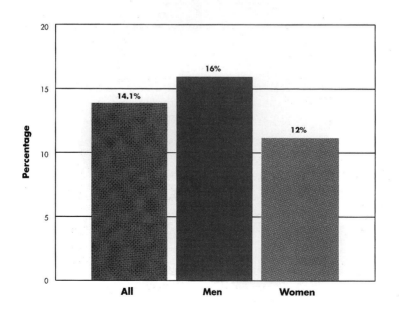

UNION MEMBERSHIP AS PERCENTAGE OF EMPLOYMENT, 1997

after year, I wondered whether women in labor were destined to be always the bridesmaid, never the bride.

At long last, women are beginning to assume our rightful place in unions. In 1995, the landmark election of John Sweeney, Richard Trumka, and Linda Chavez-Thompson to the top offices of the AFL-CIO represented a dramatic break with the past. Organizing —of all types of workers in all parts of the economy—became the number one priority of American labor. And the demand that our movement must reflect the diversity of the American workforce resounded loud and clear.

The importance of women to the future of labor had become inescapable. Two in five union members are women. With 5.5 million women members, the AFL-CIO is the largest working women's organization in the country. Now, for the first time, we're seeking to live up to that description. In 1996, President Sweeney created the first AFL-CIO Working Women's Department and invested it with a sweeping mandate: "to bring the concerns of working women into every nook and cranny of the labor movement and to turn the labor movement into an activist voice for all working women."

As predicted, we're on our way.

ALL DRESSED UP AND NOWHERE TO GO

In the traditional telling, labor's story in this country has been a decidedly male affair — decade after decade of union men slugging it out with titans of business, also all men. Our picture of the Industrial Age is of men working in mines, steel mills, and auto plants. As late as the 1970s, when I started working, the word "worker" still evoked a man in a hardhat.

But these images are wrong. Women in the textile and garment trades—not just men in heavy industry—powered the Industrial Age. And in 1970, the average worker was not a construction worker; the typical worker was someone like me, a woman at a typewriter.

Contrary to the stereotype, women have always been key to union organizing in this country. Women textile workers organized and went on a series of strikes throughout the 1880s. The 1884 strikes of women textile workers and hatmakers in New York led the head of the Knights of Labor to dub them "the best men in the order." The first union of African-American women workers was the "Washer Women of Jackson," formed by women laundry workers in 1886 in Mississippi. In the new century, women cannery workers, bookbinders, cracker packers, waitresses, packinghouse workers, salesclerks, teachers, and telephone operators organized.

A revolt of women garment workers in New York came to be known as "The Uprising of the 20,000." When 60,000 New York cloakmakers went on strike in 1910, 75% of them were women.

In 1911, the fire at the Triangle Shirtwaist Factory killed 146 women and girls, rocking the nation and providing the impetus for the creation of protective legislation. But these workers were not passive victims. The Triangle workers had gone on strike in 1909, inspiring the Uprising of the 20,000. While hundreds of shops signed contracts for better working conditions, Triangle did not. As a result, the workers' demands for fire escapes and unlocked doors went unmet.

A cut in pay for women and children textile workers in Massachusetts sparked the Lawrence Strike of 1912. Strikers created the tactic of mass picketing, with 5,000 to 20,000 textile workers forming a human chain, weaving around the mills to keep out scabs. Big Bill Haywood deemed the women to be every bit as militant as the men.

The militancy of women workers didn't stop in the olden days. Waitresses organized throughout the '30s and '40s—by the late 1940s, more than 200,000 women culinary workers were organized, with close to a quarter of these in separate, women-only waitress organizations. In 1946, the walkout of women department store workers in Oakland, California, sparked a general strike involving more than 120,000 workers. Two-thirds of the 350,000 telephone workers who went on strike in 1947 were women. And in the 1960s and early 1970s, teachers' unions tripled in membership to more than 2 million, the vast majority of whom were women.

In 1974, women in unions demanded an organized voice for themselves across unions and created the Coalition of Labor Union Women. Thirty-five hundred women crammed into a Chicago hotel, far exceeding all expectations. In the famous words of Myra Wolfgang of the UAW, "Tell [AFL-CIO President] George Meany we didn't come here

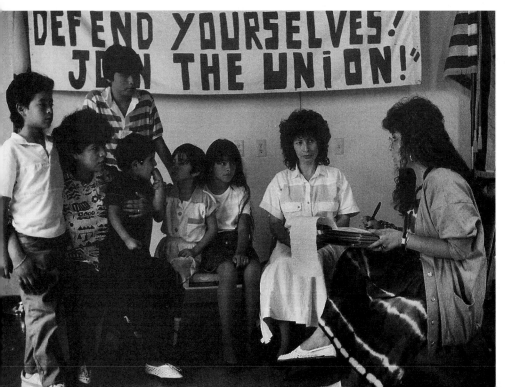

to swap recipes." At that time, the only department in the AFL-CIO headed by a woman was the library. It wasn't until 1980 that a woman was elected to the AFL-CIO Executive Council. As late as 1995, only three out of twenty AFL-CIO departments were headed by women.

Women had always worked for pay, and had served as a crucial reserve labor force at key times, such as the expansion of industry in the late 1800s and early 1900s, World War I, and the shift from manufacturing to the service sector that began in the 1970s. They had also fought for their rights as workers. But entry into the male world of labor unions remained hard and leadership roles non-existent. Women in the labor movement—all dressed up and nowhere to go.

Until now. Today, finally, women workers are coming into their own. Over the last twelve years, women have led the ranks of new recruits into America's unions. More women than men say they would join a union if given the chance (49% of working women compared to 41% of working men). Contrary to the American ethic, women overwhelmingly believe it is more effective to join together to solve problems on the job than it is to solve problems on their own.

ASK A WORKING WOMAN

How do we know? We asked. The AFL-CIO Working Women's Department wanted to restart a conversation with the nation's working women. Early in 1997, we set out to learn about what women care about the most, the language they use, and the way they think of themselves. We met face to face with working women on their jobs and in their homes and communities. We conducted focus groups. We went on a national tour, with dozens of meetings, from a school library to the 17th floor of a construction site to a hotel kitchen.

We distributed a survey with the help of 1,000 local partners—organizations from the National Korean American Service and Education Consortium to the National Association of Female Executives, from the Fenton Area Chamber of Commerce in Missouri to the Mt. Olive Baptist Church in Hackensack, NJ, and from the YWCA of Pekin, IL, to unions across the country. Fifty thousand women responded. Their stories were confirmed by a scientific poll. Women have their own view of their priorities; that view is remarkably consistent across lines of income, race, and region. The reality of their lives often contradicts what the media and political leaders would have them believe. Here's what they told us:

Women are quick to identify with the label "working women" and feel they share a set of common concerns with other women who work. This is especially true of women without a college degree, across races. Many of them choose the phrase "working woman" spontaneously to describe themselves, and they agree without hesitation that the label applies to them and most of the women they know. All look at working women as women who need money. "I look at myself," said one African-American woman. "Working woman, that's just who I am," echoed a white woman. A Latina described herself and others like her as "strong women...because we are willing to do anything. We work." "The woman has to work," one woman summed up. "It's not like it used to be."

Women feel confident about their role as workers and know their families depend on them. "I assign the work of all the guys on the team," said a crew leader at a Milwaukee auto plant. "I work hard but I don't do overtime at work," she continued, "and I don't do windows at home."

A welder took off her asbestos gloves to reveal polished inch-long nails. "I think of myself like Xena, a warrior. Very strong," a midwestern Latina said.

Flight attendants in Atlanta were angry that they are "treated like children."

A widowed Asian-American hotel kitchen worker told of putting her two children through school, recovering from a disabling back injury, enjoying ballroom dancing—and organizing the union at her hotel.

Nearly two-thirds of working women report that they provide half or more of their household income. More than half (52%) of married women contribute about half or more of their household income. Two out of five working women head their own households and 28% of them have dependent children. Political leaders may persist in painting women as secondary wage earners, but women know their pay is essential.

"Women have to decide what's more important," one Republican politician said, "raising their children or having a second car." Women see it differently. "It is very important to have a job so that I don't have to depend on somebody to take care of me," one woman said.

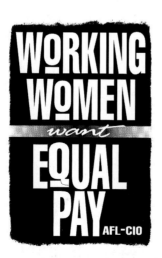

They believe they have it harder at work because they are women. "Because we are women, they pay less," was a typical statement by a woman in Chicago. "Men in my company get the promotions and women don't," echoed a woman in Baltimore. Other women mentioned the "good old boy network" which ensures that men get everything and the women get pushed aside. "They get all the perks," stated this low-income woman.

If they feel their lot as working women is unfair at work, they also believe they do more than their share at

home. "Men don't have to worry about the kids," said a white woman, and a Latina agreed: "The man comes home, takes a shower, eats and goes to sleep, and the woman is washing, cleaning, doing, doing." Some women take pride in their ability to do more than men: "A man can only do one job at a time, where women can do five. Men could only mow the grass but women could cook, do wash...and take care of the children at the same time."

Others are resigned. Asked whether men would be interested in family-friendly work policies such as flex-time, one woman replied, "I don't know if men would be interested in flexibility. My husband thinks flexibility is being willing to sleep on the other side of the bed."

For millions of working women, the most urgent concern is one that has received scant public attention. The media has been telling women for a decade that our most important problem is juggling work and family. And working women agree that we need policies that allow us to be good parents and responsible workers. But while the media has remained largely silent on the issue of equal pay for years, women have been seething about it. Ninety-nine percent of women say equal pay is important, yet one-third say they don't have it. And it's not just women who are concerned about equal pay. In survey after survey, women *and* men cite equal pay as a top solution to family income problems.

Responses to the "Ask A Working Woman" survey show the frustration working women feel about equal pay. A woman from the state of Washington wrote, "We get less pay for the job done than a man. . . . They don't pay what you're really worth." A New Jersey

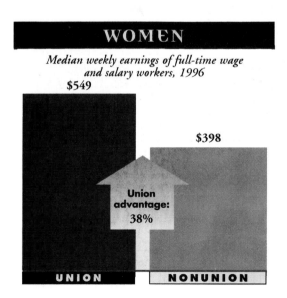

WOMEN

Median weekly earnings of full-time wage and salary workers, 1996

$549

$398

Union advantage: 38%

UNION   NONUNION

woman explained: "Women working in professions that are historically and presently comprised of women (i.e nursing) are still not being treated and paid like their male-counterpart professionals."

Women's feelings that their paychecks are essential for their families reinforce their concern with equal pay. One woman wrote, "Women need to be able to support themselves and/or their families."

The problems are even worse for some groups of working women. Half of African

American working women (50%) say they want equal pay but do not have it. Nearly half (42%) of women in pink-collar jobs—clerical and secretarial positions—say that equal pay is important but do not have it.

Despite the talk of an improving economy, most working women think things have gotten worse over the last five years. Staggering numbers of women go without basic benefits. On nearly every measure, women told us that the situation for working women had gotten worse, rather than better, over the last five years. More than nine out of ten working women say that protection from downsizing and layoffs is important, but only one-third say they are protected. Working women believe that over the last five years job security, finding affordable child care, and making ends meet are worse.

And no wonder they are having a harder time: one-third of working women lack retirement benefits, nearly a third (30%) lack health coverage, and nearly a third (29%) don't even have paid sick leave. "I work to pay the health insurance, not to take my kids to Disneyland," one woman told me. A 42- year-old clerical worker worried that "At my age, one of my biggest concerns is how I will live when I retire. No benefits makes it hard after 10 years at the same place."

We hear a lot in the media about "family-friendly" businesses, but most working women have never gotten close to a family-friendly policy. Only one out of ten working women reports getting any help from her job with child care or elder care, and two out of five say they don't have flexible hours or control over their hours. A Wisconsin woman

What's getting better and what's getting worse?

I'd like to ask you about the situation for working women now compared to the situation five years ago. For each of the situations I mention, please tell me whether you think it has gotten better in the last five years, gotten worse or stayed the same.

SOURCE: LAKE SOSIN SNELL PERRY AND ASSOCIATES

	BETTER	WORSE	SAME	BETTER-WORSE
Job security	26%	**41%**	31%	-15
Finding affordable child care*	15%	**39%**	17%	-24
Making ends meet	29%	**37%**	31%	-8
Saving for retirement	30%	**37%**	28%	-7
Health care coverage	32%	**37%**	26%	-5
Juggling work and family	29%	**29%**	37%	0
Promotions and advancement	31%	**21%**	42%	+10

*On child care, 29 percent don't know. For the other questions, the percent who responded "don't know" is 6 percent or less.
Note: Percentages may not total 100 due to rounding and "don't know" responses.

said she needs "more flexibility in work hours, so I can attend parent-teacher conferences and school events. I work second shift and don't have that option. We need my income to make ends meet. So my kids suffer."

Another woman pleaded, "Please, I need flex-time in the morning once or twice a week so I can drop my daughter off at school and see her go in the door. If this does not happen soon, my job of seventeen years will be gone." A Michigan woman wrote, "Companies have this idea that there is no other life outside of your job—six and seven day operations and ten and twelve hour days are destroying family life."

Despite America's "get ahead on your own" ethos, a whopping four out of five working women say it is more effective to solve problems by joining together. And why not? That's the way most women lead their lives. If you have to report to work early, you drop off your kid at your neighbor's. If your mother is sick, you work with your sister to share the grocery shopping and the doctor visits. Women want to use this mutually cooperative approach on the job, too. Women expect more from business (96% say business has a role to play in addressing the problems at work) and from government (79%). But they also believe working women's organizations (92%) and unions (75%) can be helpful.

The same issues and themes reverberate throughout conversations with working women, but there are some differences in emphasis. Latinas are among the most focused on family issues; Asian-Americans are more focused on discrimination. African-Americans are the most militant about organizing. Young women are concentrated in retail jobs and are more likely to want child care but not have it. Pink-collar workers see the lack of basic benefits as a major problem.

WORKING WOMEN WORKING TOGETHER

A postal worker from New Hampshire spoke for many working women in a letter she addressed to the members of the AFL-CIO:

> Thank you for sending me the survey on working women and for the attention you're giving to working women's issues. Presently, I'm a United States postal worker. The pay and benefits are great. What I find difficult to handle is when I need to stay home from work to care for a sick child. I have 2 children, ages 6 and 4. . . Both have had chicken pox, conjunctivitis, as well as the usual viral illnesses.

> Of course, I feel guilty missing work at times. I don't have a back-up person to take care of my children when they are ill. I feel torn when my children are ill. . . . They're what I'm working for. Please keep me informed.

The "Ask A Working Woman" Survey was not just a report, but a mandate. Nearly 2,000 women—most union members, many not—jammed a Washington, D.C., hotel the weekend after Labor Day in 1997 and pledged to carry out campaigns on equal pay, child care, and power at the ballot box. Valencia Baker from Baltimore begged to be let in to the over-subscribed conference by writing on her registration form, "Please! I will be active, I promise!"

Alma Richards said of the conference,"Oh, I'm hyped up, yes." Debbie Macklin said, "I mean, I'm feeling strong. It's great." And Armeta Dixon wasn't alone when she said, "I'm just so charged and ready to do something. Something substantial."

Stephanie Walker from the Greater Syracuse Labor Council wrote, "I still have goosebumps from the Working Women Working Together Conference. . . . We have heard the call and we are ready to act. . . .There ain't no stopping us now!!!" A dozen unions, state federations, and central labor councils have started or revived women's committees. A local Oil, Chemical and Atomic Workers' officer from Ponca City, Oklahoma, wrote to tell us of forming a "Steering Committee for the Working Woman." "I am encouraged and have great hope that together we will accomplish great success," she said.

The leadership of the AFL-CIO is making changes in its house. Linda Chavez-Thompson is the first woman to be elected as a top officer of the AFL-CIO. As president, John Sweeney increased the number of women department heads from 6% to 50%. Women members of the Executive Council have increased from none before 1980 to 15% today. But clearly this isn't enough. At the 1997 AFL-CIO Convention, John Sweeney called on the delegates to set and achieve an important goal. "My idea of a perfect labor movement is one that corrects its own imperfections. With all that we've accomplished over the past two years, we haven't done that when it comes to making the face of our leadership reflect the faces of our membership and of the new American workforce. I ask you to join me in a renewed effort to bring more women and minorities into the leadership of our movement at every level."

These changes are essential. Women, like other groups, don't want to join an organization if they can't see themselves in it. When asked to imagine an organization that would work on their issues, working women said they wanted "women in key places in it," and "women in top positions."

But there's little point in promoting gender without an agenda. If America's unions and America's working women are to thrive, we need a powerful program focused on issues women care about.

THE PROGRAM

The AFL-CIO Working Women's Department is pursuing just such a focused program to reach out to union and non-union women alike.

Working Women Want Equal Pay

Working at the grassroots level we can turn this private insult—the lack of equal pay—into a public issue once again. We worked with women's organizations to hold hundreds of local events on a national day of action, Equal Pay Day. We're taking legal action where necessary, direct action where we can. We've stepped up organizing and bargaining. We're supporting federal and state legislation which punishes the lawbreakers and makes equal pay available to all women. We'll force politicians to be accountable by letting working women know who's with them and who's against them on equal pay.

Working Together for Kids

We're working with child care advocates to bring the voice of working parents and the needs of child care workers into the debate on expanding and improving child care. "Working Together for Kids" will push for a big investment in child care and after-school programs and for raising the pay of child care workers. Why should child care workers earn less than poodle groomers?

We've fanned out into the community, increasing our bargaining on child care and bringing our voice into the decisions at the state and county level on how child care programs will be funded.

Ten unions in New York formed a child care coalition calling for more state funding of child care and a multi-union child care fund, the first coalition of its kind in the country. Brian McLaughlin, president of the New York Central Labor Council, who hails from the International Brotherhood of Electrical Workers, called child care a "fundamental issue. . . like the 8-hour workday, minimum wage and occupational safety and health."

Working Women Vote

We strive to be everywhere at election time, reminding the politicians that working women vote. If anything, the vote of working women loomed as even more important for 1998 and 2000 than in the past. We've hit a thousand communities with the message that working women know more than the politicians when it comes to real social policy, and it's time we were heard. The price of macaroni and cheese can be as important as macro-economics, and politicians need to respond to what we care about most.

Working Women Organize

Not only is there a gender gap in politics, there's a gender gap in organizing. More women are organizing than are men. Union campaigns in workplaces that are a majority female are more likely to win than are campaigns where women are in the minority. Women are considered by many organizers to be more likely to stick with the union in a long fight.

Imagine what unions could do if they deliberately built on their strength among women workers. Unions need to talk to women workers and listen when they talk back. Nor should we be afraid to tap into the deep well of emotion—pride at what they've accomplished, anger at being held back, passion for the well-being of their families— that these workers feel as women. Think about it. Would a good organizer avoid talking about health and safety to a group of workers who have been injured? Of course not. Working women experience injury and insult every day on the job—and they will tell you so. They don't feel at odds with men. But they do believe they have a particular experience, and unions need to acknowledge that experience and respond to it.

Women can play a key role in the union movement's campaign to make the right to organize our central theme. The right to organize should be considered a basic women's right. Because women are nearly half the workforce and contribute at least half their families' income, workers' rights are women's rights. Because women make up a majority of minimum wage workers, part-time workers and temporary workers, workers' rights are women's rights. Because half of working women are in jobs where they don't even have the right to organize, workers' rights are women's rights. The right to organize a union should be considered a civil right for all Americans—and the tie to women's rights can be a powerful argument.

A Network for Every Woman Who Wants to Make Changes on the Job

Yes, America's unions must make every effort to engage women in traditional union organizing. But we must also reach women who may not be able to participate in a union drive today—or ever. We ought to aim to engage all of America's 61 million women in conversation. We are building a grassroots operation that starts with union women and reaches beyond—to their sisters and aunts, their next-door neighbors and best friends. For every woman who wants to make changes on the job, the Working Women Working Together Network provides useful information and a chance to work for change. Tens of thousands are part of it already.

Going to the Chapel?

When I first started out as a union organizer, I had a recurring dream. I was sitting at the bargaining table, prepared to make some devastating arguments to management, but while my lips moved no sound came out. Throughout my twenty-five years in the labor movement I have often had this feeling. I am shouting, "Women are nearly half the workforce! Concentrated in the growing sectors of the economy! Special consciousness as workers! More likely to believe in collective action!" It has taken many years for the message to begin to get through.

Today, I am more hopeful than ever. Women's role in society and the workforce has fundamentally changed. The leadership of the labor movement is pushing for change. Today's labor movement can and should become the voice of working women. By joining together in the partnership that is unquestionably meant to be, women and unions will make history. It's in the stars.

NOTE

Historical information drawn from Barbara Wertheimer's "We Were There" and from Dorothy Sue Cobble

WORKING WOMEN'S VIEW OF THE ECONOMY, UNIONS, AND PUBLIC POLICY

peter d. hart research associates

This report presents the central findings from public opinion research conducted among working women in recent years by Peter D. Hart Research Associates. The supporting data come primarily from surveys conducted on behalf of the AFL-CIO, although other sources have been drawn upon in some cases. Unless otherwise indicated, the results reported in this document are among *potential union members*, defined as non-union working women (or men) who are employed in a non-supervisory capacity.

An examination of working women's opinions regarding the American economy, work, labor unions, public policy issues, and politics reveals distinctive attitudes and perceptions among this critically important group of workers. The surveys allow us to take a close look at what moves working women as a group—what they care about and what

Working Women

	Working Women	Men
Net positive to unions	+7%	-12%
Union representation election	+3%	-17%
Side w/workers over management	51%	43%
For corporate responsibility laws	58%	42%

kinds of support they seek. The research suggests that it would be difficult to exaggerate the potential significance of working women as a target audience for the labor movement. Women distinguish themselves from men among potential union members by having notably lower negative feelings toward unions, being more likely to vote for union representation in their workplace, feeling more sympathetic to workers vis-à-vis management, and more strongly favoring a range of progressive pro-family public policy initiatives.

The report first presents findings and data regarding working women's perceptions of the economy and their jobs, then explores their attitudes toward labor unions, and concludes with an examination of their perspective on politics and key public policy issues.

ECONOMY AND JOBS

Economy

A Hart Research poll conducted on behalf of the AFL-CIO in January 1998 reveals that increasing numbers of working women are satisfied with the economic situation in the country today. A solid 63 percent of working women are now satisfied with the economy. (Findings from a national survey among, 1,624 general public and union members conducted by Peter D. Hart Research for the AFL-CIO. Interviews were conducted between January 7 and 11, 1998. These data represents result among non-supervisory working women, and include both union and non-union women.) Only 28 percent were satisfied in our May 1996 survey. (Findings from a national survey among 801 union and non-union women conducted by Peter D. Hart Research for the AFL-CIO between May 14 and 16, 1996) The proportion of women dissatisfied with the economy dropped from 70 percent to only 35 percent over the same period.

The apparently rosy state of the economy at present, however, has not eliminated women's anxiety about what may lie ahead. When asked to think ahead to the future, working women are fairly evenly divided between feeling hopeful and confident (50 percent) and being worried and concerned (46 percent) about their economic and financial prospects (Peter D. Hart Research, January 1998). Among non-college-educated working women, just 43 percent feel hopeful and confident, while 52 percent are worried about the future.

Moreover, despite women's increasing satisfaction with the overall state of the economy, they still have serious concerns about economic and work-related issues that they feel need to be addressed. For example, four in ten non-union working women believe that they are not receiving equal pay for equal work, and fully 99 percent feel that this is an important issue (Finding from a national survey of union and non-union working women conducted by Lake, Sogin, Snell + Perry for the AFL-CIO between July 30 and August 3, 1997).

In a January 1998 study for the AFL-CIO, respondents were asked to rate several problems facing the country today, using a 10-point scale on which a "10" means the problem is extremely serious. Among women, the top concerns were families not being able to afford health care coverage (72 percent rate this item as an "8," "9," or "10") and HMOs and health insurance companies restricting access to doctors and quality care (70 percent). It is clear that issues involving health care are at the forefront of working women's minds today. (This will be discussed in more detail later in this report.)

Another problem that women regard as particularly serious is the disparity between wages and salaries with the cost of living (68 percent rate as "8," "9," or "10"). Indeed, just 43 percent of working women report that their family's income is high enough to put money aside for the future, while a majority (56 percent) say either that they can only pay their current bills or cannot even keep up with their bills (Peter D. Hart Research, January 1998). Working people generally feel upbeat about employment prospects today, which drives their more positive assessments of the economy, but they still believe that they need a raise.

While working men share many of their female counterparts' criticisms of today's economy, working women generally attribute more seriousness to the spectrum of economic problems that organized labor seeks to redress. The following table illustrates the issues on which the gender gap is most pronounced. Working women express great concern over the issue of working parents having trouble balancing the responsibilities of both work and family (66 percent of working women rate this as a serious problem, including 73 percent of those under age forty and 74 percent of those making less than

$35,000). They also voice concern about being unable to save enough for a secure retirement (64 percent) and the broader problem of "an economy where large corporations and the wealthy do extremely well, but average working people are just getting by" (64 percent) (Peter D. Hart Research, January 1998).

Proportions Rating Selected Issues as Serious Problems Facing the Country
(Ratings of "8" to "10" on 10-point scale)

	WOMEN	MEN	DIFFERENTIAL
People not being able to save enough money for a secure retirement	64%	43%	+21
Corporations paying huge salaries to CEOs while eliminating the jobs of regular employees	61%	43%	+18
Working parents having trouble balancing the responsibilities of both work and family	66%	52%	+14
Families not being able to afford health care coverage	72%	60%	+12
An economy where large corporations and the wealthy do extremely well, but average working people are just getting by	64%	52%	+12

Job Satisfaction

A majority of both men (70 percent) and women (64 percent) consider their job to be an important aspect of their life (although men are 6 percent more likely than are women to label their job as the most important aspect). Yet, when men and women are asked what takes precedence when they are faced with a conflict between the time demands of work and home, they reveal divergent priorities. A 52 percent majority of women say they will spend more time at home, even if work suffers, while only 36 percent would forego obligations at home in order to meet obligations at work. In contrast, we see a division of opinion among men, who are equally likely to put work first while letting home suffer (43 percent) as to put home first while letting work suffer (45 percent). (Finding from a national survey among 2,004 American union and non-union working women conducted by Hart/Teeter for NBC and the *Wall Street Journal* between September 11 and 15, 1997.)

The priority that women attach to meeting family responsibilities does not mean that they take their career development any less seriously. In a recent NBC News/*Wall Street Journal* study, working men and women were asked which of the following statements comes closer to their point of view:

> **Statement A:** What is most important to me about my job are the wages and benefits.

> **Statement B:** What is most important to me about my job are the opportunities it gives me to use my talents and make a difference

Significantly, working women and men are equally likely (55 percent) to believe that the opportunity to use talents and to make a difference is a more important part of their job than are wages and benefits (Hart/Teeter September 1997).

At the same time, in some important areas, women and men have different perceptions (and presumably, experiences) regarding the workplace. Sixty-one percent of men say that the statement "My company rewards and develops good workers" applies to them, while only 33 percent believe it does not apply. In contrast, 54 percent of women feel that this statement applies to them, and 42 percent say it does not apply (Hart/Teeter September 1997). One of the most frequently voiced work-related complaints we hear from working women is that they are often required to provide training to men who are then promoted over them. Working women's talents continue to go unrecognized in many workplaces, even at levels well below that of the "glass ceiling."

On a more general level, only one-third of working women say that they trust employers to treat their employees fairly, while a strong two-thirds trust employers only some or not much at all on this measure (a sentiment shared by nearly equal numbers of men) (Peter D. Hart Research, January 1998). The following table displays the results from a question in which non-union working women are asked whether their employer provides certain positive working conditions, and includes the five items on which these women are most likely to say their employer does *not* measure up. In only one area – raising wages when profits increase—do a majority feel that their employer does not make the grade. However, at least one-third of all working women affirm that their employer falls short when it comes to opportunities for advancement, paying a living wage, respecting the right to organize, and helping employees balance work and family. (Finding from a national survey among 1,201 general public and 811 union members conducted by Peter D. Hart Research for the AFL-CIO between April 19 and 22, 1996. These data represent results among non-union, non-supervisory working women.)

Proportions of Non-union Working Women Who Say Selected Quality Does Not Describe Their Employer

Raises wages when profits increase	51%
Provides opportunities for advancement	38%
Pays a living wage	37%
Respects the right of employees to join a union	36%
Helps employees balance their family and work responsibilities	34%

What are employees seeking in their work and in their employer? In this area, we see again some significant gender differences. For example, women assign greater value than do men to having an employer who treats employees with respect. And women are more likely than are men to choose the following items as among the most important things for an employer to do (Peter D.Hart Research, April 1996):

TREAT EMPLOYEES WITH RESPECT
12 point difference, 46 percent women/34 percent men

PROVIDE HEALTH CARE COVERAGE
12 point difference, 37 percent women/25 percent men

PROVIDE A SECURE PENSION PLAN
13 point difference, 33 percent women/20 percent men

RAISE WAGES WHEN PROFITS INCREASE
13 poin t difference, 29 percent women/16percent men.

View of Labor Unions

Over time, non-union working women have consistently displayed a greater receptivity to labor unions than have their male counterparts. As illustrated in the following table, women are not necessarily more positive toward unions, but they are less negative and more neutral toward them than are men. Among non-union working women today, unions are viewed more positively than negatively by a seven point margin, while among non-union men, the negative sentiment toward unions outweighs the positive by twelve points, a substantial gender gap. In addition, women are considerably less positive and more negative toward "large business corporations," while men are more positive toward business than toward labor.

The gender division that is evident in terms of general feelings toward unions extends into the arena of support for organizing the workplace, with working women exhibiting a particular appetite for representation. Non-union women believe that joining together (79 percent) is the preferred approach to solving problems rather than working individually (15 percent), and they are consistently more in favor of (and less opposed to) forming a union at their workplace than are men (Lake, Sosin, Snell + Perry, July 1997). As the following table shows, a 49 percent plurality of women currently would vote for union representation, in contrast to a 57 percent majority of men who would vote no. (Finding from a national survey among 1,002 general public and 614 union mem-

Feelings Toward Unions

	WOMEN	MEN	GENDER GAP (WOMEN/MEN)
1997 Hart Research			
Positive	30%	265	+4
Negative	23%	385	-15
Differential	+7	-12	
1996 Hart/Mellman			
Positive	30%	21%	+9
Negative	27%	38%	-11
Differential	+3	-17	
1993 Hart Research			
Positive	32%	29%	+3
Negative	28%	42%	-14
Differential	+4	-13	

bers conducted by Peter D. Hart Research for the AFL-CIO. Interviews were conducted between January 31 and February 4, 1997. These data represent results among non-union, non-supervisory working women.

In response to a similar question, in which they are asked whether they would vote to form an *employees association* that is not a union, women have an overwhelmingly positive reaction, with 78 percent saying they would vote for such an association. (Peter D. Hart Research, January 1997). This suggests that, while unions may carry a negative connotation for some, women are extremely supportive of the underlying philosophy and concept of collective action.

Women also are more inclined to sympathize with workers and labor unions over management than are men. When asked which side they generally favor in a dispute, women are more than three times as likely to side with labor union over management

Unionizing the Workplace

	WOMEN	MEN	GENDER GAP (WOMEN/MEN)
1997 Hart Research			
For	49%	40%	+9
Against	46%	57%	-11
Differential	+3	-17	
1996 Hart/Mellman			
For	43%	36%	+7
Against	46%	59%	-13
Differential	-3	-23	
1993 Hart Research			
For	46%	32%	+14
Against	39%	57%	-18
Differential	+7	-25	
1984 Harris poll[a]			
For			
Against	34%	26%	+8
Differential	60%	70%	-10
a This data are among non-union workers.	-26	-44	

(47 percent unions/14 percent management). Men also are more likely to side with labor unions, but by a much slimmer margin (36 percent unions/21 percent management). It should be noted, however, that this represents a significant improvement for men as a group: they were almost evenly divided on this question as recently as 1996. As expected, when a similar question is asked about management versus workers in a dispute, management loses support among both sexes, but the gender gap remains. Workers enjoy a 51 percent to 6 percent advantage among women, and a narrower, but still healthy 43 percent to 16 percent preference among men. Women also feel that it would be good rather than bad for the economy if more workers joined unions (38 percent to 30 percent), but men are more likely to feel that this would be bad rather than good for the economy (39 percent to 34 percent) (Peter D. Hart Research, January 1997).

Characteristics of Labor Unions

Women express clear ideas both about the areas in which they think labor unions are doing well, and about the areas in which they see unions as falling short. They are confident (66 percent) that unions seek reasonable agreements for their members instead of making unreasonable demands (25 percent) (Peter D. Hart Research, January 1997). Along similar lines, 61 percent go further and say that they believe unions only go out on strike when necessary rather than being too quick to strike (Peter D. Hart Research, January 1998). Less than one-fifth (19 percent) of women think that "weakness" is a description applicable to unions, whereas 63 percent find "generally strong" to be the trait more applicable to unions. Significantly, a 51 percent majority say that unions help individuals to make the most of themselves, as opposed to discouraging individual effort and initiative (Peter D. Hart Research, January 1997). Women also are generous in their assessment of union leadership: majorities believe that leaders are responsive to the members (59 percent), (Peter D. Hart Research, January 1998), that they let members make important decisions (52 percent), (Peter D. Hart Research, January 1998), and that they encourage participation by members (60 percent) (Peter D. Hart Research, January 1997).

At the same time, working women see unions falling short in some areas. Less than one-half of women believe that the following positive features apply to unions:

A FORCE FOR CHANGE
47 percent (Peter D. Hart Research, January 1997).

INNOVATIVE AND CHANGE WITH THE TIMES
43 percent (Peter D. Hart Research, January 1997).

MOSTLY HONEST
35 percent say this applies to unions (Peter D. Hart Research, January 1998).

CONCERNED ABOUT ALL WORKING PEOPLE
20 percent (Peter D. Hart Research, January 1997).

When discussing qualities that are important for a union to have, women express a clear and strong preference. Fully 81 percent of working women affirm that it is very important for a union to *work to establish strong health and safety protections in the workplace*. This quality stands out far above any other item that women consider to be important; no other concern elicits nearly the same level of support. We also see a substantial gender gap on this item: only 63 percent of working men regard establishing health and safety protections as very important, and it doesn't even rank among men's top three issues (Peter D. Hart Research, January 1997).

The gender gap extends to several other qualities that people want in a union, with women generally ascribing more importance to all the items than do men. As the following table illustrates, men and women have diverging views concerning what should be priorities for a union. The gap is particularly large when it comes to a union that "negotiates contract provisions that help working parents, such as flexible schedules and on-site daycare" (Peter D. Hart Research, January 1997).

We note, however, that one quality is nearly equally important in the eyes of women (tied for second-most important) and men (most important): "It emphasizes communication and cooperation with employers, rather than confrontation" (Peter D. Hart Research, January 1997). This is a message often fails to get through to non-union workers in organizing drives, in large part because of intense employer hostility. However, our research for a number of AFL-CIO unions convinces us that this feature of labor unions is critically important to communicate to working women (and men). Many workers fear that the tension and animosity of the pre-election period will continue under union representation. Indeed, a "yes" vote can be seen as support for perpetual war between employees and employer (and between pro-union and anti-union employees). Workers need to be assured that conflict is not inherent in a unionized workplace, and that union representation actually produces expanded opportunity for productive communication between employees and employer (on more equal footing).

Women and Repositioning Ads
In four U.S. cities during the late summer and fall of 1997, the AFL-CIO tested a series of ads aimed at improving the public's attitudes toward unions and strengthening the

Proportions Who Say Selected Qualities are Very Important in a Union

	WOMEN	MEN
It works to establish strong health and safety protections in the workplace	81%	63%
It emphasizes communication and cooperation with employers, rather than confrontation	74%	71%
It strongly defends the rights of individual employees when they are treated unfairly by management	74%	66%
It has a strong record of negotiating good health care benefits and pensions	74%	58%
It works hard to give employees a real voice on the job	74%	63%
It helps to provide training and improving members' skills throughout their careers	72%	68%
It negotiates contract provisions that help working parents, such as flexible schedules and on-site daycare	66%	47%
It has a strong record of negotiating good wage and salary increases	65%	59%
The union's leaders really put the members' interests first	65%	61%
It works for legislation and programs that help working families, like the minimum wage and Medicare	63%	62%
It provides members with information about important issues and elections, so the members can be informed citizens and voters	61%	40%

organizing environment for labor in general. Each ad featured actual union members and covered such topics as cooperation, having a voice, workplace safety, and workplace benefits. Hart Research conducted survey research among potential union members in the four target markets before and after the ads aired, and recorded increased positive attitudes toward unions following the ads. Moreover, women are among the workers that responded most favorably to the repositioning ads, confirming earlier findings that they are likely to be especially receptive to union appeals. Women react very positively to the ads overall, and their scores on key measures of attitudes toward unions increased appreciatively following the ads.

Women's overall view of unions was somewhat more positive than that of men prior to the round of advertising. Following the ads, women's positive feelings toward unions increase 7 percent, slightly less than do men's (9 percent), most likely because women's assessment was already somewhat more favorable than was men's and therefore had less elasticity. Blue- and pink-collar women's positive feelings toward unions increase quite a bit (up 8 percent), bringing these workers' score to the same level as that of their male counterparts (48 percent positive for blue/pink-collar men, 47 percent positive for blue/pink collar -omen). White-collar and professional women's positive feelings do not increase as much, but they were already at a much higher level than those of their male counterparts. (Findings from pre- and post-advertising survey conducted by Peter D. Hart Research for AFL-CIO in four target markets, including Milwaukee, WI, Baltimore, MD, St. Louis, MO, and Seattle, WA; among 2,036 non-union, non-supervisory working adults. Interviews were conducted during September and October, 1997. These data represent results among non-union, non-supervisory working women.) On the arguably more important measure of voting for union representation in their workplace, women show more improvement than do men despite their already being much more likely to vote for union representation.

Women's likelihood of voting for union representation increases by seven points to 57 percent, a margin of 20 points in favor of union representation. Men's likelihood of supporting union representation increases four points to 46 percent, narrowing the gap between yes and no voters to a two-point margin against union representation. Women in both age groups increase their margin for union representation quite a bit. Women between eighteen and thirty-four years old, although not as positive toward unions as other subgroups, give union representation a gigantic thirty-one-point margin of victory and increase their support for union representation from 53 percent to 63 percent. The greatest increase in union support among women is found among white-collar and professional workers, up ten points from a slight plurality of 45 percent voting for union representation to a 55 percent majority supporting unions. Blue- and pink-collar women are the group most likely to favor union representation, with 60 percent saying they would vote for a union (Peter D. Hart Research, September 1997).

Change in "Yes" Vote for Union

	PRE-AD	POST-AD	CHANGE IN
All Workers	47%	57%	+5
Sex			
Men	42%	46%	+4
Women	50%	57%	+7
Sex: Age			
Men 18 to 34	46%	49%	+3
Women 18 to 34	53%	63%	+10
Men 35 and over	39%	42%	+3
Women 35 and over	48%	53%	+5
Sex: Occupation			
Blue/pink-collar men	50%	49%	-1
Blue/pink-collar women	55%	60%	+5
White-collar/professional men	33%	41%	+8
White-collar/professional women	45%	55%	+10

The Ads

Each of the four ads features a union member in a context that the general public does not automatically associate with unions. The most effective ad overall shows a worker from Harley Davidson Motorcycles speaking about how the union and management worked together to revitalize the company. This ad plays well to both men and women. Two other ads are very popular with women in particular. The first centers on Erin, a single mother who is a chef at a hotel, talking about balancing family and work, respect from the employer, and workplace benefits. The second one features an African-American nurse named Arthereane speaking about how her union gives her and other nurses a voice on the job, and about how union representation is consistent with the value of quality patient care. (Peter D. Hart Research, September 1997.) (A fourth ad was less effective among all subgroups, and is being revised.)

Both the Erin and Arthereane spots feature women in roles with which many working women can identify. These ads effectively show the new face of labor. The women in these ads do not work in sectors traditionally thought of as containing "union jobs" (manufacturing and construction). Moreover, the problems they face are not extreme sweatshop conditions. Rather, Erin and Arthereane are professionals who take pride in their work and are truly concerned about making their workplace better—and their union helps them to be more productive and to have a greater say in the way things are run. In Erin's case, the union also helps in her personal life by making sure she can get leave when she needs to take care of her family. The values that these ads hit—hard work, responsibility, and family—are all key values for working women (Peter D. Hart Research, January 1997).

Impact of Ads: Proportions Who Recall Each Ad & Say it is Effective

	HARLEY	ERIN	ARTHEREANE
All Workers	25%	20%	20%
Sex			
Men	28%	16%	14%
Women	22%	24%	24%
Sex: Age			
Men 18 to 34	26%	15%	13%
Women 18 to 34	20%	24%	24%
Men 35 and over	30%	16%	16%
Women 35 and over	24%	24%	25%
Sex: Ocupation			
Blue/pink collar men	35%	18%	16%
Blue/ink collar women	24%	24%	25%
White collar/professional men	23%	14%	13%
White collar/professional women	21%	23%	24%

PUBLIC POLICY AND POLITICS

Issues of Importance to Women

Women expect corporations to be held to a high standard of responsibility as employers. A 58 percent majority of women support the passage of laws that would hold corporations accountable to their employees; only a third oppose these laws. In contrast, only 42 percent of men believe that such laws should be passed, and a slight majority (51 percent) say such laws should not be passed because government involvement would make business less competitive and cost jobs in the long run. The idea of a workplace bill of rights elicits an even more favorable reaction, and is supported by an overwhelming three quarters (77 percent) of working women. In addition, 90 percent of working women support the idea of a law requiring employers to show good cause when they fire an employee. And 91 percent want to strengthen laws to ensure equal pay for equal work. (Peter D. Hart Research, January 1997).

As mentioned earlier in this report, women attribute greatest importance to the issue of health care. For example, 74 percent believe that a strong record of negotiating good health care benefits and pensions is an important quality for unions to have, even more than feel that way about a record of negotiating good wage and salary increases (65 percent) (Peter D. Hart Research, January 1997). Women show their commitment to this issue by coming down harder than men do on the responsibility of employers in this area. Women show stronger support (84 percent) than do men (76 percent) for a proposal to require employers to provide health benefits to part-time employees, and they also are more willing than are men (69 percent to 64 percent) to require employers to provide health insurance (Peter D. Hart Research, January 1997). It is important to recognize, however, that to working women, the most important goal for improving the health care system is making coverage more affordable (51 percent), which is far more important to them than are covering those who have no coverage (13 percent), giving people more choice of doctors and specialists (7 percent), and improving the quality of health care (6 percent) (Peter D. Hart Research, January 1998).

Men and women agree on the importance of retirement security. Women show strong support for continuing coverage, protecting government programs, and helping people save. They display slightly less support for employer requirements on this issue than for health care, but these proposals still enjoy strong majority support and weak opposition among women. (Peter D. Hart Research, January 1998).

Proportions Who Support Selected Policy Initiatives

	WOMEN	MEN
Retirement Security		
Protect Social Security and restore its long-term financial health	91%	88%
Make it easier for people to continue their pension coverage when they change jobs	93%	91%
Provide tax incentives that reward people for saving for their retirement	85%	91%
Health Care		
Provide government health insurance for children whose parents cannot afford coverage	90%	84%
Allow people who retire between age 62 and 64 to purchase health insurance from Medicare	87%	82%
Provide affordable insurance to cover nursing home and other long-term care expenses	87%	89%
General		
Strengthen the laws that require employers to give women equal opportunities and equal pay for equal work	91%	84%
Require foreign companies that do business in the United States to pay their fair share of taxes	89%	91%
Crack down on imported products from countries that allow child labor and deny workers' rights	88%	83%
Increase funding for hiring teachers and modernizing school buildings	85%	84%

Political Views

Working women are a critically important constituency for pro-union candidates. Four in ten (41 percent) describe their overall point of view in terms of the political parties as Democratic, just under a third describe themselves as Republican (30 percent), and about one quarter say they are independent (24 percent). In terms of their ideological approach to issues, 41 percent of working women say they are moderates, 27 percent are liberals, and 26 percent are conservatives. Non-union men are more conservative (31 percent) and less liberal (22 percent), as well as more Republican (34 percent) in their political leanings (Peter D. Hart Research, January 1998).

Women are almost twice as likely to think that the Democratic Party (45 percent) does a better job of looking out for their economic interests than to say that the Republican Party does (24 percent) (Peter D. Hart Research, January 1998). Men favor the Democrats as well in this department, although by a 15-point narrower margin than do women. While working men were closely split between Bill Clinton and Bob Dole in 1996 (45 percent say they voted for Clinton, 48 percent for Dole), more than twice as many women say they voted for Clinton than for Dole (65 percent Clinton, 29 percent Dole) (Peter D. Hart Research, January 1997). Women also report having voted for their Democratic candidate for the House in greater numbers (58 percent) than do men (42 percent). Finally, women are more negative (42 percent) than positive (24 percent) toward the Republican leaders in Congress, while men are evenly divided (37 percent). At present, women say that they plan to vote for the Democratic candidate over the Republican candidate in the 1998 U.S. House race by a seven-point margin (33 percent to 26 percent). (Peter D. Hart Research, January 1997). Men are more likely to say that they will vote for the Republican (32 percent) than for the Democrat (30 percent) in the 1998 House race.

Political Differences Between Working Men and Women

	WOMEN	MEN	GENDER GAP (WOMEN/MEN)
1996 vote for Bill Clinton for President	65%	45%	+20
Say Democrats are better than Republicans at looking out for our economic interests	45%	39%	+6
1996 vote for Democrat for U.S. House of Representatives	58%	42%	+16

BACK TO THE FOREFRONT

Union Organization of Immigrant Workers in the Nineties

hector figueroa

As the new AFL-CIO tries to reverse thirty years of decline in labor's power, the organizing of immigrant workers, particularly those of Latin American and Asian/Pacific origin, has moved to the forefront. Member unions are taking note and taking charge. The UFW (United Farm Workers) campaign to organize Mexican and Asian strawberry workers in California is one of the major organizing projects of the new AFL-CIO. The campaign has brought new life to the farm workers' movement and has helped advance cooperation among unions, including former rivals like the UFW and the IBT (International Brotherhood of Teamsters). This UFW-IBT cooperation has been extended to organizing apple workers in Washington State. The Service Employees' International Union or SEIU's Justice for Janitors (JfJ) campaign to organize the immigrant workers that clean America's skyscrapers—and its blocking of a Washington D.C. bridge to draw attention to the conditions prevailing in the commercial office industry—helped define John Sweeney's successful campaign to lead the AFL-CIO. The JfJ campaign is now focused on organizing workers in the suburbs of some of America's largest cities by the year 2000. The campaign to end garment sweatshops here and abroad, mounted by UNITE (Union of Needletrades, Industrial & Textile Employees), is another example of the pre-eminence of organizing immigrant workers. The campaign, aimed at the big retailers who ultimately have the power to end sweatshops, spreads from New York's Chinatown to Asia to Central America. With innovative tactics, including working with community coalitions and unions overseas, the campaign has raised the level of American consumers' awareness about clothes' manufacturing.

The new leadership of the AFL-CIO is already devoting more resources than labor has ever done in the past to organize immigrant workers and to encourage affiliates to do the same. This very positive development bodes well for the growing number of Latin, Asian/Pacific, and other minority labor activists. Changes at the top of organized labor offer hope for the future of minority and immigrant worker organizing. Immigrant workers, whatever their origin, ethnicity, race, or sex have much in common with, and often struggle side by side with, U.S. workers. They also face similar challenges: increas-

ing the ranks of labor through organizing, developing new organizational forms that link economic demands with social justice and political empowerment, and reaching out to counterparts within and outside the U.S. borders. And while the U.S. labor movement is still a long way from meeting the specific needs of immigrant workers, their activist presence in the U.S. labor force captures the imagination of mainstream labor. As Linda Chavez-Thompson, Executive Vice President of the AFL-CIO has said: "When you look at any large organizing drive going on today, for the most part, they are Latinos."

GROWING WORKFORCE

Foreign-born workers are the fastest growing segment of the U.S. working class. These workers are an integral part of the labor market in a growing number of cities in various industries. Asian, Latin American, African, and Eastern European workers labor in manufacturing, service, and agricultural companies that compete in local, national, and international markets. These workers often maintain close ties to both their local community and to their nation of origin. They are key contributors to the "universalization" and the diversification of the U.S. working class. The struggle of immigrant workers in the U.S. can help define organized labor through the next century. To ignore the exploitation, labor, and civil rights violations that many immigrant workers endure undermines the living conditions of all workers and the moral and political fabric of the American labor movement.

BACK TO THE FOREFRONT

In this nation of immigrants, it is perhaps not surprising that labor activism has historically been linked to immigrant workers' struggles. Yet despite this legacy and the growing number of campaigns aimed at them, immigrant workers remain one of labor's least organized and least understood groups.

Organizing campaigns among immigrant and other minority workers often become more than just an organizing effort vis-à-vis an employer or an industry. Almost from the very outset, these campaigns take a turn towards broader demands of dignity and social justice, racial and cultural tolerance, and community empowerment. Ripe for asserting their rights as workers and residents, immigrant workers are organizing both within the trade union movement and within their communities. The ingredients that make their organizing successful are not radically different from those that empower other workers: worker-centered campaigns, sound strategies, bold tactics, community support, persistence, and determination.

Immigrant workers do not constitute a homogenous workforce. Latino workers differ from Asian/Pacific Islanders, Africans, or Europeans. And important differences exist within specific immigrant worker groups that impact on union organizing. While the reasons to organize are similar and their commitment to overcome exploitation crosses racial, national, and cultural barriers, there are important distinctions among, say, Mexican, Puerto Rican, and Central American workers, or among Chinese, Korean, and Filipino laborers. The differences based on language, national origin, gender, race, immigration status, economic sector, geography, and integration into the U.S. labor market often translate into different experiences and degrees of involvement within the labor movement and contrasting positions on key labor issues.

Still, despite these obstacles, immigrant workers are becoming protagonists in many organizing campaigns. Their ranks include workers in the garment industry, farmers, drywallers, janitors, hotel workers, and other low-wage workers. Many of these workers have engaged in massive strikes, militant action, and civil disobedience to bring public attention to their struggle to win dignity, higher wages, and decent working conditions.

An important outcome of these efforts has been the emergence of a much needed (though still small) number of trade union leaders and staff who are themselves from immigrant communities. There are over one hundred Latino and Asian/Pacific Islander labor organizers and trade unionist activists across the country, many of them active in labor-backed organizations like the Labor Council for Latin American Advancement (LCLAA) and the Asian Pacific Labor Alliance (APALA). These activists serve as an important link between mainstream organized labor and a myriad of community activists engaged in the struggle for immigrant civil rights.

ORGANIZING REMAINS A CHALLENGE

While there are many organizing campaigns involving immigrant workers, the number of unionized immigrant workers as a percentage of all immigrant workers (immigrant workers' "union density") continues to decline. For example, even though the Latino work force expanded by nearly two-thirds over the last ten years, union organizing campaigns aimed at Latinos and Latinas have failed to keep pace with the growth of the Latino workforce. While the same is true for the workforce as a whole, the decline in "union density" among Latinos, Asian/Pacific Islanders, African-American workers and recent immigrants from East/Central Europe is higher than average.

The percentage of immigrant and minority workers who are union members has fallen faster than the percentage of union membership for the labor force as a whole or for workers characterized as racially "white" by the U.S. Labor Department. Not surprisingly, the wages and working conditions of these workers have also worsened in absolute terms and relative "whites." For example, the wages of Latino workers have declined by almost twice as much as those of U.S. workers. Clearly, not enough campaigns have been launched to organize immigrant workers on the scale that is necessary to organize them.

Nonetheless, the absolute number of immigrant workers in unions has been growing fairly steadily. Precise estimates of this growth are not available, but if the growth in the number of Latino and Asian/Pacific Islander union members is any indication, the increase during the last decade has been dramatic, from a little over one million members in 1987 to more than two million members today (that's 13 percent of all union workers in the U.S.). As a result, Latino and Asian/Pacific Islander labor is increasingly more visible and carries more weight and influence than in the past. This growing movement, however, is not uniform. Its face is colored by a growing diversity of ideological and political backgrounds, ages, occupations, geographies, culture, ethnicities, and genders.

COMMON THREADS WITHIN DIVERSITY

Despite different economic experiences, immigrant workers are generally underpaid relative to white workers, under-represented in the union movement, and continue to face discrimination in the workplace. This discrimination is not isolated from the growing "anti-immigrant" sentiment in the larger community. As a result, the struggle for justice and dignity in the workplace go hand in hand with demands for immigrant rights in the community. These goals, coupled with a high disposition towards labor organizing and a significant presence within the fastest growing sectors and regions of the US economy bind immigrant workers more than their differences may separate them.

The recent experience of Latino and Latina workers illustrates well how these common goals and experience can set the stage for successful labor organizing among immigrant workers. The second half of the 1980s saw a surge in Latino labor activism. The most dramatic upsurge among Latino workers occurred among low wage service sector workers in California (especially in Los Angeles, and among low wage manufacturing workers in the Southwest, particularly in Texas and along the border. But militancy among Latino workers also increased significantly within the manufacturing and service sectors of old industrial snowbelt cities like Chicago, New York, Hartford, and Boston, and in the Southeast (including Washington D.C., Florida, North Carolina).

Latino workers are among the poorest of the labor force and are among those whose standard of living has declined the most (after brief improvements in the 1960s and 1970s). The average weekly wages for Latinos is 70 percent of that for non-Latinos. Latino workers tend to be concentrated in blue-collar and lower-skilled occupations more, and to have somewhat higher rates of unemployment than non-Latinos.

Many Latino as well as Asian/Pacific workers live in areas with expanding labor markets, particularly for entry-level positions in the service, retail, and "high-tech" manufacturing sector. As a result, the low-skill workers among these groups generally face relatively favorable job opportunities, and the prospects for organizing are good. For example, the Washington, D.C. metropolitan area is home to the largest number of Central and South Americans in the United States, and is an area of rapid job growth. The most rapidly growing job categories are janitors, cooks, and construction workers. These high growth areas have also witnessed some of the most successful recent organizing efforts among Latino workers, like Justice for Janitors, the strikes of the drywallers, and the UNITE campaign to organize garment workers.

Latin and Asian/Pacific workers who live in older industrial regions of the Midwest and the Northeast—areas once characterized by relatively high union membership—face economic circumstances very different from those living in the south. Declining union membership, plant closings, layoffs, fiscal crises in city and state governments, and high unemployment are among the challenges faced by Latin trade unionists and leaders in these areas. The need to create jobs, revitalize the inner city, organize youth, defend wages and benefits in industry-wide and public-sector contracts are key priorities of labor leaders. In light of declining membership, organizing is also near the top of the agenda for trade unions in the

snowbelt states, particularly in cities like Chicago and Milwaukee. Unions have begun to organize thousands of workers.

Several forces seem to have played a major role in the resurgence of immigrant activism. A world recession and economic difficulties in Latin America, market reforms and political repression in Asia, along with increased trade and foreign direct investment by transnational corporations had the effect of displacing millions of urban and rural workers from their countries of origin. Such forces created "global cities" with significant economic as well as cultural ties to Asia and Latin America within the United States. U.S. military intervention in Central America and the Caribbean also brought waves of immigrant workers into the United States. Displaced workers and peasants, as well as political refugees, came to the United States in large numbers and found employment in the growing service and informal sectors in manufacturing. The increased number of Latino workers in urban areas, especially in manufacturing, transportation, retail, and services, resulted in major organizing drives by unions like SEIU and UNITE. In addition, Latino and Asian/Pacific labor caucuses have increased immigrant worker representation at the local and national level in key unions.

ORGANIZING TO WIN . . . AND BUILD LEADERSHIP

Organizing campaigns involving immigrant workers are among the most publicized efforts within U.S. labor today. Experience has shown that immigrants and other "minority" workers have been quite receptive to union organizing, and their presence in organizing drives tends to increase the chance of the union winning recognition from employers. Immigrant workers, many of them employed in low-wage service and manufacturing where subcontracting, paternalistic management, and small profit margins predominate—and where union organizing is therefore more difficult—are organizing in large numbers. Latina and Asian women that clean tall commercial office buildings or sew garments for major fashion designers in America's largest cities have become some of labor's strongest and most militant supporters.

Successful organizing of immigrant workers requires commitment of resources, sound strategies, and solid institutional support. Such organizing needs to be part of a broader, national effort to increase industry and regional power among all groups of workers if it is to permanently lift the poorest segment of immigrant workers from the low wage economy and empower them in their workplace and communities. Anti-immigrant sentiments even among organized workers also need to be overcome by tying the struggle of immigrant workers to those of "native" workers. We must remember how successful union organizing among Mexican workers during the first decades of this century was abruptly interrupted by growing racism, leading to the forceful deportation of tens of thousands of Mexican workers, sometimes with the support of of organized labor. The history of organizing among Chinese workers is not radically different from that experience.

The connection between union organizing and civil right struggles is crucially important to immigrant workers. For example, many Latino and Latina union activists trace their roots to the Chicano and Puerto Rican civil right movements, the trade union struggles in Latin America, and the struggle for immigrant worker rights. Latino labor in the United States is itself the product of the complex forces that have integrated Latin America into the orbit of U.S. capitalism. How that experience shapes Latin labor trade union consciousness and influence over the rest of organized labor will be one important issue in the years to come. For example, opposition by Latin labor activists to the North American Free Trade Agreement (NAFTA) helped extend labor and environmentalist opposition to NAFTA to the U.S. Latino community. It also helped U.S. unions to find common ground with Mexican and Latin American trade unionists on the issue of linking free trade to respect for worker rights across the Americas.

Unions need to deploy organizers who can communicate with and relate to the workers. But because of the limited number of Asian/Pacific and Latin organizers and because of the mass number of workers that often need to be targeted to attain the necessary market power to lift wages and living standards, immigrant worker campaigns must be member-based. Immigrant workers need to be trained on how to do housecalls, sign fellow workers, identify leaders, and carry out other essential organizing tasks. Organizing campaigns must build organizing committees among immigrant workers that develop their ability to conduct the organizing campaign, and to negotiate and win first contracts. Worker empowerment is essential for success if organizing drives among immigrant workers is to be long lasting.

The Laborers' organizing work among asbestos removal workers, UNITE's organizing in the garment industry and among immigrant service workers in Miami, SEIU's organizing in the nursing home industry in Florida, and the Teamsters' organizing among food processing workers are good examples of member-organizing campaigns among immigrant workers. Immigrant workers need to be mobilized through bold actions and national member organizing programs, as Justice for Janitors and other similar campaigns have shown. These campaigns have tried, with growing success, to link the demands of immigrant workers in the workplace to broader demands within their communities and within their unions as well. The campaigns demonstrate that community support and coalition work are essential ingredients in any immigrant worker organizing campaign.

Also critical to any organizing effort among immigrant workers (or any group of workers) is choosing the right targets and strategy. HERE's organizing in the hotel industry and UNITE's organizing of garment workers offer examples of how immigrant organizing is most successful when conducted as part of a greater strategy to increase union density and economic power within a specific industry and geography. The pro-union sentiments and disposition to militant action by immigrant workers resonate when they are directed at the right targets—those who have the power to deliver not just union recognition but also better wages and working conditions.

EXAMPLES OF RECENT UNION CAMPAIGNS

Organizing Immigrant Service Workers

The SEIU's Justice for Janitors campaign is perhaps the most successful model to date for organizing and winning contracts for immigrant workers. Under Justice for Janitors, SEIU has managed to organize over 35,000 workers, mostly immigrants, in less than a decade. Organizing activity under this campaign has been most dynamic and successful in Los Angeles, San Francisco, California's Silicon Valley, Washington, D.C., Hartford, Detroit, Chicago, and Milwaukee. The success of the Justice for Janitors campaign, which relied on worker mobilization, community-based work, civil disobedience, and strategic campaigns—has inspired many other unions to organize immigrant workers, many of different national descent, including Latinos, Asian, Caribbeans, and Poles. Presently, SEIU is in the midst of organizing campaigns in Sacramento, Chicago, Denver, and Philadelphia. After almost ten years of struggle— one of the longest organizing efforts in recent U.S. labor history—it has successfully organized about 70 percent of the downtown commercial office market in Washington D.C.

The current Justice for Janitors' campaigns collectively represent an attempt to unionize about ten thousand workers. But SEIU's organizing of immigrant workers is by no means limited to the cleaning industry. The union remains committed to organizing immigrant workers in other industries, such as health care, ambulance service and amusement parks. SEIU's ambitious organizing projects in Los Angeles and in Las Vegas could bring justice to tens of thousands of hospital workers, including some of the highest concentrations of Filipino and other immigrant nurses in the country. SEIU's recent affiliation of New York's Local 1199 increases the union's power within the health care industry and will lead to organizing drives aimed at Asian and Caribbean health care workers in the New York metropolitan area.

The Laborers International Union of North America (LIUNA) has stepped up its organizing in the Northeast. In 1996 LIUNA won a contract and began organizing a campaign among 1,200 asbestos-removal workers (mostly Latinos and recent Polish immigrants) in New York City. This asbestos-removal campaign was one of the biggest organizing drives in New York City in several decades. The campaign not only increased the number of immigrant union members in the Laborers but also radically transformed its local union into a more democratic and militant operation. LIUNA has now extended its organizing of immigrant asbestos-removal workers to Los Angeles.

The Hotel Employees & Restaurant Employees International Union (HERE) is also organizing significant numbers of immigrant workers using community-organizing strategies. For example, the union has been organizing 7,000 workers, many of them immigrants employed at twenty-five non-union companies that circle the Los Angeles airport. The organizing campaign involved house visits to 2,000 of the workers—mostly immigrants—who live in Lennox, an unincorporated one-square-mile section of Los Angeles County right beneath the airport. This and other well-targeted drives have paid off. Recently, HERE won a "watershed" collective bargaining agreement with six hotels in downtown Los Angeles, which boosts immigrant workers' wages and recognizes important new rights for these workers, including protection and reinstatement of seniority and other rights for workers whose work authorization expires but who then correct their immigration status.

Organizing Industrial Immigrant Workers

UNITE has been organizing immigrant workers in light manufacturing, industrial laundries, and retail trades, as well as in the garment and textile industry. Recently, the union has been particularly successful in organizing Latino workers from Chicago to Florida and has actually won first contracts for immigrant workers in manufacturing and distribution in Texas.

For example, in 1995 UNITE organized over one thousand (most of them immigrants) workers at Atrium Corp., a windows manufacturer in Fort Worth. The workers were bargaining their first contract by 1997. And in New York City and Los Angeles, UNITE has established Garment Workers' Justice Centers, where non-union workers come for advice about wage-and-hour complaints, organizing committee meetings, literacy classes, and English classes. UNITE's Immigration Department (staffed by lawyers and activists) advises union members on immigration issues, conducts citizen programs, and plays an active role in coalitions for immigrant rights nationally. UNITE is also waging a national campaign to abolish sweatshops. By harnessing public horror about sweatshops, UNITE hopes to pressure retailers to take responsibility for conditions in their suppliers' factories in the United States and abroad.

The Teamsters are also becoming more active on Latino labor issues. The union represent many first-and second-generation immigrant workers in trucking and in their warehouse and distribution division. The IBT has been trying to organize tomato-processing plants like the Fresno, California-based Tomatech, which has 500 workers, most of whom are Mexicans and Mexican-Americans. The Teamsters have also been fighting an uphill battle to organize apple warehouse and distribution workers in Washington State, and are exploring a possible partnership with the United Farm Workers in those efforts.

The Ongoing Struggle of Agricultural Immigrant Workers

The United Farm Workers Union (UFW), historically one of the most inspiring and—despite its small size—influential unions among Latino trade unionists, is also successfully organizing immigrant workers. While its cause may no longer be so fashionable as it was when legendary farm worker leader Cesar Chavez exhorted urban consumers not to buy grapes, the UFW under Arturo Rodriguez and Dolores Huerta is actively organizing again. The union has expanded its organizing from its California base to Arizona, Washington, Texas, and Florida. From April 1994 through April 1995, the UFW won eight representation elections in a row and negotiated twenty-one contracts covering 3,700 workers. One of the most important contracts was with the country's largest rose grower, Bear Creek Production Co. in Wasco, California—the contract gained family medical and pension benefits, an 8 percent pay raise, nine holidays, and grievance and seniority systems. More recently the union obtained a contract for workers of the St. Michelle winery in Washington and is now contemplating two major campaigns with its former rival, the Teamsters, to organize immigrant workers employed by Washington apple growers and by California strawberry growers. Its current campaign to organize strawberry workers in California has the active backing of the new AFL-CIO leadership.

The United Food and Commercial Workers (UFCW) and the Laborers, together with community and religious groups, have formed the National Poultry Workers Alliance to organize about 50,000 poultry workers in the South. A growing number of immigrant workers can be found in the poultry industry, and the Alliance is organizing them. The Alliance won a 1996 organizing drive at Case Farms in Morgantown, N.C., where many any of the 600 workers employed there were immigrant workers from Guatemala or Mexico. They voted 337 to 183 to join the Laborers. Following that success, the union has continued to organize immigrant workers in

North Carolina's poultry industry, maintaining close ties with religious and community organizations.

CONCLUSION

Organizing immigrant workers remains a challenge for the new AFL-CIO, a challenge that must be faced in alliance with other organizations within the immigrant worker communities that are also striving for social justice, civil rights, and political empowerment for immigrants as both workers and residents in this country. The ingredients for success in these campaigns are not radically different from those needed in other situations: Leadership and membership support of organizing, including serious commitment of resources, strategic targeting, community coalition work, and bold actions that mobilize the rank and file.

A key difference, however, is that this organizing work must embrace the cultural, language, and national characteristics of the workers and their communities, which means that much of the organizing must be oriented to identify and develop leadership among the immigrant workers and be done by the workers themselves. In this respect, organizing immigrant workers not only results in more union members but also in more imaginative, worker-centered organizing strategies, and the transformation of local unions into more democratic, diverse, and powerful bodies.

When well-crafted, immigrant worker organizing is both inspiring and rewarding. It helps build our movement and sharpen our strategy and tactics—just what organized labor needs to regain its power and mission in American society.

BUILDING TO WIN, BUILDING TO LAST

The AFL-CIO Political Program

steve rosenthal

The check, the handshake, and the slap on the back have become the extent of labor's political program in far too many places. Union activists are all too familiar with the drill. First, the local union invites the Democratic candidate to a meeting with a dozen or so of its members. Then, the union's officer gives "their man" the check. They shake hands and the candidate pats the officer on the back. Someone snaps a picture for the local newsletter. Drill over.

Of course, some unions run election phone banks. And there are always some faithful members braving the rain or cold to knock on doors the weekend before the election or to pass out palm cards at the polls. These efforts, however, are becoming more rare—which is good, since they infrequently generate enough activity to make a significant difference in elections. If the Democratic candidate wins, once he gets to city hall, or the state house, or Washington, he may or may not vote for workers' issues—or promote a workers' rights agenda. Why should he? All labor has really done to help him is to contribute some money—although much less money than corporations provide—and he could be fairly confident of another check for the next election cycle anyway.

Too many unions have forgotten the simple premise that politics is about power, and that power in politics comes from two places: money and VOTES. Some organizations (primarily big businesses) have come to recognize that while they can't deliver votes, they can provide enough cash for candidates to "buy" votes. But as Al Barkan, the legendary director of the AFL-CIO Committee on Political Education (COPE) used to say, "They've got the money, but we've got the people."

Barkan was right on one count. Businesses' bank accounts will always be bigger than ours will. In spite of the media attention paid to the $35 million spent by the AFL-CIO on legislative and political activity in 1996, corporations outspent labor by a ratio of

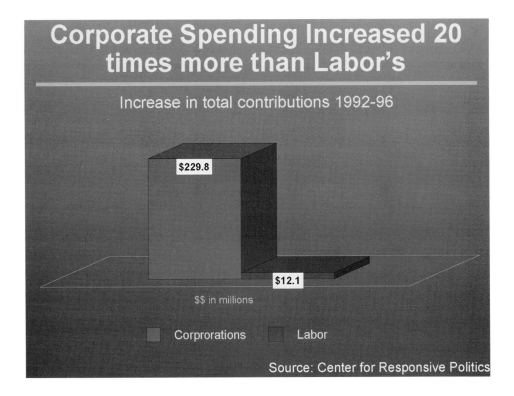

eleven to one, according to the Center for Responsive Politics. And if we consider "soft-money" contributions to political parties and other organizations, the ratio was actually twenty-three to one. That ratio has gotten greater with every election. In the 1996 election, labor gave less than $60 million of a total of $2.2 billion raised (this includes money from all unions and the AFL-CIO). From 1992 to 1996, corporate spending increased twenty times more than labor's. Our money can never compete with theirs.

And, as Barkan observed, the labor movement's strength historically has been in our ability to provide votes and organization for grass-roots political campaigns. Unfortunately, we have forgotten this resource. By not mobilizing at the grassroots, we have ceded our power to right-wing activists who have learned from our own organizing manual. In 1995, Ralph Reed, the Christian Coalition's wunderkind, proudly proclaimed, "All we are doing is what unions used to do." Yet that same year, *Fortune* magazine said, "The AFL-CIO has less clout on Capitol Hill these days than the Christian Coalition with one-tenth as many members." Sadly, *Fortune* was correct.

STICK TO THE ISSUES

Learning from the debacle of the 1994 elections, soon after the election of John Sweeney as AFL-CIO president in October 1995, the AFL-CIO began to develop a program that would capitalize on our real power—union members—for the 1996 elections. We had to decrease our reliance on our ability to provide money for candidates, and we needed to reactivate our ranks and mobilize members again to become a major part of the political process.

Our membership base was apathetic, weak, and scattered. Take, for example, the race in the Sixth Congressional District of Ohio. Before the 1994 elections, Ted Strickland, a Democrat who voted consistently with working families, represented this district. He lost the 1994 election to a Gingrichite, Frank Cremeans, by a 3,400-vote margin.

Labor used to claim that we had a lot of pull in this district because 51,000 union members live there. The fact is, however (and we've tried to keep this a secret for too long), that nationally, about 40 percent of our members aren't registered to vote. Of the members who are registered, another 40 percent don't make it to the polls. In addition, in 1994, of union members who voted, 39 percent voted Republican. So, in 1994, 7,264 union members voted for the anti-worker Republican in Ohio's sixth District race, more than twice the margin he needed to win. Between union members and their families, we should have about 75,000 union votes in that district. We should decide not only who wins the race, but also who is running and on what issues.

There were several reasons why union members voted the way they did in 1994. Members were disillusioned with the Democratic Party after the Clinton Administration pushed NAFTA and backed off a national health care plan. Union members felt they had voted for change in 1992, and had been betrayed. Many of the candidates that unions supported weren't articulating an agenda that differed from Gingrich's, and in the absence of a working-class economic agenda, the right wing was muddying the waters by pushing issues that did matter to many union members, such as gun control, a ban on gays in the military, and prayer in school.

So, union members cast protest votes, or just stayed home in 1994. There were 29 million Americans who voted in the 1992 presidential election, but didn't vote in the 1994 mid-term election. Ten million of those who stayed home were from union households. Union members and their families were actually staying at home at a higher rate than everybody else was. Across the country, union members were expressing their dissatisfaction by voting with their work-booted, wing-tipped, running-shoed, high heeled feet, pointing them in some direction other than their neighborhood polling place.

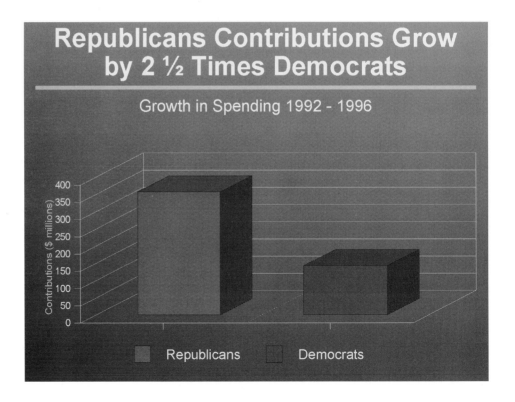

The 1994 elections showed us that we needed to take action. We weren't sure how. Many union activists wanted the AFL-CIO to issue a statement on gun control, assuring members that we didn't support candidates who wanted to take their guns. Although the instinct was correct—we did need to regain credibility with our membership—this direction was wrong. Rather than accepting the right-wing terms of the debate in 1996, we wanted to provide members with information on economic issues that impact their lives as working people. We had to alert them about the candidates' positions on fundamentals such as education, minimum wage, and health care. We then had to motivate and mobilize them on a scale more massive than we'd done in decades. Only after we had done that job would the candidates begin to address issues that matter to working people.

In order to exercise our full political clout, the AFL-CIO is creating a four-part program. First, we have to increase union member turnout in elections. Second, we must register union members to vote. Third, we must educate members on the issues so that they will want to vote. Fourth, we have to increase our base through union organizing.

To get started, we took a hard, honest look at how union members viewed politics. Similar to the public at large the vast majority of members say that they don't like politics. For them, too often "politics" has meant legislative wheeling and dealing. "Politics," in relation to the union, meant the meeting with the check and the handshake, or the letter they received from the local, which typically went something like this:

> *Dear Mary:*
>
> *John Doe is the candidate for office. John Doe is a long-time friend of labor. John Doe needs your support, so vote for him in Tuesday's election.*
>
> *Sincerely,*
>
> *Your Union President*

Although there are still many union members who would march in line and vote for the union's candidate following such an endorsement, the vast majority rightly demand more information.

Before the 1996 elections, the AFL-CIO commissioned a study by Peter D. Hart Research Associates on how union members view politics. This study documented the level of cynicism among members, and found that members increasingly reject partisanship as a meaningful way of making political decisions. Too often, members see unions as united at the hip to the Democratic Party, supporting candidates regardless of their stances on issues. Finally, the poll found that unions had lost much of their members' confidence as a source for reliable political information.

This study confirmed that members don't want to be told whom to vote for—they want to be told where the candidates stand on issues. Given the information, members want to decide for themselves for whom to vote. They essentially want their union playing the role of a Consumer Reports' watchdog, keeping watch on elected officials, reporting back on how they vote, and mobilizing members to help hold politicians accountable.

LABOR '96

The AFL-CIO worked with our affiliated unions' political directors to develop a program called "Labor '96—Building to Win, Building to Last" that addressed real issues. The program highlighted a two-step plan. The first step was to educate members about political issues through a host of channels, including paid television ads, mailings, discussions at the workplace, and talks with the candidates. Instead of mailing a letter urging members to vote for labor's true-blue friend, we sent out leaflets that compared the two candidates and their positions on issues such as education, health care, the minimum wage, retirement, and workplace and consumer safety. One leaflet had the headline: "What's at stake for working families in the 1996 elections." Members were then left to make their own informed choices.

The second step was to mobilize workers. We found that once we discussed the real issues with members and told them where candidates stood, they were more motivated to be part of labor's campaign. In order to jump-start the activity, we developed a program to reach out district by district, union local by union local. Across the country, unions dedicated a total of 135 staff members or activists to educate members. Ideally, these coordinators lived in one of the 120 congressional districts where they were working. They went through a week-long training on the basics of internal union organizing and publicizing labor's message. Then, we kicked off Labor '96 in each area with a meeting of local labor leaders.

The results were stunning. For example, we won Ohio's Sixth District—the same district where union members helped elect the anti-worker candidate in 1994. In 1996, our candidate, Strickland, came out of retirement and won against the Gingrichite. Labor '96 played a big role in this victory. We increased union members' registration by 800 people, and union household turnout went up from 58 percent to 70 percent. This time, 68 percent of union members voted for Strickland, making the union margin 8,300 votes, well exceeding the 6,000 vote margin by which Strickland won. It was the exact opposite of what happened in 1994.

We won similar victories all across the country with Labor '96, such as in the run-off race in the Ninth District of Texas. Nick Lampson challenged anti-worker Republican Steve Stockman. This district is different than many in the South, because labor does have a large presence (over 25,000 members). With the Labor '96 structure, we mobilized hundreds of union members to knock on doors and to run phone banks to turn out

What's at stake for working families in the 1996 elections?

North Carolina Congressional District 2

If you're like most working Americans, you're concerned about living standards, affordable health care, retirement security, education, and workplace and consumer safety. That's what you told us in meetings and polls. You also told us you want your union to provide information on these issues—information that will help you make the right decisions on November 5. We heard you, loud and clear!

	REPUBLICAN **DAVID FUNDERBURK**	DEMOCRAT **BOBBY ETHERIDGE**
WAGES, TAXES & THE ECONOMY	Supports tax breaks for the wealthy. Voted NO on raising the minimum wage (H.R. 1227). Voted YES on tax loopholes for millionaires (H.R. 1215). Supported cuts in Earned Income Tax Credit for families (H.R. 2491). Voted for $245 billion in tax cuts (H.R. 2491), disproportionately benefiting taxpayers earning over $100,000, along with cuts in Medicare and other vital programs.	Promotes tax fairness for working families. Opposes tax loopholes for millionaires. Supports policies to promote economic growth, incentives for corporations to keep good jobs at home, more student loans and training for the jobs of the future, and a minimum wage families can live on.
HEALTH CARE	Voted for $270 billion in Medicare cuts along with tax breaks for the wealthy (H.R. 2491). Voted to cut Medicaid (H.R. 2491) and eliminate federal standards for nursing home care (H.R. 2491).	Preserves Medicare and Medicaid. Opposes cuts in Medicare and Medicaid to pay for tax breaks for the wealthy. Supports maintaining nursing home care standards for seniors and their families.
RETIREMENT SECURITY	Puts retirement income at risk. Voted to allow corporations to raid pension funds without notifying employees (H.R. 2491). Voted to cut Medicare by $270 billion and raise premiums for seniors by $400 in the year 2002 (H.R. 2491). Voted to cut seniors' heating, food, and community services.	Pension protection is a top priority. Opposes deep cuts in Social Security or Medicare to finance tax breaks for the wealthy. Opposes provisions to allow corporations to siphon off employee pension funds. Opposes increasing retirees' out-of-pocket health-care costs.
EDUCATION 	Cuts school and education programs. Voted to cut $10 billion from the student loan program and $3.6 billion from other education programs including Head Start and Safe-and-Drug Free Schools (H.R. 2491). Supported eliminating the Department of Education and cutting job training programs (H.R. 2127).	Supports good schools and job training. Wants to invest in children and their nutrition, safety and education. Will strengthen public schools and support Head Start, school lunch, and Safe and Drug-Free School programs. Will fight to preserve access to student loans and provide job training.
WORKPLACE & CONSUMER SAFETY	Opposes job safety laws. Supported cutting OSHA's budget and enforcement of job safety laws (H.R. 2127). Voted to stop EPA enforcement of key food safety provisions (H.R. 2099) and to weaken the Clean Water Act (H.R. 961).	Fights for safe communities. Supports working families' right to information about hazards that can affect their health and safety. Will fight special interest attacks on clean water and air and safe food regulations. Will enforce environmental laws and stiffen punishment of corporate violators.

Information gathered from DCCC Candidate Principles, statements, and other sources

BOBBY ETHERIDGE SUPPORTS WORKING FAMILIES. DAVID FUNDERBURK DOESN'T.

VOTE NOVEMBER 5

BOBBY ETHERIDGE IS ENDORSED BY THE WORKING MEN AND WOMEN OF THE AFL-CIO. FOR MORE INFORMATION:

the union vote. We took full advantage of the fact that Texas has early voting, which means voters can cast their ballots up to a month in advance of Election Day. Each of the big unions individualized plans to get their voters out early. Over half the union members in the district voted, sweeping out Stockman. Lampson went to Washington elected on a working families' agenda, and has been a solid vote, since supporting a program of economic progressivism.

In Washington State, the state labor federation led the Labor '96 program. Union members passed out 75,000 issue-focused flyers in 220 worksites, and canvassed neighborhoods to turn out the union vote. At plant gates, in front of hospitals, and in one-on-one conversations in the breakrooms, union members were educating each other on where candidates stood.

The Atlanta Central Labor Council mobilized hundreds of union members from dozens of unions in a non-partisan, get-out-the vote operation. Union members volunteered in record numbers and their efforts made a visible difference. At 2 p.m. on Election Day, for example, the Terry Mill district had only had 46 percent of their expect-

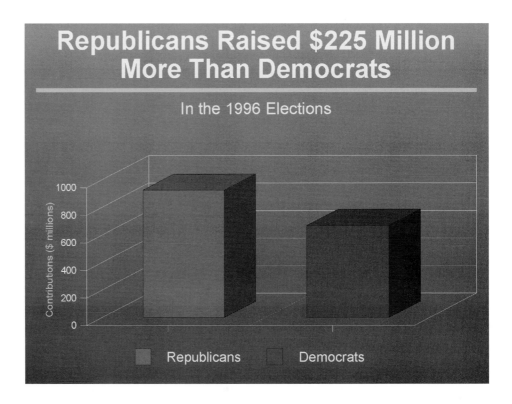

ed turnout. So union teams fanned through the neighborhood, knocking on doors and leaving a sea of blue hangers on mailboxes reminding people to vote. A sound truck blared through the neighborhood with music and encouragement to go to the polls. By 6 p.m., 81 percent of expected voters had made it to the Terry Mill voting place. Turnout in largely African-American neighborhoods alone reached 56 percent that day where it had never before topped 40 percent.

The story was the same across the country. Union members helped mobilize voters and also turned out to vote in record numbers. In 1992, during the last presidential election, 19 percent of the total voters were from union households. That number jumped to 23 percent in 1996. While turnout overall declined by 8 million votes, union household turnout increased by 2.3 million—an astonishing accomplishment. Union members voted at an even higher rate than everyone else did.

They did so conscientiously. The number of union household voters who voted for the Gingrichites dropped from 39 percent in 1994 to 35 percent in 1996. Over a million union voters switched from voting Republican in 1994 to voting Democratic in 1996. A staggering 61 percent of white men in union households voted Democratic compared to only 35 percent of white men in non-union households.

Labor '96 retired eighteen anti-workers members of the House, and cut the Gingrich margin by half. Even Majority Leader Dick Armey understood that voters' anger nearly cost him his job: "The best kept secret of the 1996 elections is . . . if just 9,759 voters had switched their votes in ten districts where Republicans won razor-thin margins, Bill Clinton would have a Democratic majority in the House today. That's too close for comfort."

Labor '96 helped bring workers' issues to Capitol Hill. In 1996, we helped fill nineteen seats with legislators who opposed fast-track trade authority. These were seats held by pro-NAFTA legislators in 1993. There are another twenty Republican members of Congress who have been forcing their party's leaders to take "Contract with America" type legislation off the table because they don't want to be put at odds with newly mobilized union members in their districts. When we educate and mobilize union members, politicians are forced to follow.

PLANS FOR THE FUTURE

Labor '96 can serve as a model for how we elect worker-friendly politicians. It also offers a model for how to get politicians to focus on issues that really matter to working families. We must continue to challenge our old assumptions and examine our past political practices.

For years, we've pounded our chests, saying that we have the biggest membership of any organization in the country, but it's not enough to be the biggest. We've got to build a lasting structure through which we can mobilize our members to get registered and to vote for candidates who support working people's issues. We need to make the case to members that political mobilization makes a difference. That means that we've got to start providing members with relevant materials about issues pending before legislative bodies, mobilizing by writing letters, making phone calls, attending accountability sessions with elected representatives, and staying involved in politics for the long haul. This work is extremely labor-intensive, requiring a real commitment of union resources and time to do it right.

The Steelworkers have begun to put together a grassroots legislative and political organization that is proving quite effective. The union's "Rapid Response Team" is aimed at reaching members on the shop floor. When a Steelworkers' local has 3 percent of their members signed up to participate in the program, the international union gives it a fax machine. When there is a key vote in Congress, faxes get blasted out from Steelworkers' headquarters in Pittsburgh into union halls across the country. Then, faxes

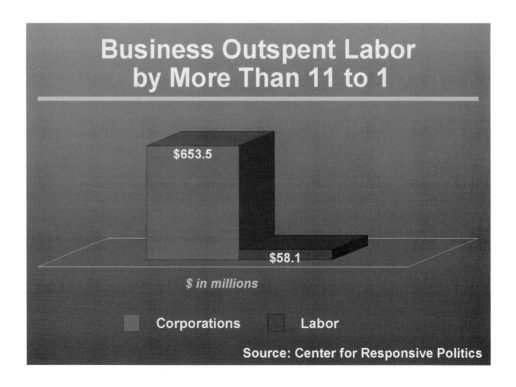

go from the union halls into workplaces. The "Rapid Response Team" members (these are volunteers) stand in the mill with a stack of papers, talk to members, and get them to write letters to their congressperson. Sometimes, volunteer organizers bring cell phones to the shop floor to barrage elected officials' offices with calls. Many Steelworkers have developed ongoing dialogues with their members of Congress. The international union in Pittsburgh gets copies of every letter, logs them in, and collates them by local and district. To stress the importance of this union program, it is run directly out of Steelworkers' President George Becker's office. Awards are given each year to the locals and districts with the highest degree of participation.

This kind of action can have a real impact on Capitol Hill. When the program was just getting started, one congressman received three letters from Steelworkers, and complained to union lobbyists that he was "inundated" with letters from union members. If three letters make a congressman feel inundated, imagine how those congressional offices are buzzing when they receive three hundred letters—or three thousand.

We need to challenge our assumptions. Instead of simply putting out a letter of support for a candidate, now we put out voter guides that examine political issues in-depth. Instead of holding a get-out-the-vote rally with union members on behalf of our supported candidate the day before the election, we now hold issues' rallies weeks before Election Day. These rallies are useful in signing up volunteers to work for the weeks leading up to the vote.

In the 1997 governor's race in New Jersey, the Mercer County Central Labor Council turned out 500 union activists for Election Day through these new practices. Each activist got a bag of literature, a walking map of a neighborhood, a list of voters for whom he or she had responsibility to turn out, a flashlight, and a boxed dinner. Labor's candidate won the county by 15,000 votes in 1997. Our candidate lost the same county by 10,000 the last time around with far fewer union members on the street. Labor's impact on this race was indisputable. A poll conducted the day after the 1997 election in New Jersey confirmed that union grassroots' activity is paying off. Among those union members who received the expanded program of member-to-member contact, materials distributed at the workplace, and additional mail and telephone contact, 23 percent more (or a total of 79 percent) claimed to have voted for the union-endorsed candidate. Sixteen thousand first-time union voters were added to the rolls in New Jersey in 1997. Focus groups and polls were used to try to determine the best arguments to use with unregistered members. We sent them mailings, which we followed up with phone calls and worksite visits. Some unions provided stewards with lists of unregistered members and urged them to register new voters. President

Sweeney has said that we will register four million union household voters by the 2000 election.

But once we have registered union members to vote, mobilized them, and educated them, we still need to increase our base. We've got to organize new union members. Politics might help us. After a 1998 meeting with a group of workers who have been trying to organize unions in the face of employer harassment and intimidation, Vice President Al Gore remarked, "The right to organize is a fundamental right. In America, it is too often violated. This must change." If Al Gore can say workers have a right to a union, certainly local politicians who seek union support can say it also. There's a whole list of things we can ask politicians to do to support the right to organize. We can ask them to deny government contracts to employers who break labor law and we can ask for support for bargaining rights for workers. Politicians can attend our rallies and picket lines and they can write letters of encouragement to workers who are forming unions. Representative Glen Poshard of Illinois frequently sends letters to workers in his district who are in a workplace that is organizing, urging them to vote for the union.

We can ask elected officials to urge employers to be neutral in a campaign or to recognize a union based on a majority showing on union cards. Politicians can be part of local workers' rights boards. They can encourage other elected officials to support us. Like Representative David Bonior, they can get arrested in an act of civil disobedience alongside workers, or like Representative Maxine Waters, they can house call workers who are preparing to vote in a union election. We must begin to demand more from the politicians we support. We must make them understand that by helping to increase union membership they are helping to increase their electoral base.

And we must raise the bar by which we judge candidates. We first have to define the issues that are important to workers, and then we have to ask ourselves whether the candidates support those issues. While many members are frustrated with labor's links to the Democratic Party, the way to regain our members' trust is not, as some suggest, to endorse more Republicans who only support workers on a few issues. The answer is to endorse fewer Democrats who give tepid support to our issues. We must actively work for those candidates who strongly support working families' agenda.

Our final step is to influence who runs for office from the first day of the campaign. Our elected officials at all levels of government do not look like Americans. Twenty-six percent of the members of Congress are millionaires, and 181 are business people or bankers. Sixty-five percent have advanced degrees, in contrast to the less than 1 percent of Americans who do. Of the 1,843 Americans who have served in the U.S. Senate, 1,813 have been white men. There have been only twenty-six female senators, four African-American senators, and three Latinos. Our representatives are just not like us.

We are beginning to change this. Under our National Labor Political Training Center, thousands of union members across the country are being trained to run campaigns and to run for office. Working with state federations from Washington State to Maine, we are developing a corps of skilled campaign activists able to run professional campaigns, and a corps of union members who are beginning to run all offices—from school board and county commission to state legislature—including eventually, for Congress. The AFL-CIO has started a program called "2,000 in 2000," aimed at running 2,000 union members for elected office in the year 2000. We hope to not only change the terms of the debate on Capitol Hill, but eventually also change the debaters themselves.

Nothing unions are doing today is really new. Labor had the same tactics in the 1930s and 1940s when our political power was at a peak. The only difference then was that we mobilized without faxes, laptops, and cell phones. But we mobilized and workers were empowered to make a difference on issues of economic importance to us. By mobilizing, we transformed a nation with programs like the New Deal and the Great Society.

Labor's goal has to be more than simply building a machine to elect Democrats. If we do that, we've lost. Our goal must be to build a base of working families that is organized around issues, a base big enough to demand politicians' attention. By accomplishing this, we will begin to give more power to working families and begin to equalize the balance between corporate interests and the interests of the rest of us.

It is a political issue that children whose parents work every day for a living can't see a decent doctor. It is a political issue that our paychecks won't pay the bills. As labor, we must design an agenda that makes politics serve working Americans and their families. Anything less is simple partisanship, and that's never been what this movement was meant to be about.

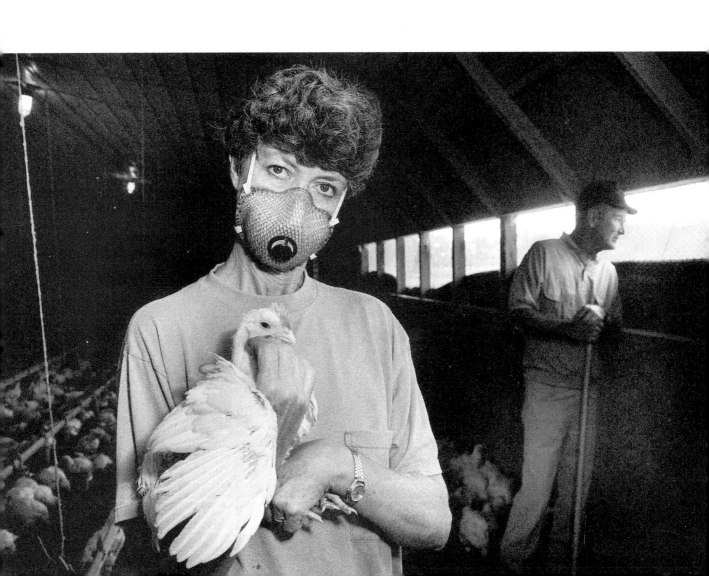

INFORMING AND EMPOWERING AMERICAN WORKERS

Ten Rules for Union Political Action

geoffrey garin and *guy molyneux*

Peter D. Hart Research Associates has conducted extensive public opinion research among American union members over the past few years, for the AFL-CIO and many of its international unions, on members' political attitudes and their view of union political action efforts. In February 1996 the first edition of "Ten Rules for Union Political Action" was published, laying out recommendations for a model of labor political action centered on *informing and empowering members.* Labor's issue and electoral work in 1996 (and since) reflected that orientation to a very substantial degree, and subsequent research documents an increase in member support for union political action. In this revised edition of "Ten Rules" we draw upon additional research conducted in 1996 and 1997 to update and sharpen the recommendations. The central focus, however, remains on informing and empowering the individual men and women who make up the American labor movement, so that they may have an effective voice in the political process.

INTRODUCTION

Opinion research reveals a union membership that supports unions' active engagement in the political process, and is generally in sync with organized labor's political and legislative priorities. The survey evidence on this point is clear and consistent:

> Three quarters agree that "unions need to invest time and money in politics and legislation today, to counter the influence that corporations and wealthy special interests have."

> Seven in ten union members say they are more likely to vote for a candidate who "is supported by the AFL-CIO and national unions, and has strong pro-union positions on the issues."

> In 1996, members said by ratios of 7 to 2 that Newt Gingrich and the Republicans were bad for average working families, and that Bill Clinton and the Democrats were good for working families. And 86 percent agreed with labor's positions on the minimum wage and Medicare.

When asked to explain in their own words why union political engagement is important, members volunteer that unions should be fighting for the sake of their members to protect workers' rights, and to give working-class people a voice in the political process.

While members demonstrate a broad understanding of the need for union political involvement, they voice concerns about the way unions have sometimes pursued political goals. The research points to two fundamental tests that members have for judging union political action programs. A good program—one that promises to mobilize members behind the union's legislative and electoral goals and earn the members' respect—must meet these two standards. *Members want political action to be, first and foremost, about them and their needs, not about candidates or political parties.* Unions need to make clear that their criteria for making political and legislative decisions concern the best interest of members and other working people. Members too often perceive unions as pursuing an "insider" strategy of trying to gain influence by cultivating relationships with party leaders or with specific candidates. Because members believe the political system is generally corrupt and hostile to the interests of working people, they have little confidence in insider strategies. They want an approach to political action that gives working men and women a voice in a political debate that now excludes them. *Second, political action should focus on informing and involving the members, so that they can be politically empowered.* Union members feel politically powerless today, and the traditional candidate endorsement model of labor political action does not work to empower them. What members want most of all from their union is more political information—and then to be trusted to make the right voting decisions—rather than simply receiving endorsements that often seem like "marching orders." Members understand that knowledge is power, and unions will win members' appreciation and respect by giving them the information they need to be smarter.

Union members are essentially calling for a new model of labor political action. The point of departure for this model must be issues that affect working people, rather than candidate endorsements. Unions must conduct politics in a way that includes and empowers the members. Most important, members need reassurance that their interests lie at the heart of unions' decision-making. Today's unions must make clear at every opportunity—to their members and to all working men and women—that they do not constitute just another special interest group, but rather a movement that seeks to empower America's workers.

Ten specific "rules for union political action" follow that address the concerns and desires we heard expressed by the membership, and point the way toward a model of labor politics built upon the core principles of educating and empowering working people.

TEN RULES FOR UNION POLITICAL ACTION

1. Issues come first, candidates and parties second.

2. In election campaigns, unions need to provide members with *information*, not voting instructions.

3. Presenting information in a credible and objective manner is critical for overcoming members' cynicism and distrust regarding politics.

4. Unions must downplay partisan rhetoric in favor of stressing their role as an *independent* voice for working people.

5. Unions should be "watchdogs" who approach politicians with a healthy skepticism and work to hold them accountable.

6. Members want unions to represent them as *workers,* by addressing issues that directly affect them on the job and by advancing a populist economic agenda.

7. Union political action should always be "of, by, and for" the members.

8. Mobilization is not fundamentally different from persuasion—informing members is also the key to increasing participation.

9. Members will best be reached by modern communication methods.

10. Effectiveness is enhanced by addressing the concerns of specific union audiences, instead of relying on a "one-size-fits-all" approach.

THE 10 RULES

1. Issues come first, candidates and parties second.

From the members' perspective, issues are the foundation upon which political action programs should be constructed. Working to elect pro-worker candidates is a legitimate union activity, but only as a means to the end of winning on important issues—not as an end in itself. Union political action decisions should always be driven by a fundamental commitment to represent members' (and workers') interests on the important issues that affect their lives.

Consequently, unions need to consistently let members know what issues the union believes are important, where the union comes down on those issues, and why. Today, members often have very low levels of knowledge in these areas, so sustained education is vitally important. In fact, members themselves readily acknowledge that they need information from their unions. They recognize that they cannot hope to keep track of legislative and political developments on their own, and that the union has the resources and expertise to follow issues and make judgments in a way they cannot.

Members are very distrustful of information that comes from politicians, and are even skeptical of much they see in the mass media, so they are looking for *independent* sources of information. Labor communications should therefore emphasize unions' independent perspective, and play off of workers' general skepticism. The goal is to convey the sense that this publication (or piece of mail, or web site) has been created by people concerned about the members' interests—*and not any other political agenda.* Union publications should feel more like a kind of "Consumer Reports" for working people, providing an objective and independent view on important employment and economic issues. One encouraging finding in the research is that most members already believe that their union generally provides accurate and truthful information—a significant accomplishment in today's cynical environment.

Members believe that unions' electoral evaluations and endorsements should be based on candidates' positions on major issues, after careful examination of all candidates' records. It will also help to have continuity between the issues that the union works on prior to election season, and the issues used to make endorsement decisions. If members have heard consistently all year that the union considers Medicare and health and safety to be top priorities, and the union then explains its endorsements in terms of candidates' stands on those same issues, it makes it more plausible that candidates are indeed being judged on an issue basis rather than on party affiliation or some other criteria.

2. In election campaigns, unions need to provide members with *information,* not voting instructions.

Again and again, members tell us that *information* is what they want most from their unions. The endorsement model of union political action—in which the union signals its approval of given candidates—is rejected by most members. Members state quite clearly that they do not want to be told for whom to vote, but this is often what they feel they get from their unions today. They perceive endorsements as "instructions" on how to vote, to which they react with indifference or even resentment. Some also suspect that endorsements are driven more by unions' institutional interests than by what is best for members.

Before members will respect endorsements, they want to see the issue positions, voting records, and other factors that lead to them. When we distribute union campaign literature that is comparative in nature, i.e., that shows the positions of *both* candidates on key issues, members respond very favorably. Saying this is precisely the type of information they find helpful and want from their unions. To be sure, they recognize that such literature is designed to build support for one of the two candidates—there is no illusion of impartiality, nor is perfect neutrality what members expect—but they do want to be assured that this information was the basis for the union's endorsement, and was not assembled subsequently to justify an endorsement based on other factors.

The power of such issue-focused electoral communications stems from two factors. First, it demonstrates that the union's campaign involvement is built upon a foundation of issues of legitimate importance to the membership. Second, by giving members factual information, instead of just relaying the union imprimatur, the union conveys trust and respect in the members' intelligence and good judgment.

As long as information is provided, most members do not object to the union also making a formal candidate endorsement. But it may often prove more effective to use language that suggests the union is offering guidance rather than commands. And many members' first choice would be to have the union just evaluate the candidates, provide the information, and then leave it to individual members to make the final call.

3. Presenting information in a credible and objective manner is critical for overcoming members' cynicism and distrust regarding politics.

When members say they want to receive detailed information on candidates from their union, they of course want that information to be accurate and fair. Although members tend to trust the accuracy of materials from the union more than many other sources, there is considerable skepticism regarding anything dealing with political matters. So it is important to develop direct mail pieces, pamphlets, and other materials that are credible. Consistently, the single most popular approach with participants in our focus group discussions is union voter guides that evaluate all candidates for a given office. Members appreciate side-by-side comparisons of the candidates that include their positions and records on key issues. Such comparisons suggest that the union actually evaluated both candidates, and didn't simply make a partisan choice.

It is very important to avoid extreme characterizations that appear implausible to members. For example, some voter guides rate the candidates, using a numeric scale or letter grades. When members see that one candidate has received a zero (or "F") on every issue, while another gets only 100s, the ratings are not believable—and this undermines the fundamental appeal of the voter guide approach. Small additions can enhance credibility. Documenting the sources of information provided in footnotes gives many members more confidence in the accuracy of what they are reading. Listing a 1-800 phone number has the same effect, because the union appears to be out front and willing to stand behind the claims it is making.

4. Unions must downplay partisan rhetoric in favor of stressing their role as an *independent* voice for working people.

Partisanship (in *either* its Democratic or Republican variety) is generally seen in a very negative light. In focus group discussions, when members read message statements or see television ads that seem to center on the parties, they tend to tune out and stop paying attention. Americans generally believe that excessive partisanship is one of the greatest failings of the country's political system, and members do not want their unions to be drawn into it.

Speaking to union members within a nonpartisan framework will therefore be essential to successful union political action. Members recognize that their union may end up endorsing Democrats more often than Republicans, even if it makes decisions on a strictly non-partisan basis. But they want reassurance that unions' support for Democrats is a consequence of a *prior commitment* to workers and their families, not just a reflection of a pro-Democratic bias (which they suspect is often at work). Stating clearly that your only agenda is standing up for working men and women and defending workers' interests is the best way to maintain a strong connection to an intensely anti-partisan union membership.

Speaking to members in ideological terms is generally no more effective than a partisan approach. Union members are no more likely than other workers to describe their own views as liberal, and are more likely to feel that the Democratic Party is "too liberal" (39 percent) than to think it is "too conservative" (8 percent). More generally, it is important to recognize that *union members' political inclinations are much more populist than liberal.* For example, it will usually not be effective to criticize a candidate for being "too conservative" (which does not trouble many members). You are much better off critiquing candidates for being "anti-worker," "anti-union," or "representing wealthy special interests, at the expense of working people."

5. Unions should be "watchdogs" who approach politicians with a healthy skepticism and work to hold them accountable.

It would be hard to overstate how cynical union members are about politics and politicians, and how far removed from their daily lives most of them perceive contemporary politics to be. At the heart of the problem is a pervasive distrust of politicians, whom members see as pursuing narrow personal or partisan agendas at the expense of the public interest. Workers believe that politicians will say anything to get elected, but then frequently turn around and do something quite different. This is a major reason why members believe that union political endorsements are ineffectual today.

Labor must show that it recognizes the danger of betrayal by politicians, and that it will hold accountable those it supports. Even as unions attempt to restore members' belief that involvement in politics is important and necessary, they must speak to and acknowledge this deep political disaffection—or risk forsaking their credibility with many members. When we tested video presentations designed to persuade members of the importance of union political action, the single most effective one tapped directly into their political cynicism. A key passage read this way:

> Members of Congress are so different from ordinary working people that we have to get commitments from them before we elect them, and then we have to watch them like hawks once they're in office to be sure they remember to represent *us.*

Members are very attracted to the idea of unions as "watchdogs" that will try to keep the politicians honest, instead of being on the inside of the system. It is the divide between average working people and a corrupt, business-dominated political system—not the one between Democrats and Republicans—that members see as the central fault line in politics today. Since partisanship can't be your political framework for communicating with members (Rule #4), this is an effective replacement. As you describe the fundamental problem which union political action seeks to redress, it is the absence of a strong voice for working people in a corrupt political system, not an imbalance of power between the two parties.

In this context of disaffection, a forceful style and language that suggests that unions are *fighting back* on their behalf is very effective with many union members (especially men). One of the high points, in terms of focus group response to arguments for political action, occurred when a union organizer said the union was going to "fight like hell" for the members. It also is important that labor positions itself as a force for change, not as a defender of the status quo. In addition, union communications need to feel, look, and sound different than traditional political advertising whenever possible. The less the messages sound and look like a continuation of the traditional partisan political dialogue, the more they will be heard by the members. This is especially important in September and October, when people are seeing and hearing so many campaign messages.

6. Members want unions to represent them as *workers,* by addressing issues that directly affect them on the job and by advancing a populist economic agenda.

The focus of labor's agenda should be primarily work-related and economic issues, as unions have clear standing with the members to discuss these issues in a way that is less true of other policy areas. Members instinctively trust unions to represent their interests on matters directly relating to their job, and this is where labor issue advocacy meets with near-universal support. On issues like workplace health and safety regulation, the forty-hour work week and overtime pay, and pension protection, members not only accept the active engagement of their unions—they demand it. Most members are also comfortable with the idea of unions representing their economic interests beyond the workplace, although this sentiment is not unanimous. Speaking out on such issues as Social Security, Medicare, the minimum wage, and tax fairness is generally thought to fall within the proper sphere of union involvement. Because large corporations and the wealthy are understood to have such hugely disproportionate political influence, unions are viewed as offering a valuable counterweight on economic matters, to the benefit of working families. Note, however, that the mandate to address non-work-related issues is not limitless—most members feel it is inappropriate for unions to take positions on controversial social and cultural issues (such as abortion or gun control).

In seeking to represent members' economic interests, it is important to focus on concrete measures that can help improve their lives. The focus group and survey results find many issues to be compelling, including raising the minimum wage, defending Medicare, providing greater educational opportunity, and protecting workplace health and safety. Consistently, the most powerful issues relate to the fundamental "pocketbook" concerns of the membership, while issues that appeal to compassion for the economically vulnerable are somewhat less effective.

Members also are receptive to the idea that they themselves should give more weight to their identity as workers when they make voting decisions. They feel comfortable with unions' working to cultivate this notion among members. One of the most compelling messages tested in the focus groups was that "if we don't start thinking as *workers* when we enter the voting booth, big corporations and the rich will continue to win out over working people."

7. Union political action should always be "of, by, and for" the members.

Political action decisions, such as endorsements, have more impact when they are seen as emerging from—and responding to—the membership and its concerns. Members should see that the internal decision-making process for union political action is consistent with the core goal of empowering working people. Unions cannot credibly speak about politically empowering working people if members are not seen as having a say in the union itself. As much as possible, rank-and-file members should have visible opportunities to be involved in the process, such as through membership surveys or public candidate forums. Members don't expect the union to make decisions by referendum—they understand that union leaders have important information and expertise to bring to bear—but they do want some role for the membership. In addition, the evaluation and endorsement process should be as *transparent* as possible. If members know how and why the union has reached an endorsement conclusion, they will have vastly more respect for it. Even those members who do not ultimately vote for the union-backed candidate in a given race will feel better about their union if they know members had a say in the decision.

Furthermore, political action is not just something the union does "for" members— it should mean mobilizing and involving the members themselves. Members believe union political action should be about *empowering the members to make a difference*. The starting point is asking people to do more: letter writing, signing petitions, calling elected officials. Members surely won't get involved if they are not asked, and union surveys show that many have never received a request for participation. Many members will, of course, still remain uninvolved, but even those who do not respond will feel better knowing that the union welcomes their participation.

Many members recognize that organized labor can only truly be strong if workers get involved, and they recognize that workers' detachment from politics is ultimately self-defeating. They are willing to have their current cynicism and complacency challenged, and support unions' efforts to encourage political engagement. One of the most effective issue ads run by the AFL-CIO in 1996 showed workers speaking at a public meeting on Medicare in Boston. In part, members responded to the substance of the testimony, but what made this ad powerful was showing real people speaking out, and taking their message—via television—to a wide audience. By doing that, the Federation literally gave average people a chance to be heard, which is exactly what members are looking for. By the same token, one of the most compelling pieces of political direct mail we tested told members that on election day, "You're in Charge."

8. Mobilization is not fundamentally different from persuasion—informing members is also the key to increasing participation.

Members strongly support union efforts to encourage them to vote on election day. Regardless of partisan identification, they feel this is an important and legitimate union activity. They especially appreciate appeals that explicitly say that the union wants them to vote, *even if they do not support union-endorsed candidates*. Expressing this concern about members' participation, even if it does not serve the union's immediate electoral agenda, impresses members tremendously. It suggests that the union's commitment to empowering individual members is fundamental and genuine.

Traditionally, mobilization is thought of as a fundamentally different activity than persuading members to support particular candidates. However, research suggests that the most important barrier to participation is members' low level of knowledge. People who do not feel they know much about the issues in a campaign, or where the candidates stand, are reluctant to walk into a voting booth. It is intimidating, and they worry that they will make the wrong decisions—so it seems safer to stay home. Members who feel well-informed, in contrast, participate at a very high rate. Consequently, the best way to increase membership turnout is to educate them about the issues and candidates, so that they feel like—and in fact are—well-informed voters. Postcard reminders and other direct encouragements to vote are helpful, but the only way to significantly affect turnout of union members is to raise their level of political knowledge. In other words, the key to mobilization turns out to be the same as for persuasion—providing members with a steady flow of accurate and fair information.

9. Members will best be reached by modern communication methods.

We know from our research for many AFL-CIO member unions that labor newspapers and magazines effectively reach only a portion of the membership. Unions will need to employ a variety of other communication strategies in their political action efforts, including direct mail and radio and television advertising. Union members have consistently given good ratings to the AFL-CIO's issue-oriented television advertisements, both in focus groups and in surveys. They appreciate the content, especially the focus on conveying information about important legislative issues, but they also are proud to see *unions* speaking out, being active, and trying to make their presence felt. Some even express the hope that this will improve unions' larger public image, which in turn will make them stronger at the bargaining table as well as in the political sphere.

Focus group discussions of political direct mail provide some important insights into how to make these communications effective:

> *Use powerful visual images in union communications.* Members have little interest in messages that arrive in standard envelopes, but find those with more colorful and graphically-oriented presentations to be quite compelling.

> *Positive images and information are important.* Members get tired of seeing unhappy people, complaining about economic problems. Negative information is often an essential part of your message, but don't let this dominate your communications efforts.

> *Humor is effective, especially when delivering negative information.* With members often feeling deluged by political mail (from both candidates and groups), it's important to differentiate your communications and grab people's atten-

tion. Humorous images and clever tag lines often do the trick. It is also an effective way to deliver negative information against a candidate, as it seems less mean-spirited.

Speak to members' core values. The union should not get so caught up in talking about policies that it forgets to talk about the fundamental values that drive union political commitments. You may need to educate members about changes in the OSHA budget or pension coverage regulations, but always communicate the underlying values: strong families, respect for hard work, keeping promises, doing the right thing, and representing members.

Employ accessible language. Fight the tendency to employ insider-speak, such as the formal name of legislation or agency acronyms. For one thing, most members won't know what you're talking about. Such jargon also serves to reinforce members' impression that the union is part of a distant, impenetrable political culture that has little to do with their lives. Messages should be plain and clear: talk about the 40-hour week, not the "Fair Labor Standards Act"; talk about how often a candidate takes the side of working people, not about "COPE ratings."

10. Effectiveness is enhanced by addressing the concerns of specific union audiences, instead of relying on a "one-size-fits-all" approach.

When you can, target messages to specific union audiences, instead of relying on a "one-size-fits-all" approach. It is often possible, especially with direct mail, for unions to reach targeted subgroups among the membership. Opinion research indicates that this can potentially be very effective. Some of the most relevant targeting options involve gender, sector, and age.

In many situations, unions should consider employing separate messages for *men and women.* A political direct mail piece addressed specifically to women, for example, was selected by nearly every female focus group participant as something she would be most likely to open and read. On the legislative front, communications with women might highlight education cutbacks and child care, while men might hear about tax cuts for the rich and U.S. jobs moving overseas. Even on a single issue, such as the 40-hour week, research has shown that men and women respond to different arguments for labor's position.

Sector of employment is also an important distinction. Construction trade members care passionately about preserving Davis-Bacon and other prevailing wage laws, while other union members rank this as a lower concern. Workers in manufacturing industries care more deeply than do others about foreign trade issues. Public employees understand that political figures are their "employers," and can be appealed to much more in terms of the direct impact of politics on their incomes, conditions of employment, and retirement security.

In a diverse labor movement, sensitivity to *language differences* is essential. Spanish-speaking union members, for example, express deep appreciation when they see Spanish language literature in focus groups. Even those who are themselves comfortable reading in English are glad to see their union recognizing the need for non-English educational materials.

The research also consistently shows major *age variations* in political attitudes among union members. Unfortunately, younger members are less politically knowledgeable and less likely than are older members to say they have received political information from their union (many of them are probably not even on union mailing lists). Clearly, reaching out to the young trade unionists who are the movement's future, and educating them about labor's economic perspective, issue priorities, and political preferences is a vitally important task today.

If labor only addresses the most broadly-held concerns of workers, some of the most powerful mobilizing issues will be overlooked. A more targeted approach, therefore, is often the right way to go.

Postscript: The Impact of Labor '96.

The first edition of "Ten Rules" (February 1996) included these words: "We believe that a revitalized labor political action program built around addressing these desires of the membership can reengage members in politics, strengthen unions, and ultimately reshape American politics. The AFL-CIO and its member unions are well positioned to fill this leadership void." This optimistic forecast was put to the test in 1996, when the AFL-CIO and many unions took new approaches to legislative and political work that were generally consistent with these recommendations. Surveys provide strong evidence that the labor movement reaped considerable rewards from the energy and innovation of 1996, with big increases in union members' turnout rate, votes for pro-union candidates, and, perhaps most importantly, support for union political action:

> A post-election survey found that union members familiar with the AFL-CIO's legislative issue campaign viewed it positively by a nearly five-to-one margin;

National exit polls showed that union members' turnout increased over the 1994 level, and their support for union-backed candidates also increased;

A January 1998 national survey of union members found dramatic increases in members' satisfaction with unions' approach to political and legislative affairs (up fourteen percentage points), trust in unions to take the right position on important issues (up twelve points), and strong support for unions overall (up fourteen points).

As impressive as these figures are, there is no reason to believe they represent the ceiling of what can be accomplished in the area of union political action. On the contrary, 1996 could very well be just the beginning. As unions become more disciplined and sophisticated at pursuing a strategy based on the fundamental principle of informing and empowering members, they should make still greater advances in providing a real political voice to working Americans.

TWO FOR THE YEAR 2000

kelly candaele

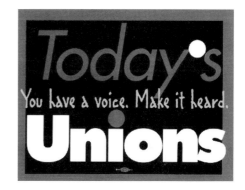

The AFL-CIO has initiated a program to elect two thousand union members to various political offices throughout the country by the year 2000. Implicit in this bold program are the assumptions that within labor's ranks is a wealth of political talent that should enter campaigns and that candidates who are explicitly pro-union can win. This positive assessment of the ability of self-identified union members to capture political office runs counter to prevailing wisdom among pundits and political professionals. The "special interest" tag of unions, so the argument goes, is too difficult to overcome for candidates closely aligned with organized labor. But in Los Angeles, two recent elections conducted in close cooperation with local unions and the Los Angeles County Federation of Labor were successful in putting union activists into office.

One of those elections was my own. I ran successfully, with the strong support of my own union, the American Federation of Teachers, for a vacant seat on the Los Angeles Community College Board of Trustees. Trustees are responsible for policy in a nine campus college district. The second election put Gil Cedillo, past General Manager for SEIU Local 660, a county employee union, into the California State Assembly. The backbone of both campaigns were local unions who aggressively communicated to and turned out their members, but more importantly, who organized with a new attitude and approach to political action. What follows are some brief suggestions drawn from these two campaigns that might help other union political activists prepare to run and win.

The first critical decisions is finding the right candidate to run for office. While this might seem like common sense, there are countless examples of unions putting forward candidates without considering an individual's background, political skills, or motivations. "I think I could do a good job," is not strong enough reason to devote membership resources and time to a campaign.

The American Federation of Teachers, College Guild, has for years cultivated candidates for Board of Trustees offices. Unlike most unions, they have not surrendered the candidate selection process to business or to other conservative ideological interests. They have looked for qualified candidates who know union issues and have sought out an ethnically diverse group of candidates to support. Their sophistication in recruiting and nurturing candidates has been rare in the labor movement, but in Los Angeles that is beginning to change.

Both Cedillo and myself came to our respective campaigns with decades of union and community involvement behind us. We both came from union organizing backgrounds and knew that campaigning required discipline and the ability to cross institutional boundaries to solicit broader community support. As organizers, we've had to deal with the practical realities of creating and sustaining majorities.

Years of experience debating policy issues within our respective unions also prepared us for the inevitable campaign controversies over economic and social policy. We knew that union work was a citizenship school for working-class people entering political life. It's important that candidates who come from labor recognize and draw on that valuable resource.

Early in our campaigns we decided that for principled and political reasons, we would use our union backgrounds as a strength rather than as something to soft-pedal. Although we relied on the assistance of campaign consultants, we knew that we, as individuals, were primarily responsible for the issues and directions of the campaigns.

I had to campaign throughout Los Angeles County, in the relatively progressive areas of West, South Central and East Los Angeles, as well as the more conservative San Fernando Valley. Even in the San Fernando Valley, where some voters were suspicious of my union ties, I spoke of the productive value of a close relationship with the faculty and support staff on the college campuses. When attacked by other candidates as being a "tool" of the unions, I responded that I was proud to have their support and that our educational mission would be enhanced by faculty who felt empowered and respected for their work. I stated in community meetings that "one of the things you do to show respect for employees is to pay them well." I found that confidently asserting a seemingly unpopular position garnered respect, and at times even votes, in areas where a suspicion of unions was prevalent.

Cedillo's Assembly District includes downtown Los Angeles, Koreatown, Little Tokyo, and parts of east Los Angeles, an area reflecting the social and economic contradictions of the city—high-rise financial muscle juxtaposed with some of the poorest precincts in the county. One of Cedillo's strongest allies was Miguel Contreras, new chief of the Los Angeles County Federation of Labor. Contreras, a strong backer of National AFL-CIO President John Sweeney and an advocate for militant unionism, came out of the United Farm Workers with the belief that critical allies in the broader community (including immigrants) could help revive a moribund labor movement. Those allies could also be helpful in electing union candidates to office.

A decisive moment for the labor/immigrant alliance in Los Angeles came in 1994 when the local Federation of Labor joined a highly visible campaign to defeat Proposition 187, the attempt to exclude illegal immigrants from health care and public education. At that time, Contreras was Political Director of the Federation. Labor's move sent a strong message to the immigrant community that most unions saw new immigrants as potential allies rather than as threats to economic security. After Cedillo secured the endorsement of the Los Angeles Labor Federation, Contreras aggressively organized labor's political arm and articulated one of the main ideological themes of the campaign: that the battle in this election was between Governor Pete Wilson and an emerging Latino majority in Los Angeles.

In a move reflecting both Contreras's and the AFL-CIO's commitment to working closely with community groups previously shunned by labor's hierarchy, unions reached out to the "One Stop Immigration Center," and "La Hermindad," two prominent immigrant rights groups, to help shape a pro-worker/immigrant message and to bring seasoned activists into the campaign. Six hundred volunteers were recruited to walk precincts during the final days of the election.

The immigrant groups targeted 9,000 voters who had registered for the first time within the fourteen months leading up to the close of registration. Each one of those new voters received five pieces of mail and three door hangers. In an Assembly District with one of the lowest turnout ratios in the state, 45 percent of the new immigrant voters targeted went to the polls.

In both of our campaigns the message directed to union members differed from past approaches. According to David Rolf, an SEIU official who ran Cedillo's day-to-day field operation for the California State AFL-CIO, the message to the 7,000 targeted union members in the district reflected the ideological changes that John Sweeney brought to AFL-CIO political operations. "We no longer insult our members intelligence," Rolf said, reflecting on the positive election results.

Standard practice in previous Los Angeles campaigns was to send out thousands of "slate cards" listing the union endorsed candidates. The slate card would occasionally be accompanied by a letter from a local union president letting the member know that "the union" had determined which candidates were worthy of his support. Often, no other information was provided. "Our research and focus groups with our own members told us that they weren't listening when we simply told the rank and file how to vote," Rolf said. "We had to change our approach so our members actually cared about what we did."

John Sweeney initiated that change while still International President of SEIU. He instigated a thorough review of union operations through a "Committee On The Future," which looked seriously at the dynamics of American politics, economics, and culture, and concluded that the union movement had to change or die. When Sweeney was elected to head the AFL-CIO, part of that study became "Ten Rules for Union Political Action," a hard critique of how ineffective labor's political arm had become (see previous chapter.) For years, according to the report, unions had been telling members how to vote, but avoiding an extensive conversation about the real economic and social issues that impacted their lives. In the absence of serious discussion and political education, radio talk show hosts, political buccaneers, and conservative think tanks that controlled the terms of political debate filled the ideological vacuum. When asked, rank-and-file members stated they were much more concerned about where candidates stood on issues affecting their paychecks, their health care, and their jobs than they were about which elected officials or Democratic and Republican Party bigwigs had endorsed them.

Cedillo was a candidate perfectly positioned for labor's new approach to political action. He actually had a record in the community and he wasn't afraid of taking strong positions. The mail sent to union members focused on his fight as a union leader to save the large county hospital in the district when other elected officials wanted to close it down or turnover a downsized version to private sector operators. Mailers featured real union members talking about real issues without the usual "your union is supporting so and so" refrain. One piece confronted the issue of institutional endorsements head on. It showed a picture of a homecare worker and read, "My vote does not belong to a candidate, an elected official or even the leader of my union. It belongs to me. And here is why I'm voting for Gil Cedillo."

"Cedillo had a track record," Rolf pointed out. "He was a union leader, he had spent years negotiating health care benefits and he fought to preserve a hospital that was critical to the community. We didn't send our members pictures with him with his arm around some politician. We talked about issues that were important." The labor/community strategy paid off. Cedillo won virtually every precinct against an incumbent member of the Los Angeles school board who was expected to dominate the race.

And in my Community College race, I emphasized to voters the class and ethnic nature of our colleges. I talked about access and opportunity for working-class and poor students and spoke constantly about the need for inexpensive child care and transportation. I did not offer "education" as an abstraction, divorced from the broader struggle for economic justice, or as the panacea for social problems.

At least in Los Angeles, local labor looks less like the movement Gompers shaped and more like the militant turn-of-the-century union, the Industrial Workers of the World. The infamous IWW reached out to immigrants, itinerants, and other-low wage workers on the so called "fringe" of the economy. The IWW, a left-wing challenger to the centrist AFL, took in workers that the craft-union-dominated AFL had turned their backs on. Clearly, Contreras and a growing list of elected officials aligned with organized labor are, like the IWW, wagering their organizational and political capital on the conviction that new immigrant workers can be organized and brought to the polls in decisive numbers.

Cedillo and I also worked closely with academics and intellectuals who translated their scholarly work into practical proposals for action. A number of academics helped shape the content of my campaign. University of Wisconsin Professor Joel Rogers provided valuable policy information on how unions and business in Dane County, Wisconsin joined with local community colleges to train workers and to upgrade their skills. The real-life information provided a context for linking the work of progressive organizations and policy activists with the needs of our students and the changing mission of our colleges. Progressive academics helped put intellectual and policy meat on the bones of a campaign for an educational position, which in the absence of serious thinking could have succumbed to liberal clichés about education being the only engine of upward mobility.

Finally, Cedillo and I were both helped by the general sense of labor renewal starting at the highest levels of the AFL-CIO. Successful political campaigns derive from hard work, some luck, and inspiration—the ability to convince people that you are worthy of their support. The labor movement must take the idealistic impulses that often initially attract people and bring them into politics. Finding members who are willing to run, training them and providing a base of support can provide a sense of mission to a process that is still dominated by "check-book politics." A union PAC writing a check is a lazy way of being political. Building a union that relates to politics in a dynamic way takes work. The cynicism currently pervasive in politics can only be overcome by making political life a cause again.

Gil Cedillo and I felt we were not just two people running for office but were engaged in a broader project that linked politics with the future of the American labor movement. The values and accomplishments of the labor movement shaped our families' history and the trajectory of our work lives. Now those same values are shaping the battles that we fight as elected leaders.

PUBLIC POLICY AND THE TWO-THIRDS MAJORITY

marc baldwin

The 1990s are proving to be a difficult time to advance rigorous policy work. Take Medicare for example. In the 1996 elections, Republicans insisted that their budget didn't cut Medicare because baseline funding increased. Never mind that inflation cut the purchasing power of that spending below current levels. Never mind that independent analyses showed that the cuts would result in significantly increased spending among private employers as their costs rose to shore up cuts in public systems. Never mind that urban hospitals were forecast to close as a result. For months the American public was treated to the spectacle of supposed experts spouting the partisan inanity that taking billions of dollars out of Medicare would "protect and strengthen" the program. Into this inauspicious environment of serious policy debate, the AFL-CIO Public Policy Department was launched.

CHANGING POLICY ENVIRONMENT

We can't talk about the changing structure and output of AFL-CIO policy work without putting them in context. It is unfair, for example, to assume that the AFL-CIO before President Sweeney was uninterested in policy development. Characterizations of "Big Labor" that assume our policy and legislative work were always motivated solely by short-term, narrow interests are badly mistaken. The AFL-CIO has always had a commitment to policy work that went beyond the next congressional committee meeting or federal budget. The memoirs of Nelson Cruikshank give a personal glimpse of AFL-CIO policy intervention from the New Deal to Carter (*The Cruikshank Chronicles*, Archon Books: 1989). The AFL-CIO Social Security Department under Cruikshank played a pivotal role in winning Medicare. And former AFL-CIO President Lane Kirkland's first job with the AFL (before the AFL and the CIO merged) was in the research department. He also ran the Operating Engineers' research and education departments before becoming executive assistant to George Meany. The new policy department is thus the latest incarnation of a long history. It is as evolutionary as it is revolutionary.

What drives the creation, construction, and direction of the latest policy effort is an evolving policy environment. The environment that led to President Sweeney's victory simultaneously created the impetus for expanded, redirected policy work. These changes can be traced to four environmental changes. First, throughout the 1980s, U.S. income distribution grew increasingly polarized. The declining middle class, expanding bottom of the wage scale, and transformation of labor markets took most Americans by surprise after decades of constant economic improvement. The existence of the "anxious class" is now taken for granted, but its appearance in economic life and the depth of its penetration into all occupations and industries is a very recent phenomenon. Labor was caught flat-footed. Our bargaining strategies, policy arguments, and political tactics were all based on incremental improvements and stable alliances. President Sweeney's personal history of organizing at the bottom of the income ladder gave him a powerful sense of the nation's economic transformation and the need to rethink our responses.

Second, income polarization had at least one clear cause: the declining power of unions to capture and redistribute productivity gains. By the late 1990s, the stagnlation of the 1970s had been completely wrung out of the economy. Tight labor markets no longer gave rise to increased wage pressures. The deep recession in the early 1980s, the corporate assault on unions, and global production strategies put heavy downward pressure on wage demands. By 1995, the grotesque inequities of ballooning CEO pay, declining worker wages, and footloose global companies were too much for union members

and the general public to stomach. AFL-CIO affiliates wanted a stronger labor movement response and, to get it, they needed better information and more policy work.

Third, the composition of the labor movement changed. The industrial shift toward
public sector unions was clear in national survey data. Between 1978 and 1997, the public sector portion of all unionization went from 17 to 42 percent. The expansion of public sector unionism led many AFL-CIO affiliates to pursue bargaining units in this area.
At last count, the Public Employee Department of the AFL-CIO had thirty-five international unions as members. This trend is important because policy work and bargaining
support go hand in hand where unions represent workers who administer public programs. New programs mean new funding streams, new job classifications, and new
issues to understand. The growth of public sector membership logically led to increased
affiliate activity around policy development. More specifically, the unions with most representation in the public sector—the Service Employees (SEIU) and the American
Federation of State, County & Municipal Employees (AFSCME)—had led the charge to
transform the AFL-CIO in 1995. Both unions have large policy shops that integrate bargaining, legislation, and organizing.

Finally, all of the above factors highlight the most important environmental influence on the changing nature of AFL-CIO policy work. Union membership did not just
move to new sectors. It declined. Declining union membership forced the AFL-CIO and
its affiliate unions to achieve new alliances. The way we do politics changed the way we
do policy. As membership declined, our capacity to independently influence many policy decisions also declined. Labor must increasingly reach out to new industries and occupations for membership and to diverse organizations for political support. As some
specific examples below show , the increased desire and need to reach out to new constituencies has fundamentally changed our policy structures and outputs.

POLICY CAPACITY AND THE LABOR MOVEMENT

The 1980s were a period of dramatic expansion of right-wing policy capacity. The growth
of these networks is well documented elsewhere[1]. By combining a vast network of well-
funded foundations and aggressive policy shops, the Right was able to capitalize on electoral success at both the federal and state levels. Obviously, the labor movement can
never match the financial capacity of corporate America. But it is striking to see just how
far behind we had fallen by the mid-1990s.

The labor movement's internal policy capacity reflects the primary agenda of the
affiliates, namely, successful collective bargaining. At the time of President Sweeney's

victory, only the AFL-CIO had policy departments that were solely engaged in policy development and legislative support. The policy departments of affiliate unions all have collective bargaining responsibility in addition to their legislative advocacy support. Most have "research" departments, which have some policy responsibility. Fewer than five affiliates have separate "policy" departments. Policy capacity outside the labor movement, serving labor's interests, is similarly limited.

There is an extensive network of "progressive" policy outfits in Washington and, to a lesser extent, in the states, but these organizations are, for the most part, ambivalent toward organized labor. The Economic Policy Institute is the exception which proves the rule. Although EPI is frequently described in the press as "labor-funded" most of its support comes from outside the labor movement. Limited policy capacity has caused many unions and labor-oriented legislators to turn to individual academics with labor orientations to support their work.

Even within the AFL-CIO, policy work has been distressingly unorganized. Before the reorganization, the Employee Benefits Department, the Economic Research Department, and the Safety and Health Departments all had responsibility for significant policy work in areas with potential overlap. They went about their business with minimal contact with each other. Worse, departments had limited means to ensure information flowed where it was most needed: outside Washington. The policy department now works closely with the new Field Mobilization Department to produce information for state and local campaigns, the Legislation Department to provide content for legislative discussions, and the Organizing Department to build the case for unions. A new position within the AFL-CIO—Assistant to the President for Government Affairs—coordinates policy work across all departments through regular strategy meetings. The story of the reshaping of AFL-CIO policy capacity is thus the story of reshaping both policy output and policy delivery.

POLICY IMPERATIVES

Unlike academic policy researchers, we don't have the luxury of exploring whatever interesting research agenda we might care to. The labor movement exists in a hostile environment, with pressing, immediate demands. To ensure that immediate needs are channeled toward longer term goals, our work is organized around three themes:

1) Improve the environment for union organizing

2) Define an independent, issue-based policy agenda

3) Pursue progressive, majoritarian policy initiatives to unite the bottom two-third of Americans.

Our research and writing has to promote unionization. Several AFL-CIO programs work toward that end. The Union Cities effort promotes community organizing among the local AFL-CIO bodies, the elected Central Labor Councils. As part of Union Cities, the Public Policy Department has developed materials on the union advantage in wages and benefits and, more broadly, promoted the notion that expanded unionization bene-fits everyone in a local area.

And with the Organizing Department and Organizing Institute, we develop similar arguments in the "right to organize" campaigns. We directly support federal and state leg-islative efforts through the Legislative Department and Field Mobilization Department.

AFL-CIO policy output runs at two speeds. On one hand, we are called upon to inter-vene in high level policy forums. We debate anti-union researchers and hostile studies in traditional academic and policy forums. On the other hand, our work must also be convincing to workers without economic training. Along with working papers, we do talking points. We write draft letters to editors. We work with our Education Department to make economic arguments accessible. As unionization has declined, our work is increasingly focused on rebuilding the union perspective on issues and convincing work-ers who are not yet union members that our arguments are right. And while we develop arguments around specific legislative efforts, we also try to keep an eye on the future. When we fought against "fast track" for trade agreements, we were fighting an immedi-ate battle, and beginning to advance a more visionary trade policy. Small gains around health care are won in the context of a bigger debate about economic security. A victory against privatization of some programs in one state is an opportunity to educate voters and union members about economic power, social insurance principles, and solidarity. Despite having a minority of friendly state governors and an openly hostile majority in Congress, our work is oriented, at least in part, toward developing sweeping policy reforms which may be years away.

But we must still attempt to advance a majoritarian politics. With unionization below 10 percent in the private sector, we can't win big legislative victories on our own. To be sure, we still chalk up wins around bills that support specific unions and address the con-cerns of specific union members. But the only way to really move policy is to reach out. Said differently, the best way to defend ourselves in a hostile policy environment is to take the offensive. Taking the offensive means advancing a broad, progressive policy agenda for all working families, unionized or not. The income polarization, lost job security, and family pressures of the 1980s have created a vast two-thirds majority of workers susceptible to a unifying message. Although specific issues may change over time, the overarching need to increase financial security, improve the mix of work and family, and restore the balance of power in the workplace will be facts of life for years to come.

These concerns are neither readily addressed by the Right nor truly understood by the New Democrats. The Right's obsession with market solutions (particularly when they benefit specific allies within the market) can never convincingly address market failures. Similarly, the desire of New Democrats to find "win-win" solutions and to welcome business partnerships means they can never fully address issues where employers are clearly part of the problem, like declining employer-sponsored insurance and under-investment in workplace training. New Democrats have a blind spot where employer mandates are needed. Incentives, voluntarism, and cost-benefit analysis drive New Democratic politics. These approaches will never lead to the kind of transformation of economic relations that working people need. In the long run, workers need an improved context for organizing and mobilization of a new majority around an independent policy agenda.

KEY ISSUES FOR THE 2/3 MAJORITY

Several recent campaign efforts show how AFL-CIO policy work is used in practice. These campaigns illustrate both the range of output (briefing papers, press events, larger studies) and the vehicles for delivery (other AFL-CIO departments, editorial boards, allied groups).

Minimum Wage

The recent modest increase in the minimum wage was a pivotal event on the policy agenda of the new AFL-CIO. To many observers before the battle, the decline of the minimum wage over the years was not seen as a union issue. Few union members earn the minimum wage. Few union contracts have any relation to the minimum wage. It is a mistake to assume that no union members were directly affected by the increase, but the fact remains that in part because it had declined so significantly, the minimum wage increase had have little direct impact on union members. Yet the move to raise this threshold galvanized AFL-CIO activity.

Why did the issue inspire such action and, ultimately, lead to a stunning victory? The answer lies in the transformation of the labor market. People understood, regardless of their personal wages, that the floor was falling out of the labor market. Wide-spread pub-

Poverty and the Minimum Wage

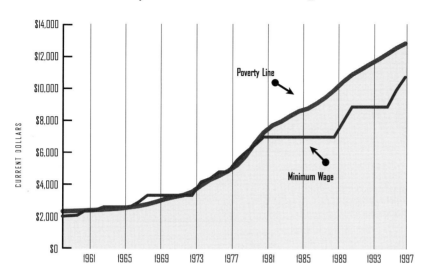

Unions Raise Wages

Median weekly earnings of full-time wage and salary workers, 1996

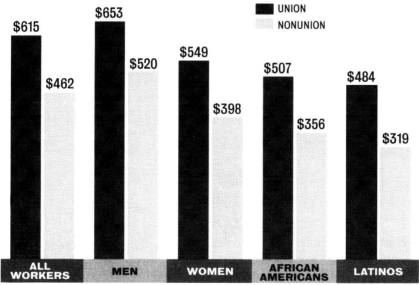

Source: U.S. Bureau of Labor Statistics

lic support for raising the minimum wage spoke volumes about Americans' sense of fairness, their skepticism about economic performance, and their willingness to question free market economic assumptions. For the AFL-CIO and affiliate unions, this awareness presented a timely opportunity to draw a sharp line between the New Right and workers—all workers, not just union members.

The contribution of policy work was small compared with the grassroots mobilization that led to victory. But our arguments were key in illustrating labor's broader agenda. Two aspects of the minimum wage fight were important. First, several economists developed a wage profile analysis showing that economic benefits beyond those of workers who directly receive a minimum wage increase. Employers who pay just above the minimum wage often increase wages to remain above the threshold. This wage increase, in turn, leads to further upward pressure throughout the labor market. By highlighting the benefits to all workers of raising the bottom, these analyses promote solidarity and argue for organizing activity among low-wage workers. Second, several economists produced new studies showing tiny employment effects when wages increase. Opponents had claimed that raising wages would reduce employment as employees became more expensive. In countering this argument, minimum wage advocates created an opportunity to confront neoclassical economics, bigger issues about distribution, and myths about the effect of wages on employment.

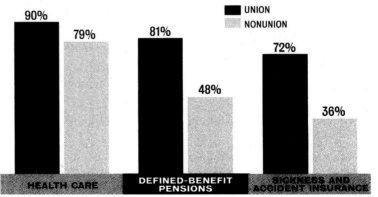

More Union Workers Have Health and Pension Benefits

Percent of full-time employees covered by selected benefit programs in firms with more than 100 people, 1993

■ UNION
▒ NONUNION

90%   79%   81%   48%   72%   36%

HEALTH CARE   DEFINED-BENEFIT PENSIONS   SICKNESS AND ACCIDENT INSURANCE

Employee status for workfare workers

If the minimum wage fight seemed afield from labor's core concerns, the situation of former welfare recipients must seem remote. But the Public Policy Department played a pivotal role in building a coalition of labor and human service advocates that pressed federal agencies to defend welfare-to-work workers from employer abuse. In the aftermath of the 1997 welfare legislation, some Republicans began pushing to limit workplace protections for welfare-to-work workers. They began arguing that these workers are not really workers, but are performing community service. The AFL-CIO and allied groups fought back. Their fundamental message: all workers, regardless of their previous status, have a right to respect and dignity. By refusing to allow one group of workers to be treated as second-class citizens, the fight to defend welfare-to-work participants was a springboard to larger policy questions about the rights of employees, the need to create jobs, the need to improve working conditions for all low-wage workers, and the need for a national strategy to reduce poverty, not just to reduce welfare.

Months of policy development and advocacy were undertaken at the staff level, building alliances between unions and anti-poverty advocates. The AFL-CIO ran advertisements and held press events, highlighting the connection to the minimum wage. In Los Angeles, the AFL-CIO Executive Council passed a resolution in support of union organizing among these new workers.

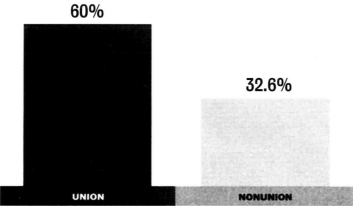

Union Workers Have Greater Job Security
Percent of workers with the same employer for 10 or more years

60%

32.6%

UNION NONUNION

Source: AFL-CIO analysis of April 1993 Current Population Survey Data

The effort to build coalitions around employee rights for welfare-to-work has had two important lasting consequences. First, the coalition, which was built at the national level, has worked effectively on state issues. Shortly after the victory around employee status, Texas proposed a sweeping privatization of key human services. The public sector unions faced job losses and human service advocates had fears about privacy, adequacy of services, and the fairness of private contractors. Relationships built at the national level resulted in useful alliances in the state. Together, the needs of low-income residents and the interests of union members prevailed. Second, again at the local level, the effort to defend former welfare recipients from abuse has become linked to interest in "living wage" ordinances. These ordinances go beyond minimum wage efforts to propose a higher, living wage standard for city contracts and other employer agreements. By arguing that employment should reduce poverty, not just reduce welfare payments, the AFL-CIO and allied groups set the stage for this campaign work.

Fast Track Trade Authority

In 1997, President Clinton pursued "fast-track" authority—to send trade agreements to Congress for yes-or-no votes, without amendments. The fast-track fight, like the North American Free Trade Agreement before it, brought out the best and the worst of the labor movement. The best was international solidarity, manifest in the effort to see trade agreements that raise protections for all workers rather than those that degrade protections to the lowest common denominator. The worst was xenophobia.

To promote unionization, define an independent path, and unite a majority of working people, the AFL-CIO framed the fast-track debate in terms of a global shift in bargaining power between workers and employers. This shift plays out domestically within companies, and internationally within companies that operate in the United States and in countries with fewer labor protections. The debate was not just about a specific legislative effort, but about declining living standards and resisting efforts that fuel that decline. Trade issues unite all workers—both the higher wage manufacturing workers who feel directly threatened and lower wage workers who know that labor standards are vital.

Follow-up on issues have included child labor and sweatshops. These issues resonate strongly with Americans, and they have significant coalition-building potential given the moral outrage they inspire and their direct impact on some sectors with lower-wage union members. Current international economic issues like International Monetary Fund reform, labor standards in international agreements, and the Multilateral Agreement on Investment are inspiring detailed debate in fast track's aftermath. Labor's victory was cause for celebration and for introspection. Winning the fast track battle has proved that organized labor and the AFL-CIO Policy Department have an important role to play in shaping the debate about the role of the United States in the international economy.

The United Parcel Service Strike

The UPS strike was a pivotal event in U.S. labor history, and it drove home one particular lesson in relation to policy work: all the working papers and press events in the world pale before a good mass mobilization. Propaganda, on a national scale, does have powerful educational potential. We did make a modest contribution to the UPS effort: we helped frame and spread the message, which the mobilization carried, and, in the aftermath, we explored the potential for further solidarity with contingent workers.

Ask any American what the UPS strike was about and the reply will be: part-time work. Like the minimum wage, the concerns of the part-time workers at UPS struck a chord with all American workers. "Part time" became a proxy for uncertainty, declining income, and lower benefits.

The struggle crystalized the effects of decades of increased competitive pressure and economic anxiety. Part of our role was to show the cause and effect relationship—and to show that real people were really suffering. So we produced analyses of declining health and pension benefits, located information on trends in contingent work, and noted the growth of the temporary help industry. We always saw these specific trends in the context of declining living standards and declining bargaining power, so that when AFL-CIO leaders spoke about the strike, they could confidently relate specific UPS issues to the national degradation of wages, benefits, and job security.

THE NEW AMERICAN MAJORITY

It may be too soon to tell, but the rebirth of activism in the labor movement suggests a new period in industrial relations. From the immediate post-War period through the 1970s, the United States saw rapid productivity gains, increased unionization, and rising living standards. After 1973, as many have noted, a U-turn in wages and benefits gripped American workers as reduced union strength and an increasingly open economy shifted the balance of power toward capital. The 1980s were the culmination of that revanchism as employers, the White House, and international lending institutions fought back against workers' gains. Unionization, which had been slowly declining, plummeted. The forward march of labor was truly halted.

Now, by fits and starts, the labor movement is moving forward. Stronger coalition alliances, new strategies, a more functional organization structure, and a new optimism have fostered extensive activity. Organizing has taken center stage. Policy support is being brought to bear around legislative, community, and organizing activity. In an era when the balance of power has shifted strongly toward capital, the new American labor movement is beginning to strike back.

NOTE

1. Thomes Edsall, *The New Politics of Inequality*; E.J. Dionne, *Why Americans Hate Politics*; Patricia Sexton, *The War on Labor and The Left*

A NEW INTERNATIONALISM

Advancing Workers' Rights in the Global Economy

barbara shailor

THE FLIGHT TO BANGLADESH, FEBRUARY 1998

Weighted down with briefcases overflowing with paper and files, Clayola Brown, a Vice President of UNITE (Union of Needletrades, Industrial & Textile Employees) and I are making our last stop in a two-week journey that has taken us through the Philippines, Thailand, and now Bangladesh. Anxious to sleep, we are interrupted by the small talk of another American traveler.

"So what brings you girls to this part of the world?"

Too tired to engage and eager to avoid the inevitable, "What hotel are you staying at?" question, I just sort of nod.

"Yeah . . . I'm with Tommy Hilfiger . . . I'm coming here a lot. Not much to do . . . but a great place for business. . . . So really . . . what are doing here? You on vacation?"

"Vacation—in Bangladesh?" I think to myself, "There is only one travel book on Bangladesh available in English, *The Lonely Planet*, and it doesn't exactly describe Dhaka as a tourist haven."

"Well, actually we'll be looking at garment factories," I respond.

"No kidding. Wow, so am I. So what company are you with?"

"I'm with the AFL-CIO and Clayola Brown is a Vice President of UNITE, you know the Union of Needle and—"

"Ah ha. Oh yeah, right, yep. I know, I know."

We can go to sleep now, certain we won't be disturbed again, at least not until we awake to the realities of Bangladesh when we interview young children and women who sew the clothes sold in shopping malls across America.

THOSE DARK SATANIC MILLS

Tommy Hilfiger and the GAP and Wal-mart and K-mart and every major clothing manufacturer are fleeing from the higher-paid workers of Hong Kong, Thailand, Indonesia and China, and are looking for the newest, cheapest, least regulated source of labor that they can find. Today, that it is in Bangladesh. Where manufacturers head next and how they operate is the story of 21st-century capitalism yet untold.

The ready-made garment industry accounts for almost 70 percent of the export earnings of Bangladesh. Over 2,100 factories employ 1.3 million workers, 85 percent of whom are women. Local employers urged their government to devalue its currency in order to compete with other Asian countries caught in the downward spiral of deflation. Is $23 a month too much to pay these young women workers as they try to compete in the endless race to the bottom?

Where is the bottom?
Is the bottom Karanigonj, Bangladesh where children as young as seven work twenty hours a day in the garment industry? Many children are not paid, receiving only rice for their labor, many are sick, some almost blind. Many suffer from jaundice. A small boy hammers rivets into children's jeans designed for youngsters his own age. His fingers

are bruised by the hammer when he misses the rivets. He says that he is beaten when he makes mistakes.

Or is the bottom perhaps Burma, a nation ruled by a military regime that has murdered thousands, and now keeps its economy afloat through a combination of drug trafficking, forced labor, and joint ventures with U.S.-based multinational companies like UNOCAL?

Or is it Indonesia, where for years workers have struggled under the repressive reign of Suharto, and where Muchtar Pakpahan, head of the independent trade unions, waits in his hospital bed to go back on trial for treason for organizing a union not controlled by the government and corporations? Millions of workers are losing their jobs while the regime continues to subsidize family businesses. Will the IMF insist on banking reforms but ignore human and political reform?

Or Russia, where millions of workers go months at a time without wages? Their unpaid salaries now total billions of dollars. At one point, the government used pension funds to pay workers. Suicides and social unrest mark the unraveling of the social fabric, and signs of the complete collapse of the Russian economy loom on the horizon.

Or the Northern Mariana islands, which, for over a decade have profited from their status as a commonwealth of the U.S.? Manufacturing produces hundreds of millions of dollars of goods—mostly textiles and apparel—which bear the "Made in the USA" label, and are actually made by the 40,000 Asian "guestworkers" who are forced to work in some of the worst shops, cheated out of pay, housed in rat-infested labor camps, and forced to give up their rights.

Around the world, the plight of workers in the bottomless pit of economic processing zones is eerily similar. Employers seek the most desperate, pliant, and vulnerable workers for jobs in some of the least accountable factories and most exploitative working conditions. Young women are separated from their family homes and brought to live in cramped and dangerous factory dorms where thousands have died in fires. Employers use amphetamines to make these young workers in the maquiladoras and economic processing zones work longer and faster.

Throughout Central America companies find the suppression of unions facilitates outsourcing in the export processing zones. For example, despite serious organizing in the Dominican Republic's thirty-two economic processing zones, only nine collective bargaining agreements have been signed. The hundreds of thousands of workers, mostly young women, who manufacture clothes for U.S. companies, are forced to work overtime without toilet facilities, and are physically abused and intimidated. Thousands have been fired, beaten and threatened for just siding with the unions, but the working conditions are so appalling that even violence can't completely dissuade workers from joining.

And while Africa has not yet seen its young women locked behind the gates of economic processing zones, governments continue to brutally repress workers rights. In Ghana, Uganda and Lesotho union activists and leaders have been shot. In Swaziland and Kenya, campaigns of union repression, harassment, and intimidation have been underway for years. In Sudan and Congo, strikes lead to detention, arrests, and torture. Nigeria has been singled out as one of the most brutally repressive regimes in the world, yet still has the support of the multinationals.

Not only young women suffer. Globalization has given rise to increasing rates of child labor worldwide. Children have been put to work making the clothes and toys that American children will wear and play with. Around the world an estimated 250 million children between the ages of five to fourteen are working; half of them full-time. In fields and factories and brothels, these children have been forced to relinquish their childhoods. They suffer from crippling arthritis, from chemical exposure, from sexual abuse, and malnourishment. They die from accidents in the mines and on construction sites.

THE INTERNATIONAL TRADE UNION CHALLENGE

It is now commonplace to understand that we work and live in a global economy that is dominated by elite corporate giants. These multinationals are the driving force of the economy, restructuring production and distribution lines, moving jobs and money across the world at an unprecedented pace. The fundamental struggle of our time is to make this global economy work for people: to secure basic worker rights, environmental and consumer protections, workplace health and safety standards, and anti-trust and financial regulations to hold great corporate powers accountable.

At the beginning of this century we witnessed a similar struggle when great trusts and industrial combines forged our national economy. Then, as now, rapid industrialization produced massive accumulation of wealth and power, generated booms and busts, displaced workers and farmers, and sparked upheaval and protest. The progressives of that era joined in a struggle to organize unions, to extend democracy, and to impose new rules that protected people—from food and drug regulations, a ban on child labor, a minimum wage, and progressive income taxes, to labor laws, social security, and consumer and environmental standards. These reforms did not come easily. They were not granted by the generosity of the corporate CEOs. They met fierce resistance. Fierce strikes, and mass movements were required.

Now capital has loosened the boundaries again by going global. And so are we. The time to act is now.

A NEW INTERNATIONALISM:
ADVANCING LABOR RIGHTS IN THE GLOBAL ECONOMY

The AFL-CIO is presented with an historic challenge and opportunity to put forward a new internationalism and new global solidarity. The intersection of solidarity, self interest and commitment connect workers' struggles. We envision a program for the global economy that will share the benefit of economic development with working people. Fundamental to that vision is the need to organize new workers into unions, so that they strengthen their ability to bargain collectively with their employers, to speak effectively to their governments, to represent themselves at the new international institutions, and to achieve justice and dignity in their communities the world over.

In the United States, the AFL-CIO is working to change the rules of the global economy. We are working with our affiliates to educate and mobilize our membership on the inclusion of workers' rights in trade and investment agreements. Most recently, the vic-

tory over fast-track trade negotiating authority marks the first major setback to the neoliberal economic model.

We continue to work with trade unions in both industrialized and developing countries on campaigns to include basic international labor rights in regional trade agreements and in the Multilateral Agreement on Investment. The goal of these efforts is to ensure that the promotion of trade and investment goes hand in hand with enabling workers to exercise their basic rights. We do not advocate a global minimum wage—but we do want to stop governments and companies from trying to gain competitive advantage through repression, discrimination, abuse, and exploitation.

BUILDING BRIDGES

The AFL-CIO has been reaching out to build new strategic links not only with the traditionally international organizations representing workers worldwide, but with regional and industrial organizations working to create campaigns as well. For the first time, the AFL-CIO met with the European Trade Union Confederation and the European Industrial Councils in Washington, D.C. We organized this session for the purpose of educating American unions on the European Directive, which stipulates the conditions under which a multinational company must form and finance a European Works Council. Over 1,200 companies, 220 of which are based in the U.S., are required under European law to provide European workers with a structure and process non-existent in most of the world.

We convened meetings of the General Secretaries of the International Trade Secretariats to meet U.S. counterparts in to strengthen and coordinate our industrial work. We organized the International Confederation of Free Trade Unions' (ICFTU) first multinational working group meeting in the U.S. to engage in multinational strategies and to develop multinational campaigns.

We invited the presidents of the labor federations from all the G-7 countries to meet at the AFL-CIO in 1997 to present a workers' program for global growth and prosperity to President Clinton and to members of the Cabinet prior to the world leaders' meeting in the United States.

We are bringing unions and NGOs together on a regular basis to plan campaigns on issues such as corporate codes of conduct, investment agreements, regional trade issues, privatization, human and worker rights violations, child labor, non-discrimination, and the strengthening of fundamental worker rights. We are reaching out to union leaders from Canada, Mexico, Brazil, South Africa, Japan, Hong Kong, Korea, and Malaysia.

Transcending the rhetoric of solidarity, there are real opportunities to shape both government policy and cross-border campaigns.

We have demonstrated and picketed in front of embassies and consulates for our brothers and sisters in Indonesia, in South Korea, in Nigeria, in Argentina, in China, and in Brazil. American workers turn out by the hundreds and thousands to protest against a global system that does not work for working people. AFL-CIO officers, local union leaders, and activists—firefighters, teachers, machinists, truck drivers, janitors, carpenters, seamen, city hall clerks, farm workers, auto workers, steelworkers, secretaries, longshoremen, retail clerks, nurses, miners, flight attendants—union members from every sector and every union have turned out in support of the rights of workers in countries around the world.

American workers increasingly understand that their fate is intimately connected to the fate of workers the world over. The simple truth is that the global economy cannot grow if workers in the United States and Europe are losing jobs and income, and workers in Indonesia or Nigeria or Guatemala or China or Romania are repressed, paid poverty wages, forbidden to form unions, and unable either to purchase the products they make or to support their own families. Economic stagnation, widespread poverty, environmental corruption and degradation are global problems. The response to these problems is too often to blame the poor, the immigrant, and the worker. But it is the protection of those workers and the expansion and safeguarding of those workers' rights that are fundamental to sustainable economic gains. Broad-based, sustainable solutions to the problems that we face today require strong political and economic institutions, including labor unions. Self-sustaining unions that are not controlled by government or corporate interests and that are democratic, accountable, transparent, and truly represent their members are the best global partners that American workers can have.

The AFL-CIO's new Solidarity Center is designed to assist unions in the developing world in building their capacity to become strong partners. Through cooperative design and implementation of concrete projects, unions will better represent their workers in international institutions and with their own governments, at the bargaining table and in organizing. The Solidarity Center was established July 1, 1997 when in consultation with AFL-CIO affiliates, a new Board of Directors, and the International Department were consolidated with the four international institutes. Jointly funded by the AFL-CIO, the U.S. Agency for International Development, and the National Endowment for Democracy, the Solidarity Center works to help unions build their capacity to create broad-based economic development, so that all workers can freely create representative organizations and processes to defend their rights and to protect their interests. Child labor, export processing zones, health and safety violations, labor law violations, and the often violent repression of trade union organizing exist in every region of the world. Our consolidated center working with AFL-CIO affiliated unions, NGOs and the International Trade Secretariats provides coordinated global programs to aid and assist unions the world over.

CROSS-BORDER SOLIDARITY

The AFL-CIO, through our affiliated unions, represents more workers employed by multinational corporations than any other labor federation in the world, making the

American labor movement uniquely positioned to provide leadership and a vision for the international trade union movement. It is increasingly clear that the realities of the global economy dictate that we can only secure and strengthen American workers' right to organize and to bargain by extending our help to secure the right to organize to workers the world over.

Decisions can be made by a few multinationals who change tactics and direct new strategies far faster than any other organization anywhere on earth. There is no question that the success or failure of making these companies deal with unions world-wide will, in large part, determine the fate of trade unionism and capitalism as we know it in the twenty-first century. It is only the constant maintenance of our relationships in the trade secretariats through frank and open dialog and a shared understanding of solutions that gives workers a fighting chance against corporate power. We believe we have both the practical need and the moral responsibility to connect our workers at General Electric in Alabama with the workers at General Electric in Indonesia—workers prohibited from bargaining and jailed for organizing. We must connect the respect and dignity of our members at Boeing in Seattle with the hardships of workers earning thirty-five cents an hour producing 737s in Xian, China. Mexico is another example, where, with a broad range of unions, we are developing programs and support for work. The need for cross-border solidarity is paramount, as the Han Young workers fired for trying to organize, the maquila workers fired for being pregnant, and the Latina workers at La Conexion Familiar in California who gained enormous support when a case was filed by the Mexican unions show us. The more specific and the more concrete our work becomes, the easier the fight for workers' rights will become for our members and for our unions, and the more understandable our struggle will be to the press, to the politicians, and yes, even to the companies.

THE FLIGHT

As Clayola Brown and I boarded the plane, just a few days later, we were inspired and renewed by all that makes one hopeful about the human condition and the future of generations yet to come. Nazma Akhter, a former child worker who started in the factory at the age of twelve and worked for seventy hours a week for a monthly salary of eight dollars, is now International Director of the Bangladesh Independent Garment Workers' Union.

The Bangladesh Independent Garment Workers Union (BIGU) was founded after almost two years of organizing, and began when a band of women discovered embezzling in their union and decided to form their own instead. Since its founding, BIGU membership has expanded to over 30,000 members and activists. Having withstood a brutal attack on their headquarters when men emptied their rifles, doused the union's attorney with gasoline, ransacked the offices, and threatened further brutality and even killings if the union continued its work, BIGU continued to organize. And in July 1997, BIGU won a long and difficult political and legal battle when they were officially registered as a legitimate union. Local unions are now registered in fifteen factories, while another five have applications pending. The union operates three schools for children who are former garment workers, three health clinics, and three counseling centers that provide education and training in a variety of topics, including literacy and labor education.

BIGU is much more than just an isolated story of women of extraordinary courage confronting the odds and forming one union, in one industry, in one small and desperately poor country, half-way around the world from the corporate boardrooms and shopping malls of America. BIGU is the human stop sign on the road to the bottom.

NEW AGENDA

Corporations need more accountability, not more license. Financial markets need more regulation, not less responsibility. Workers need to be empowered, not weakened. The problem is not that governments are too strong, but that they are too weak. Companies and countries that want to get out of the race to the bottom are afraid to pursue alternative paths. It will take the pressure of international political will to create change.

We must make many changes in order to stop the downward spiral of human degradation. The attitudes of unions must change. We can no longer focus on the short term interests of existing members, but we must devote more of our energies to the longer term interests of all working people. At a policy level, we must make new rules to ensure the global marketplace works for working people, so that companies compete by their ability to produce products of value, not by their willingness to impoverish their workers or to despoil the environment. We need new boundaries on financial markets that favor long-term investment over short-term speculation. We need an end to incentives that favor companies that slash and burn over those that build and grow. Basic social guarantees—health care and social security, the right to form and to join unions, the right to due process on the job—

must be strengthened. Greater investment in and commitment to education and training is vital.

These are but the first steps. We need new energy, leadership, ideas, and a bold new political agenda. Success demands that we make our mission the creation of a vibrant global economy that will lift up working people throughout the world, rather than drive them down. That mission is essential to any sound economic policy, and is a basic moral measure of who we are.

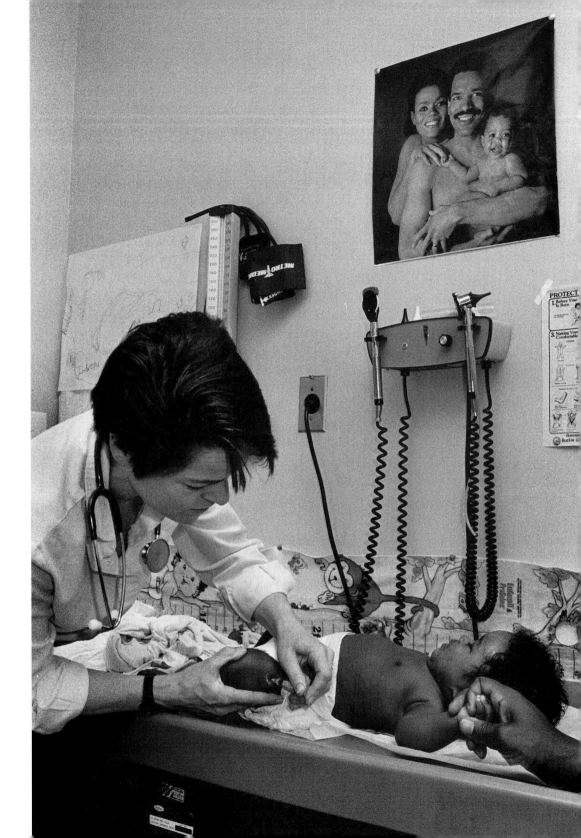

THE ROAD TO UNION CITY

Building the Labor Movement Citywide

amy b. dean

Richelle Noroyan is a twenty-five-year-old college graduate living in Santa Cruz, California. But, despite her education, all Noroyan's diploma ever bought her was a succession of seven dollar an hour jobs in the region's booming high-tech industry.

Several miles away, Alejandro Rodriguez and his family live in San Jose. For four years, Rodriguez, a refugee from Nicaragua, worked as a shipping clerk at Hewlett-Packard. But two years ago, the giant computer maker subcontracted Rodriguez's job—and those of his co-workers—to a large temporary employment firm that provides few of the benefits HP offers its full-time employees. Though neither Noroyan and Rodriguez may know it, both represent the greatest challenge—and best hope—facing the American labor movement: the workers of the new economy. But winning their support and that of millions of other workers like them requires a re-engineering of the labor movement and a fundamental redefinition of its relationship to the communities in which it operates.

U.S. Unions and the New Economy

Globalization, new technologies, and a rapidly changing workforce demography have given way to a strange new economic landscape. Union leaders have long recognized the effect these forces could have on workers and their families and, over the course of the last twenty-five years, have offered a few responses to the challenges facing U.S. industries in the new economy. In 1964, for example, Walter Ruether of the United Auto Workers lobbied for a federal commitment to produce an American-made alternative in response to the growing demand for imported Volkswagens. In the time since Ruether proposed his federal response to auto imports, foreign trade has accelerated greatly, making the U.S. economy almost three times more dependent on it than it was in the early 1960s. The impact on workers and their unions has been catastrophic in many industries, and even the toughest restrictions on imports or the introduction of new technologies provide little resistance to the new world order. While many predicted that the end result of globalization and new technologies would be massive, permanent unemployment, time has proven that instead, many of the jobs lost in manufacturing and other industries have been replaced by jobs not unlike those held by Noroyan and Rodriguez. An earlier generation of Americans once looked for jobs in metal-bending industries, but today's workforce is more likely to seek jobs in information technology, the public sector, and health care. By the year 2005, there will be more than seven times as many Americans working as systems analysts than as tool and die makers. The number of workers employed in technical and related support positions will increase by more than 20 percent. Jobs in service occupations will expand by more than 18 percent. Yet while almost three-quarters of U.S. workers are already employed in these sectors, fewer than 13 percent are union members today. And no less significant to U.S. unions than these new kind of jobs is the economy that is creating them.

The New Localism

The growth of health care giants such as Columbia/HCA and Kaiser Permanente suggests the era of large corporate employers is anything but behind us, but big business is hardly the big employer it once was. As Alejandro Rodriguez's experience underscores, many firms, particularly in the information technology industry, prefer to subcontract tasks that may have previously been performed in-house. Unlike U.S. Steel, which operated its own coal mines, or Ford Motor, whose massive Rouge Assembly Plant was even built with resources from its own steel mill, a distinguishing characteristic of new businesses is their reluctance to invest in plants and personnel of their own. Instead, these firms depend on an intricate network of subcontractors who, in turn, regularly contract out work of their own. Similarly, as Richelle Naroyan's experience suggests, even professional and technical workers, who may have once built careers by working for only one employer, now find themselves working for several on a part-time or temporary basis. In the health care industry, for example, nurses and other technical employees routinely work as independent contractors. The fact that many of the new economy's workers will find employment at several firms in their community rather than at a large, multinational corporation presents a unique challenge for the U.S. labor movement.

Organizing the workers of the new economy means targeting a host of smaller local employers rather than a handful of large ones, as well as making union membership attractive to those workers who will frequently change employers. For example, many of the needs experienced by these workers, such as portable pension and health care benefits,

UNION MEMBERSHIP FOR VARIOUS AGE GROUPS, 1997

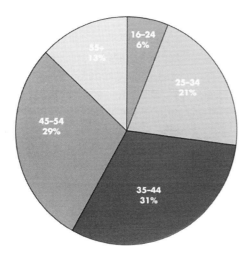

job training and placement services, can be—and often are—provided through unions. Yet, doing so requires organized labor to become far less centralized and more interwoven with local community services than it is currently.

As federal power "devolves" to the state and local levels, representing workers in the new economy demands that unions become more integrated in local decision-making processes than they have ever been in the past. Where economic development strategies may have once been shaped by officials advocating shortsighted tax and land use policies in the hope of attracting investment, community development in the new economy depends on physical infrastructure and the availability and quality of human resources. Thus, even in a global economy, communities still have the ability to encourage the growth of some industries (and not others), as well as to establish the terms and conditions of growth. As the only institution whose mission is to represent the interests of workers and their families, unions must have more significant responsibility or role in shaping local economic development.

To represent effectively workers like Norayan and Rodriquez, unions will need to adopt structures as flexible and, as in many respects, as decentralized as the new economy itself. Some are. One of America's oldest unions, the International Association of Machinists & Aerospace Workers (IAM), has launched an innovative training program to help both local Machinist leaders and their employers decentralize decision-making to help transform companies into "high performance" workplaces. Other unions, once accustomed only to more traditional forms of collective bargaining, are seeking to become relevant to contingent workers by reinventing themselves. They can take their cue from unions in the performing arts, entertainment, and construction industry. One of the most promising initiatives is the Communications Workers of America's (CWA) effort to establish employment centers. Such centers combine placement services with skill certification, creating a labor market intermediary valued by both employees and employers in which the union has a major role in training, workforce development, and placement.

A Culture of Decline

There is, of course, no single explanation for the labor movement's failure to organize the unorganized either in the new or old economy. Many union leaders often point with good reason to the shortcomings of U.S. labor law. But the decline of union strength can hardly be blamed on weak labor laws alone. Challenging organized labor's culture of decline is fundamental to growing unions in the new economy. While most national labor leaders understand the importance of change, local leaders must take some responsibility for the real work of rebuilding union strength. It is here, in communities across America, where the new economy is taking shape and where the day-to-day political battles that will shape the future of U.S. workers will be fought. And, not incidentally, it's here, too, where over 80 percent of organized labor's resources—and all of its members—can be mobilized to meet that challenge.

For the better part of a decade, the process of grassroots change has been gathering momentum in cities like San Jose, Atlanta, Seattle, and Milwaukee. In these and other communities, union activists frequently sidestepped the AFL-CIO in the 1980s and early 1990s to organize local Jobs with Justice coalitions or other initiatives to win new allies for unions in the community. These coalitions, composed of unions, religious leaders, civil rights activists, and others, helped compensate for the labor movement's declining clout in contract negotiations and local politics. In the wake of labor's defeat in derailing the 1993 North American Free Trade Agreement (NAFTA), union activists in a number of communities joined together with environmentalists and other coalition partners, again without AFL-CIO sanction, to demand greater accountability to labor by Democrats. In Baltimore, Minneapolis, Boston, Chicago, and Los Angeles, unionists and community organizers also joined forces to battle for "living wage ordinances" to boost the incomes of some of the city's poorest workers. But while evidence of a new, creative movement for economic justice could be found in many communities throughout the U.S., it ultimately took the Sweeney insurgency to galvanize organized labor's renaissance .

The New AFL-CIO

Though the drive that sent John Sweeney, Richard Trumka, and Linda Chavez-Thompson to the AFL-CIO was sparked by a general desire for change, the programs they've initiated have actually borrowed heavily from the labor movement's past. In several important respects, the Sweeney program is reminiscent of the early days of the Congress of Industrial Organizations (CIO), when the cause of unionism and social justice were seen as one and the same in many communities. However, where the CIO of the 1930s helped engineer massive organizing drives that targeted industries, Sweeney's AFL-CIO instead may become a catalyst for organizing entire regions.

Unlike the CIO's John L. Lewis, whose own United Mine Workers financed union organizing drives in steel and other "new" industries, Sweeney inherited the helm of a mature federation whose member unions often act as a loosely knit collection of International Unions, many of which often perceive their affiliation with the AFL-CIO as optional and not critical to survival. In contrast to the autocratic Lewis, Sweeney works with the presidents of individual unions as partners and leads through consensus, seizing the initiative where he can. Fortunately, where Sweeney and the "new" AFL-CIO have been able to seize the initiative is where it counts the most: at the local level.

Though even some of its friends describe the AFL-CIO as a mammoth Washington bureaucracy, it is also a collection of individual state-level federations and 600 central labor councils (CLCs). These semi-autonomous state federations and CLCs, many of which predate the AFL-CIO itself, all have their own histories and unique traditions. In one Midwestern state, labor leaders still take care to assure "balance" in the state AFL-CIO's leadership by selecting one officer from a union originally affiliated with the AFL, and another whose union was part of the CIO (never mind that the two rival federations

merged in 1955). Despite this arcane tradition, that federation, like many others, has long been an effective voice for working families in lobbying state government.

At one time, CLCs were the cornerstone of much of the American labor movement, when the distance and meager resources of national unions made routine servicing of their local affiliates difficult, if not impossible. It was a time when the absence of effective labor laws demanded that union activists band together for their very survival. In 1934, for example, the AFL's Minneapolis, Minnesota Central Labor Union, joined with the Teamsters in a series of strikes so effective that the state's governor finally declared a "state of insurrection" and imposed martial law. In the years since, the activities of most CLCs have hardly been as noteworthy. Indeed CLC leadership wasn't always based on merit. Prior to a 1996 leadership change, for example, the twenty-five members of the executive board of the Cleveland, Ohio Federation of Labor, included no fewer than eight retired union officials, among them the CLC's president who had long since been ousted by members of his own union. Not surprisingly, only four of the twenty-five members were women, and, in a city whose workforce is now largely African-American, only two of the twenty-five were black. And Cleveland is anything but unique. Lacking any clear mission or goals, CLCs in many communities have devolved into little more than social clubs for local union leaders, largely dormant organizations barely capable of organizing blood collection drives for the Red Cross, let alone the workers of the new economy.

The Road to Union City

The first indication that Sweeney and his supporters understood the urgency of rebuilding union power at the local level came during their 1995 campaign. In the months leading up to the AFL-CIO's convention, Sweeney's team moved swiftly to take advantage of an obscure provision in the AFL-CIO Constitution providing each CLC with one convention delegate. Though the individual votes of these delegates would have no effect on a roll-call vote, Sweeney realized that the presence of hundreds of additional supporters on the convention floor could be an important factor in his behalf. The effort to solicit support for Sweeney from CLCs often turned into fierce battles that bitterly divided local labor councils. Yet this effort also gave rise, for the first time ever, to an identifiable group of CLC leaders backing change at the AFL-CIO.

In 1996, with Sweeney's support, these CLC leaders became the nucleus of a twenty-two member Advisory Committee on the Future of Central Labor Councils. Working with the AFL-CIO's staff, the members of the committee surveyed the current activities and goals of CLCs, but more importantly, debated strategies for the ways in which CLCs could re-engineer themselves to be effective organizations that could improve opportunities for unions to be successful in organizing and bargaining at the local level. Committee members understood that CLCs could become a vital force to promote organizing, to educate and to mobilize community support for workers' rights, and to give labor a stronger voice in the political arena. After all, over the years many committee members had helped move their own CLCs in this new direction. But they also understood that, to be successful, they had to provide a framework that CLCs could use to plan and to measure their performance and progress. That framework became the Union Cities initiative.

The Union Cities initiative is a straightforward set of eight goals that the AFL-CIO presented as a challenge to CLCs and other labor bodies:

> Shifting 30 percent of their resources to organizing. Currently, CLCs have essentially no role in promoting union growth. By urging them to commit one-third of their resources to organizing, the AFL-CIO has challenged them to assist unions to win new members. Some CLCs have responded by coordinating multi-union organizing "blitzes" (which are quick, intense organizing sessions where organizers either visit workers at their homes or at the plant gates or outside of the worksites), training volunteer member organizers, and generating political and community support for first time organizing drives and contract fights.

> Mobilizing union members to participate in demonstrations and other "rapid response" efforts against anti-union employers. In order to compensate for the weakness of U.S. labor laws, CLCs are retooling and adopting new strategies to pressure hostile businesses and public officials who refuse to respect workers' rights. CLCs are urged to set a goal of mobilizing at least 1 percent of local union members to participate in these activities.

> Organizing to elect pro-worker candidates for office and holding them accountable once they are elected. As opposed to maintaining a more reactive stance, CLCs are urged to actively recruit candidates for political office, assist in their election, and in many cases union members themselves for elected office.Promoting local economic development efforts that create jobs and honor community values. Given the growth of the new economy at the local level, CLCs are being encouraged to become directly involved in local economic development initiatives as advocates for workers and their families.

> Sponsoring the AFL-CIO's new economics education program geared to union families. Winning the fight to gain strong contracts and organize new mem-

bers is impossible unless union families understand the scope of the economic changes shaping their workplaces and communities. CLCs can now play a critically important role in raising the awareness of union families about these and other issues by sponsoring the Federation's innovative new economics education classes.

Urging local governments to pass measures supporting the right of workers to organize. By challenging local governments to support workers' rights, CLCs can help generate a local climate more conducive to union organizing.

Working to insure greater ethnic, racial, and gender diversity in all CLC operations. As has often been noted, the failure of the labor movement to reflect the diversity of the American workforce has seriously undermined its ability to attract new members. As the most visible voice of the labor movement at the local level, it is particularly crucial for CLCs to challenge the widespread notion that unions are principally the domain of white males.

Encouraging CLC's to work with unions to achieve a 3 percent growth rate by the year 2000. In the past, the AFL-CIO has presented CLCs with few goals to measure their progress. By setting a target of a 3 percent growth rate by the year 2000, the Federation has created a standard CLCs can use to measure their progress.

In essence, the "eight steps" to becoming a Union City are intended to create the local environment necessary for unions to, once again, be successful in organizing and bargaining. Union Cities achieves this goal first, by bringing local unions together within a region to set objectives and to develop a strategic action plan to build their power and promote new growth. Second, by putting their Union Cities plan into action, a once sedentary local labor movement will become reinvigorated and once again be able to demonstrate the depth of its public support. Third, the local labor movement will then be able to form the broader alliances necessary to put the issues of economic equity and social justice front and center in the community as a whole. To date, more than one hundred CLCs representing almost half of all U.S. union members have endorsed the effort. Perhaps even more important than their endorsement, though, is the fact that even by considering it, union leaders, activists, and rank-and-file members are finally coming together to discuss and to initiate strategies at the local level to reverse the labor movement's decline. Though some local union leaders may say the call to dedicate 30 percent of their resources to organizing is unrealistic, the reality is that, up to now, few outside of a handful of labor activists and academics have even discussed the question of how much unions should contribute to organizing. By setting new goals, Union Cities has already succeeded in democratizing a discussion that had previously excluded the vast majority of union leaders and members. And, if our experience in San Jose offers any guide, the debate being fostered by Union Cities will inevitably help organized labor live up to the challenge of organizing in the new economy.

By committing itself several years ago to a program not unlike Union Cities, San Jose's South Bay AFL-CIO Labor Council was able to move well beyond then-traditional boundaries of the labor movement. By engaging our own membership and the community, our CLC came to better understand what it would take for workers, like Richelle Naroyan and Alejandro Rodriguez, to begin to see organized labor as part of their future, not just their past. To reach out to these workers, we launched a new kind of coalition—Working Partnerships USA—to build bridges between organized labor and workers in the new economy. Through Working Partnerships, we are "reinventing" our own local labor movement with an eye toward offering high tech workers the representation and services they truly need, not the kind the labor movement believes they should want. While Working Partnerships USA may not be a model for CLCs in every community, it has enabled ours to become a far more relevant voice: one that resonates with working families as a whole, and not just organized labor's institutional base.

The left has traditionally mistaken localism for conservatism, but if the next generation of American unionism is to take root, it will be by rejecting "big labor" in favor of more decentralized, flexible approaches: a unionism contoured to respond to each region's unique economy and workforce. History may someday show that by launching Union Cities, John Sweeney did more than breathe new life into old central labor councils. He may have triggered an irreversible process that finally enabled the American labor movement to organize the workers of the new economy.

THE "AMERICA NEEDS A RAISE" CAMPAIGN

The New Labor Movement and the Politics of Living Standards

david kusnet

In his acceptance speech after winning the presidency of the AFL-CIO, John Sweeney said four simple words, "America needs a raise." While this phrase appeared only once in Sweeney's speech, it was included in most of the next day's newspaper reports—a rarity for a speech by an AFL-CIO president. The jaded and dwindling labor press corps recognized that these words signified a new message for the AFL-CIO. The slogan summed up an unacknowledged reality: most Americans' living standards were stagnating. And, if the new AFL-CIO leadership kept addressing this issue, they could do what most labor leaders hadn't done for a generation or more: speak to—and for—working people about their economic condition.

During Sweeney's first year as president, the AFL-CIO linked its legislative, organizing, bargaining, and political work under the umbrella theme of "America Needs a Raise," and began conducting a new conversation with unrepresented workers in their communities.

These efforts lifted the labor movement's public profile, helped convince Congress to increase the minimum wage, injected economic issues into the 1996 elections, and spurred efforts already underway to raise the minimum wage in many states and cities. But the "America Needs a Raise" campaign also demonstrated the difficulty of mobilizing low- and moderate-income Americans around economic issues in an era when most people seek to solve their problems through individual striving, political leaders concentrate on "upscale" constituencies, and the news media avoid "downbeat" stories.

Raising the Unspoken Issue

Labor's new leaders were addressing what had been virtually a taboo topic in public debate. With rare exceptions, for twenty years or more, stagnant living standards had been a problem most people intuitively understood but the nation's elite stubbornly denied. The hourly wage of the typical worker had been in free-fall since 1973, starting with blue-collar men but spreading to 80 percent of workers all across the occupational spectrum. Meanwhile, the mainstays of middle class economic security were also crumbling.[1] Employer-provided health benefits were eroding, with companies shifting costs to employees through higher co-payments, deductibles, and premiums. Company pension

Value of the Minimum Wage

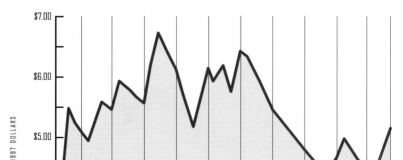

plans were dwindling or disappearing, to be replaced by 401(k) plans without employer contributions.[2] And jobs themselves were becoming less secure, as massive layoffs began in production work in basic industries early in the 1980s and later hit white-collar and managerial employees during the recession of 1991 and 1992. Increasingly, full-time jobs were replaced by part-time positions without health care, pension benefits, or any promise of future employment.

Even when the business cycle rebounded, ordinary Americans benefited little, if at all. From late 1992 through 1993—as unemployment levels held steady and major corporations from IBM to Chase Manhattan kept shedding workers through corporate "downsizing"—the upturn was dubbed the "jobless recovery." By 1994, job creation swelled and wages stagnated, leading to the "raise-less recovery." And, well through 1995, the recovery was still unusually regressive, increasing corporate profits and stock prices, but aggravating middle class insecurities and economic inequalities. During the recession of the early 1980s, the news media covered the plight of laid-off industrial workers, but, once the economy rebounded later in that decade, little attention was paid to the fact that average hourly wages, adjusted for inflation, had not returned to 1979 levels.

Meanwhile, liberal political leaders did little to emphasize the problem. The Democratic nominees in the 1984 and 1988 elections, Walter Mondale and Michael Dukakis, both said "The rich are getting richer and the poor are getting poorer," but devoted surprisingly little attention to the plight of the middle class. In the last two weeks of his campaign, when Dukakis finally made a populist appeal with his new "On Your Side" stump speech, his support increased from 41 percent to 46 percent of the electorate.

Largely because it hit white-collar and middle-management employees as well as production and service workers, the recession of 1991 to 1992 and its lengthy aftermath generated a different response. Every year from 1991 through 1993, 5 percent of working men and 4 percent of working women were permanently displaced from their jobs. Growing numbers of Americans concluded that the problem was not just cyclical but structural: the economy was settling into an uncertain new world where wage increases were rare, and middle class security was a distant memory. To stay even, low-to-moderate income Americans resorted to a variety of "coping mechanisms." Both parents—and, often, teen-age children as well—worked outside the home. Husbands and wives worked overtime and took second and even third jobs. In spite all their efforts, families ran up their credit cards and plunged into debt.

By 1992, these insecurities were producing a new political response. With his attacks on trade and immigration, the right-wing populist Pat Buchanan won more than 35 percent of Republican voters in his challenge to incumbent President George Bush in recession-ridden New Hampshire. Later that year, by blaming political gridlock and standing apart from both major parties, corporate maverick Ross Perot appealed to alienated voters.

Meanwhile, the eventual Democratic nominee, Arkansas Governor Bill Clinton, addressed economic issues in ways that working Americans recognized. Unlike other self-styled centrists, Clinton based his appeal on the populist view that middle class living standards were stagnant. He borrowed the Economic Policy Institute's formulation that "Most Americans have been working longer and harder for less," and the sociologist William Julius Wilson's emphasis on race-neutral economic programs, such as investments in education, training and technology, which would benefit working people from all backgrounds. He criticized corporate excesses—from exorbitant executive salaries to companies that shipped American jobs overseas—and he raised an issue that was even more unmentionable than stagnant wages: economic inequality. Skillfully melding social and economic anxieties, he warned that "America is growing apart when we should be growing together," a turn of phrase that implicitly linked economic inequality with social breakdown.

But soon after becoming president, Clinton spoke less often about stagnant living standards and increasing inequality. As he shifted his emphasis from public investment

The Minimum Wage Supports Working Families

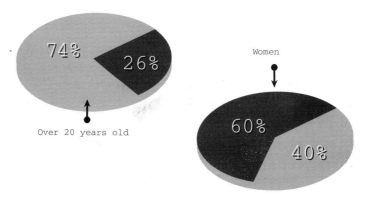

74% 26%

Over 20 years old

Women

60% 40%

to deficit reduction, Clinton also retuned his rhetoric to reassure Wall Street. Gone were the attacks on self-serving business behavior and most of the appeals to hard-pressed wage-earners. Instead, he claimed credit for the millions of new jobs the economy was creating—"taking ownership of the economy" was the phrase often used by his staff—but ignored the fact that many workers needed several of these jobs in order to afford the living standard that one job used to provide.

In November 1994, many of the same voters who had elected Clinton either stayed home or voted Republican, costing the Democrats control of both houses of Congress. Examining exit polls, the political analyst Ruy Teixeira found that the swing voters had been those whose living standards were still stagnating: the Democrats had declined ten points among high school dropouts, eleven points among high school graduates, and twelve points among those with some college education.

Still, Clinton and most members of his administration continued to emphasize the progress of the national economy, not the plight of working families. The lone dissenter was Labor Secretary Robert Reich. In a speech shortly before Labor Day, 1994, he predicted "the revolt of the anxious class." After the elections proved him prophetic, he become even more outspoken about lagging wages and growing income inequalities. By 1995, Democratic leaders from both houses of Congress—particularly House Democratic Leader Richard Gephardt, the party's second-ranking House leader David Bonior, and veteran Senator Edward Kennedy—had also began to speak of economic anxiety. In two cover stories in *Business Week*, labor reporter Aaron Bernstein explored what was happening with "Inequality" and "Wages," and, in a seven-part series in the *New York Times*, economics reporter Louis Uchitelle and several colleagues chronicled "The Downsizing of America."

One voice was absent from the national discussion that included the Labor Secretary, the business press, and even Patrick Buchanan. That missing voice belonged to the leader of the nation's labor federation. By early 1995, a growing number of labor activists, including the presidents of major national unions, had become discontent with AFL-CIO president Lane Kirkland. There were many reasons for dissatisfaction—some beyond Kirkland's control—from the continuing decline in union membership to labor's defeats on the North American Free Trade Agreement, striker replacement, and health care reform. But there was another reason as well: Kirkland avoided the news media, particularly television news and interview programs. Thus, labor was losing a rare opportunity to emerge as a voice for working Americans, unrepresented as well as organized. And Kirkland's AFL-CIO was failing to dramatize an important point: Rebuilding the labor movement was essential to restoring the middle class. John Sweeney said later that year, "I decided to run for president of the AFL-CIO because organized labor is the only voice of American workers and their families and because the silence is deafening."

A Conversation with American Workers

Taking the helm of the AFL-CIO late in 1995, Sweeney promised to begin a conversation with American workers about living standards and economic security. The discussion would take many forms, including aggressive media outreach, community meetings, and even door-to-door canvassing in working class neighborhoods. The strategy was that once working Americans heard unions addressing the realities of their lives, they would consider joining unions again.

Much of the conversation was conducted with leadership groups—from the national news media to business executives and liberal intellectuals. The soft-spoken Sweeney addressed various audiences, including the National Press Club and business groups such as the Association for a Better New York, decrying the decline in living standards and repeating the phrase, "America Needs a Raise." Soon labor's new leaders enjoyed frequent and friendly coverage. Ted Koppel of ABC's *Nightline*'s Ted Koppel declared, "Labor is back."

The most ambitious effort at kicking off the conversation with working Americans was a series of town hall meetings in twenty-six cities, which the AFL-CIO conducted using the now-familiar slogan, "America Needs a Raise." The hearings offered the opportunity for the AFL-CIO and its local affiliates to gain new visibility at the grassroots, energize local activists, jump-start existing organizing campaigns, and—most difficult but also most important—reach out to unrepresented workers who might later become interested in organizing unions in their workplaces. Putting together hearings in twenty-six cities in a matter of months demonstrated the energy and resourcefulness of the AFL-CIO's new leadership and staff. Well before each town hall meeting, AFL-CIO organizers met with potential allies, such as African-American, Latino, women's, religious, older Americans', and consumer organizations. These groups would often recruit speakers and audiences for the public meetings, and community leaders would often chair the hearings. At the public meetings, a cross-section of working Americans testified to the full range of anguish and insecurity that was commonplace in 1996. In Seattle, Deanna Bell, a sixty-two-year-old home care worker, explained: "I work 165 hours a month at my job, and I still have to do a paper route to maintain my own home and to support myself." In Birmingham, a day laborer, Wayne Bryant, told a hushed hearing: "I'm homeless, but I'm not trying to hurt someone, rob them, or create problems. I was working for $4.25 an hour, but I couldn't pay my bills, buy groceries, gas, pay the electric bill, buy food, and take the kids to get clothes or to the hospital. I need to make more, so I can live a productive and successful life."

These uncertainties reached well into the middle class. At a hearing in Columbus, Ohio, a fifty-eight-year-old man named Dave Meyer told how he lost jobs as a middle manager at Rockwell International and McDonnell-Douglas after both companies relocated. Battling age discrimination, he couldn't get anything much better than jobs that paid six dollars an hour. In Manhattan, corporate executive Kenneth McNutt told how he had been downsized out of his job at a construction company: "I'm not here to whine, but I am here to say that we've got to start talking. We can't deny any more that there's a huge change in the market economy and how it drives us."

While the hearings raised labor's public profile in many communities, their lasting impact depended largely on activities that were already underway. In Detroit, the town hall meeting heard from striking workers from the *Detroit News* and *Free Press*, and in Denver, the meeting provided a forum for workers locked-out by the state's largest grocery chain and workers downsized by US West. In Chicago and in several communities in California, the town hall meetings generated support for living wage initiatives, and in Los Angeles, unrepresented garment workers compared their meager wages and minimal benefits with the pay scales and other gains won by union members in their industry. In many other communities, however, the town hall meetings did little to generate new activity immediately, although they may well have helped to change the climate of opinion about unionism.

The Year of Income Politics?

All this happened at a rare moment in recent American politics when voters were willing to accept populist explanations for their own economic anxieties and the behavior of major corporations. During the first few months of 1996, just as labor's new leaders began speaking out, AT&T announced mass layoffs, media outlets from the *New York Times* to *Business Week* published major stories about downsizing, and Pat Buchanan beat Bob Dole in the New Hampshire primary.

Thus, Gephardt declared early in 1996 that the era of deficit politics and divisive social issues was coming to an end and "the era of income politics" was beginning. Public opinion surveys early in 1996 supported this view. In surveys conducted for the AFL-CIO, 57 percent of Americans said they were dissatisfied with the way the economy was performing. Seventy percent were concerned that they might not be able to afford health insurance, 68 percent worried that they wouldn't have retirement benefits, 57 percent said prices were rising faster than incomes, and another 57 percent were troubled by part-time jobs replacing full-time jobs. Seventy percent said that the fact that "corporations have become too greedy" is "very responsible" (53 percent) or "fairly responsible" (an additional 17 percent) for the nation's economic ills. Emboldened by this climate of opinion, Congressional Democratic leaders, including Kennedy, Bonior, and Gephardt, pushed for an increase in the minimum wage, federal charters, and to tax incentives to encourage responsible corporate behavior.

While Labor Secretary Reich was sympathetic to these efforts, President Clinton and other administration policy-makers played a double game. Seeking to build business confidence, Clinton and his economic team emphasized positive aspects of the recovery. In his 1996 State of the Union Address, just weeks after the AT&T layoffs were announced, Clinton did not refer to corporate downsizing and declared the economy was the healthiest in three decades.

But Clinton also understood the political impact of economic insecurity, presenting himself as a defender of popular social programs like Medicare against the Republican-dominated Congress. As early as 1995, he had acceded to pressure from Kennedy, Gephardt, and Bonior and supported an increase in the minimum wage. In so doing, he rejected the advice of his allies in the centrist Democratic Leadership Council, who opposed the idea not only as bad policy but as bad politics, offering advice that made embarrassing reading not long afterwards. For example columnist Morton Kondracke wrote: "DLC officials think that, if Clinton calls for a minimum wage increase in the State of the Union—as White House aides indicated he is inclined to do—it could wreak the same political damage as his 1993 vow to veto any health care bill that did not provide universal coverage." And he warned that support for a minimum wage hike would "brand him [Clinton] as an 'old Democrat.'" (In fairness the DLC did support tax cuts for the working poor through the Earned Income Tax credit).

With Clinton's support, raising the minimum wage became the major initiative upon which the administration, the labor movement, and the Congressional Democratic leadership agreed. Far from offending middle class voters, as the DLC had warned, the issue became a touchstone for whether the political system would address the economic anxieties of workers earning well above the minimum wage.

By 1996, more than five years had passed since the last increase in the federal minimum wage, and its purchasing power had plummeted to a forty-year low. While middle class voters loathed the welfare system and looked down on long-term welfare recipients, they sympathized with low-wage workers and understood how difficult it was to support a family on only $4.25-an-hour. And, for many, the frozen minimum wage was symbolic of the economy's undervaluing of workers and their jobs.

Early in 1996, a *New York Times/CBS* poll found that 84 percent of all Americans—including Reagan Democrats and Republicans and Independents—favored raising the minimum wage. For the unions and their allies, the challenge was to increase the urgency of the issue and to make the Republican-dominated Congress listen to its constituents. And the "America Needs a Raise" campaign was the perfect vehicle for accomplishing these goals.

During the Easter/Passover recess, the AFL-CIO broadcast TV and radio spots in thirty congressional districts whose representatives were doubtful about increasing the minimum wage. The spots stressed a simple point: Could you support your family on $8,800 a year? When they returned to Washington, anticipating how powerful the issue would be, twenty-two House Republicans defied their party leadership and introduced their own bill to raise the minimum wage. On April 30, the AFL-CIO began another series of radio ads in twenty-nine congressional districts urging people to call their Representatives and demand a vote on raising the minimum wage. Through phone banks, the AFL-CIO reached more than two hundred thousand union members in these districts to urge them to contact their Representatives.

While Republicans used a variety of delaying tactics, many ultimately decided not to buck public opinion in an election year. On July 9, twenty-seven Republicans joined all forty-seven Senate Democrats to pass the minimum wage increase by a 74 to 24 vote. And, on August 2, a majority of Republicans (although not their leaders) as well as every Democrat joined a 354 to 72 vote in the House of Representatives to raise the minimum wage. Clinton's signature cleared the way for an estimated 10 million minimum wage workers to get a long-overdue raise: fifty-cents-an-hour on October 1, 1996, and another forty-cents-an-hour on September 1, 1997, for a total of $1,800 a year for full-time workers.

Meanwhile, at the state and local level, there were a series of successful initiatives to raise the minimum wage above the federal level, especially for companies receiving government contracts or other public benefits. For example in Baltimore in 1995, a community-labor coalition prevailed upon the City Council in 1995 to pass an ordinance requiring city contractors to pay $6.10 an hour (and fifty-cents-an-hour more by 1996). Similar ordinances were enacted in cities including Milwaukee and Los Angeles, but, in citywide referenda in 1996, voters in Denver and Houston rejected proposals to raise the minimum wage in their cities above the federal level. California voters enacted an initiative to raise the minimum wage, but Missouri voters rejected a similar initiatives.

Taking Income Politics "Off the Table"

With the departure of Clinton's 1992 campaign team, Reich had few allies in his efforts to address economic anxieties. Clinton's new political team, particularly the former Republican consultant Dick Morris and pollster Mark Penn, counseled economic happy-talk and an emphasis upon upscale suburban voters. Morris boasted of taking the issue of economic anxiety "off the table," saying "While the budget battle raged, Mark Penn and I were fighting a lonely battle within the administration about how to describe the status of the economy . . . Mark and I campaigned to discourage economic pessimism and make sure that the administration spoke optimistically and positively about economic news."

For his part, Reich recalled that the political and economic team tried to muzzle his public utterances, with Morris making a menacing visit to his office and Treasury Secretary Robert Rubin warning him that the phrase "corporate responsibility" was "too inflammatory." And Clinton's lengthy acceptance speech at the Democratic National Convention failed to mention the increase in the minimum wage that he himself had supported.

Clinton's strategy for responding to economic insecurity was subtle and successful. His Republican rival, Bob Dole, was entirely unable to exploit lingering economic anxieties, having declared, after losing to Buchanan in New Hampshire: "I didn't realize that jobs and trade and what makes America great would become a big issue in . . . this campaign." So, understandably if unfortunately, Clinton did not choose to initiate a debate over the incomplete success of his economic policies. But his attacks upon the Republican Congress on issues from Medicare to the minimum wage implicitly recognized that most Americans still felt an acute sense of economic vulnerability.

Clinton's inferential response to economic insecurity provided a measure of common ground with the labor movement and Congressional Democrats. Gephardt and his allies put aside their earlier calls for corporate responsibility and adopted a less controversial "Families First" agenda for the campaign that did little to move beyond administration positions on such issues as education, health care, and child care. During the fall campaign, the unions, too, muted the "America needs a raise" campaign, concentrating their efforts on re-electing Clinton and returning Democrats to control over the House and Senate. With Clinton winning a three-way race with some 49 percent of the vote—and the Democrats making substantial gains but failing to retake the House with a similar share of the electorate—post-election surveys showed that Democrats at every level had substantially regained the "volatile voters" who still suffered wage stagnation, were losing the fear of layoffs, and felt threatened by Republican attacks on Medicare and other safeguards for the middle class.

Looking Forward

During 1997 and the early months of 1998, the economic recovery deepened, labor markets tightened, and working Americans—particularly low-wage workers who benefited from the boost in the minimum wage—finally began to get a raise. But, even by Labor Day, 1997, real average wages remained lower than their all-time peak in 1973. And anxieties about corporate downsizing, cuts in health and pension benefits, and consumer debt burdens remained. So did the public sentiment that corporate America was still refusing to share its profits with working Americans.

In place of the slogan "America Needs a Raise," the AFL-CIO pursued a wider "Working Families Agenda." This included expanded health care and child care, fair pay for working women, and "the right to organize"—a theme that decried the weakness of federal labor laws and enforcement mechanisms and corporate violations of even these feeble protections by firing an estimated 10,000 union supporters a year. The issue has been picked up by national leaders, particularly, Vice President Gore.

But Clinton reached a bipartisan budget agreement with Congressional Republicans that seemed based on the view that working people's living standards had righted themselves, and that the large-scale public investments that Clinton had promised in 1992 were no longer necessary.

Yet economic insecurity fueled support for labor in two important battles. In their strike against the United Parcel Service during August, 1997, the Teamsters stressed that the company was replacing full-time jobs with part-time positions without health and pension benefits. The slogan—"Part-time America won't work"—was as resonant as "America needs a raise" had been a year earlier. More than 70 percent of Americans supported the strike, building pressure upon UPS to reach a favorable settlement.

Similarly, while the Clinton Administration and Congressional Republicans supported fast track" trade legislation, most Americans opposed it. With an unusually effective campaign by the AFL-CIO, Congressional Democrats and a significant number of "Buchanan Republicans" mobilized so much opposition that the Administration chose not to submit fast track to a vote. Thus, by the beginning of 1998, Clinton returned to the stance that had served him well in 1996. Prodded by Kennedy and Bonior, he called for another raise in the minimum wage—a measure that once again enjoyed overwhelming support in the polls. In an especially shrewd initiative, Clinton urged the expansion of Medicare to allow workers in their mid-to-late fifties to "buy into" the program, a proposal that recognized the vulnerability of older workers to cuts in their health benefits and to layoffs as well. Borrowing from the "working family" agenda of congressional Democrats and organized labor, Clinton also called for expansions in child care. This agenda enabled Clinton to win high ratings for his 1998 State of the Union Address, gaining support not only from his Democratic base but from swing voters as well.

Meanwhile, for a revitalized AFL-CIO, the questions remain: Which themes will prove as compelling to most people and the news media as "America needs a raise" had been in 1996? And how can we use these themes to continue the conversation with working Americans and to advance the work of organizing communities, workplaces, and entire industries? The "America Needs a Raise" campaign, through its successes and its failures, revealed how essential, and how arduous our work will be.

NOTES
1 *State of Working America,* EPI, 1998, p.31
2 Ibid. pgs. 146-47

PART-TIME AMERICA WON'T WORK

The Teamsters' Fight for Good Jobs at UPS

matt witt and rand wilson

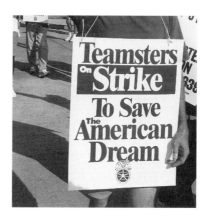

Eleven days into the 1997 strike by 185,000 Teamsters at United Parcel Service, UPS driver Deborah Burdette appeared in a white wedding gown at the picket line outside the company's distribution center in Anderson, South Carolina. After she and her fiancé, Joel Phillips, walked down a makeshift "aisle" outside the center and exchanged vows, her coworkers saluted them, not by throwing rice but by waving their picket signs. "Part-Time America Won't Work," said some of the placards. "We'll Fight For A Secure Future," said others. TV cameras were there to capture the scene for local and national news broadcasts, and a wire story and photo were picked up in many newspapers around the nation. Through this media coverage, millions of Americans heard once again the message they had been getting for weeks from Teamster members at UPS, that the strike

179

was a fight for all working families against the corporate shift to more "throwaway," low-wage, part-time, temporary, or subcontracted jobs without pensions or health coverage.

While having a picket line wedding was unusual, the event was in many ways typical of the Teamsters' successful contract campaign at UPS. It involved members and their families in actions to build unity and to send a message to management. It also educated the public through the news media, with members themselves doing most of the talking. The contract campaign was perhaps the best example of a new emphasis on membership involvement and community coalition building that began when new top leadership took office in the Teamsters Union in 1992. Facing huge corporations in a global economy and an often hostile political and legal environment, Teamster leaders knew that winning gains for working people could no longer be accomplished just by a few pickets outside a plant gate.

The UPS workers were the largest group in the Teamsters Union and one of the ten largest private sector work forces in the world. Looking ahead to the 1997 contract negotiations, they knew they were in for a tough fight. The company's long-time slogan, "The Tightest Ship in the Shipping Business," reflected a management style that prized heavy-handed control over employees. The work force was sharply divided, with 40 percent of the members holding well-paid, full-time driver jobs and 60 percent holding lower-wage, part-time positions as loaders and sorters. UPS had gained the union's permission in the 1960s to start using part-time workers, and in 1982 won agreement from top Teamster officials to freeze starting part-time pay at eight dollars per hour. Now, the company wanted to move even further in that direction, demanding a greater shift to part-timers, more subcontracting, and a company takeover of Teamster members' pension plans. With annual profits of more than $1 billion, the company had a huge war chest with which to fight for its goals. No union could match that kind of money. But Teamster members at UPS had been working for years to build up the "people power" it would take to fight back.

The first skirmishes in the 1997 contract battle actually took place soon after the previous contract was settled in 1993. In February, 1994, UPS raised its package weight limit from seventy to one hundred and fifty pounds without negotiating with the union over the necessary safety precautions. To the company's surprise, the International Union encouraged members to protect themselves by staying home from work on the day the new weight limit went into effect. Within hours, UPS changed its tune and signed an agreement with the union providing that no Teamster could be required to handle over-seventy pound packages without proper lifting devices and help from another member. At a company where there had never been a national strike, the one-day safe-

Teamster 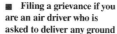 Update

MAY 5, 1997

BLOW THE WHISTLE ON UPS

On May 22, Teamster members across the country will "blow the whistle" on subcontracting, supervisors working, and other ways the company tries to undermine our job security.

Special Teamster whistles will be distributed at rallies. The noise we make will send a message to management that we're standing together for improved job security.

For information on the rally in your area, talk to your steward or contact your local union.

You can also help fight for a secure future by:

■ **Filing a grievance when you see supervisors doing Teamster work.** New language in the 1993 national contract expanded members' right to collect money from the company when you catch supervisors doing Teamster work.

■ **Filling out a postcard available from your Teamster steward whenever you spot UPS subcontractors.** The Teamsters National Negotiating Committee will use this information to fight for better language on subcontracting in the next contract.

■ **Filing a grievance if you are an air driver who is asked to deliver any ground packages.** Also help enforce contract language (Article 40, Section 1, (a) 8) that obligates UPS to pay the regular package car driver rates if an air driver picks up ground packages. The only exception to this is if the air driver is making an air pickup after the regular driver has been at the customer's premises and the customer has an exception ground package for shipment.

WE'LL FIGHT FOR A SECURE FUTURE

INTERNATIONAL
BROTHERHOOD OF TEAMSTERS
25 LOUISIANA AVE. NW, WASHINGTON, DC 20001

Teamster Proposals Target Subcontracting

Teamster members are uniting behind a package of national contract proposals that would make our jobs more secure.

A key goal is to stop subcontracting of Teamster jobs. The low wages and benefits paid by some subcontractors create pressure to hold down our wages and benefits.

Subcontracting of feeder driver work reduces job opportunities for package car drivers who want to become feeder drivers and for part-timers who want full-time work.

In addition to stopping subcontracting, union proposals would:

■ Require UPS to negotiate with the union over new technology and equipment in order to protect jobs and guarantee that future work will be done by Teamsters.

ty walkout sent a strong signal to management, Teamster members, and local union leaders that the company could no longer trample workers' rights without a fight.

Two months later, Teamster drivers and dock workers at major trucking companies showed the union's commitment to reversing the national shift to throwaway jobs by launching a three-week national strike that stopped the freight haulers from introducing UPS-style, low-wage part-timers.

The next year, UPS announced that it was unilaterally implementing a new "Team Concept" program. Draped in the rhetoric of labor-management "cooperation" and "trust," the program would allow the company to replace the seniority system with management favoritism and to set up "team steering committees" that could bring about workplace changes without the involvement of elected union representatives. Management and its high-priced Team Concept consultants were caught off guard when the union launched a full-scale membership education campaign showing the differences between the company's promises of "partnership" and the program's fine print that undermined the union contract. In addition to conducting training sessions at local unions, the International Union sent every union steward a video and print materials on the theme, "Actions Speak Louder Than Words," to share with other union members. If the company wants "teamwork," the materials urged members to ask, why doesn't it negotiate with the union to create more full-time jobs, stop subcontracting, and improve job safety? Faced with a union membership that was armed with the facts, the UPS eventually agreed to end the Team Concept program. Like the fight over package safety, the union's campaign to defend workers' rights helped build membership unity heading into the 1997 contract negotiations.

More than a year before the July 31, 1997 contract expiration date, the International Union began sending bulletins to every UPS member's home, highlighting the importance of Teamster families' involvement in the upcoming contract campaign. Nine months before the contract deadline, every member received a survey asking them to help shape the union's bargaining priorities. But Teamster leaders knew that the most effective communication takes place in person. That's why UPS management sends out frequent messages about productivity and competitiveness for supervisors to go over with employees in "Pre-Work Communication Meetings." To counter that system, Teamsters Parcel Division Director Ken Hall asked all Teamster local unions to set up "member-to-member" communications networks. Under these networks, each steward or other volunteer was responsible for communication with approximately twenty workers. The International Union deployed education staff and field representatives—some of them UPS rank-and-filers—to help locals get the networks established.

In the months leading up to crunch time in contract negotiations, the networks were used to organize membership participation in a series of actions that built unity among full-timers and part-timers and gave the news media and community organizations the opportunity to hear directly from UPS workers about their concerns. On March 10, the day before the two sides exchanged opening proposals at the bargaining table, Teamster members held rallies in seven key cities, attracting heavy media coverage that highlighted Teamster members' key issues: more full-time jobs, an end to subcontracting, major pension and wage increases, and stronger job safety and health protection. Union leaders knew these rallies had hit the right nerve when UPS negotiators complained about them early on the first day of bargaining. "The union has never had actions like this so early in the negotiations," they said. "What's going on?"

Before the next negotiating session two weeks later, the union doubled the number of rallies. And during April, Teamster UPS members conducted a coordinated campaign to document the company's record as one of the nation's worst job safety violators. More than five thousand members filed safety grievances using a special "EZ Grievance Form." These were featured at local "Don't Break Our Backs" rallies where injured UPS workers spoke.

On May 22, union members held hundreds of local "Blow The Whistle on UPS" rallies to highlight practices such as subcontracting that undermine workers' job security. Thousands of members blew shrill plastic whistles outside UPS facilities to signal their unity. On the same day, rallies were held by unions representing UPS workers in seven European countries as a result of Teamsters' coordination with the International Transport Workers' Federation. The specter of international solidarity actions was particularly threatening to UPS because it had invested billions of dollars in trying to become a major delivery provider in Europe.

In June, Teamster members launched a series of actions to highlight the need for more full-time jobs. "Half a Job is Not Enough," a widely distributed union research report for UPS workers, the media, and interested academics, explained that over ten thousand UPS workers who already worked

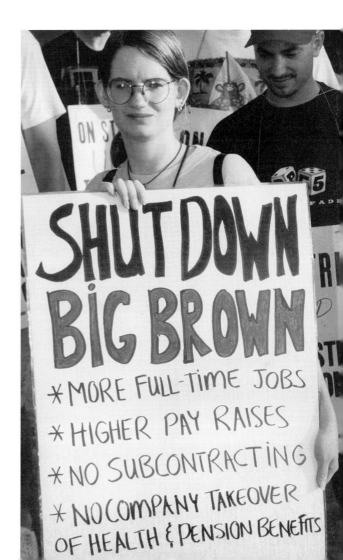

more than thirty-five hours per week were considered by UPS to be holding two "part-time" positions and therefore did not receive full-time wage rates.

More than one hundred thousand Teamsters signed petitions telling UPS that "We'll Fight for More Full-Time Jobs." Part-time package sorters and full-time drivers marched together in public demonstrations in cities like Memphis and San Francisco. They also held membership rallies throughout the country, using the theme that "whether you're part-time or full-time, it's union time at UPS." At a rally in southern California, part-time air package driver Ellen Ortiz told hundreds of UPS workers and their families, "I'm a single mom with two kids and no safety net. I had to tell my son 'no' when he asked for a new pair of shoes because his were falling apart. I'm tired of not being able to afford even the basics for my children."

In July, the union sent each steward an audiotape to share with other workers. It included excerpts from a tape top UPS negotiator Dave Murray had sent to supervisors a few months earlier. On the tape, workers could hear Murray saying that not only was eight dollars an hour an adequate part-time wage, but in many areas it would be "a fine full-time wage." On the tape, the UPS negotiator also criticized Teamster leaders for communicating with members throughout the negotiations. "In the past," Murray said, "commitments were made to not speak to the members or the employees for whom the contract is being negotiated. The reason this was usually viewed as a wise position for both parties was that the communication of positions taken during negotiations often raises the expectations of those people who ultimately could be voting on the ratification of the agreement." After each comment by the UPS executive, the union tape included short responses from rank-and-file members. "I know that they're making money on our backs," said part-timer Adrian Herrera from southern California. "Even if they would give us raises, they'd still make a hell of a good profit."

By mid-July, with management continuing to ignore workers' proposals at the bargaining table, members voted by 95 percent to authorize a strike if necessary when the contract expired. Strengthened by months of demonstrations of membership support, Teamster negotiators refused to let management's concession demands become the focus of bargaining. On July 30, UPS made a "last, best, and final offer" that demanded more shifting to low-wage, part-time jobs; more subcontracting; company control of workers' retirement money; and lower wage increases than in the past. The company offered to create only 1,000 new full-time jobs by combining existing part-time positions during the proposed five-year agreement.

To show good faith, union leaders agreed to negotiate for three days past the deadline. Management's response was to demand that its final offer be put to a membership vote, but Teamster negotiators had no intention of letting a substandard agreement be shoved down workers' throats. On August 3, Teamster members had no more options and the strike began.

UPS launched a million-dollar ad campaign aimed at making management appear reasonable to UPS workers, customers, and the news media. But months of union education, communication, and action had paid off. More than 99 percent of the workers stood strong on the picket lines. When reporters searched them out for interviews, they heard one consistent message, bolstered by up-to-the-minute information that strikers were getting from a toll-free hot line, the Teamster internet web page, a special electronic "listserv" mailing list for active members, and national conference calls that gave every UPS worker the chance to go to their local union hall and hear their chief negotiators answer questions. "The whole world's going to part-time," Mark Dray, a twenty-five veteran of the company, told the *Minneapolis Star-Tribune*. "Used to be the American dream was to get a good job and own your own home with a white picket fence. Now it's hoping you win the lottery." Part-timer Mike McBride told the *Cleveland Plain Dealer*, "This strike is not for today and it's not for this week. It's about ten years down the line. If we don't stand up, we might as well pack our bags up."

In some areas, UPS strikers traveled their regular delivery routes to visit customers and explain why it became necessary to interrupt service. These visits strengthened the positive image most drivers already had with their customers. Meanwhile, working people all over America made the Teamster fight their own. The UPS pilots, who belong to an independent association, refused to fly. In Seattle, 2,000 people formed a human chain around a UPS hub. More than two thousand telephone workers marched in Manhattan to show their support. U.S. Senator Paul Wellstone of Minnesota, Reverend Jesse Jackson, and other national and local politicians walked picket lines.

The new leadership of the AFL-CIO provided a major psychological boost by arranging millions of dollars in loan pledges from other unions to maintain strike benefits for as long as necessary. The importance of this support was dramatized in workers' own voices at a news conference with Teamsters General President Ron Carey and AFL-CIO President John Sweeney. Rachel Howard, a part-timer who had been waiting eight years for a full-time job, explained that "there are many weeks when I've logged more than sixty or sixty-five hours. But UPS calls me a part-timer and pays me part-time wages. I have a son who is 15 months old," she said, as tears came to her eyes. "This strike is for him. And I'm willing to sacrifice for as long as it takes to make sure he has a future." Ezekiel Wineglass, a driver with thirty-three years of experience, talked about UPS's demand to take control of members' pension funds, "When the union pension plan gets extra money, they give it to the people who earned it in the first place. I know the company won't do that. They'll take that money and put it in the pockets of the CEOs." Voices like Howard's and Wineglass's helped build public support for the strikers that was reflected in a two to one margin in a Gallup poll. That, in turn, played a key role in encouraging the White House to reject demands from UPS and Republican leaders to invoke the Taft-Hartley law and force an end to the strike without a settlement. "If I had known that it was going to go from negotiating for UPS to negotiating for part-time America, we would've approached it differently," UPS vice chair John Alden later told *Business Week*.

On August 15, the Teamsters announced that August 22 would be a national Action Day for Good Jobs, with support activities planned in communities all across the country. Seeing that the strike was building momentum as it headed into the third week, UPS management caved in on every major issue. The company agreed to create 10,000 new full-time jobs by combining existing part-time positions—not the 1,000 they had insisted on in their July 30 "final" offer. They would raise pensions by as much as 50 percent—and do so within the Teamster plans, not under a new company-controlled plan. Subcontracting, instead of being expanded, would be eliminated except during peak season, and then only with local union approval. Wage increases would be the highest in the company's history, with extra increases for part-timers. The only compromise by the union was to accept a contract term of five years instead of the four-year term of the previous agreement.

After the contract was ratified, Teamsters Parcel Division Director Ken Hall announced a campaign to help local unions and members make sure UPS lived up to all the new gains it had agreed to. "We want to keep members involved," Hall said. "We want to keep building the union at the worksite. And we want to be sure that we're even stronger the next time UPS thinks about taking us on."

While UPS workers enjoyed the improved job security, pensions, and full-time opportunities they had won, many said the strike had taught them broader lessons about corporate greed and the need to get involved in fighting back. In a speech to a group of students at Stanford University months later, rank-and-file UPS driver Keith Barros summed up the experience of many: "I never used to get involved in much of anything but my own private life," he said. "I could just go to work, come home, watch football, and everything would be just fine. I hope I represent a number of less-outspoken people who are part of an awakening movement to get involved in where we are going as a society.

"Find a way to help this world and the people in it," he urged his young audience. "We owe it to our children who will have to live with what we have done."

FAST TRACK DERAILED

david glenn

In the early morning hours of November 10, 1997, after a marathon weekend of arm-twisting and horse-trading, the Clinton administration and the Republican congressional leadership finally conceded defeat in their efforts to renew presidential "fast-track" negotiating authority for trade agreements. Roughly 80 percent of House Democrats were standing firm against fast track, and a substantial number of Republicans had also defected.

The failure to extend fast track—which would next have been used in an attempt to broaden the North American Free Trade Agreement (NAFTA) to include Chile and other South American countries—came as an enormous shock to the Washington establishment and to the nation's pundits. As late as mid-October, nearly every published commentary predicted that fast track would pass Congress by a comfortable margin. In the wake of fast track's defeat, the press quickly filled with howling editorials that generally included the words "protectionism," "dinosaur," and "hysteria." The nation's guardians of opinion might not have been so stunned if they spent more time in places like Jamestown, Kentucky. During the very week of fast track's congressional collapse, the Fruit of the Loom company announced plans to lay off nearly a thousand non-union workers at its plant there, taking their jobs to Mexico or the Caribbean. "I'm a United States citizen, I'm losing my job," one of these workers told a reporter. "How is NAFTA so great?" The press might also have found it instructive to visit Tijuana, where, at the moment of fast track's defeat, workers at a Han Young auto parts plant were fighting for recognition of their independent trade union. The struggle at Han Young has highlighted the emptiness of NAFTA's promises: prosperity continues to elude the working class in Mexico, whose average wages have dropped by 25 percent in real terms since NAFTA was ratified. And corruption of various sorts is still epidemic in the administration of Mexican labor law, regional authorities in Baja have conducted a range of suspect maneuvers in their efforts to deny the Han Young workers a truly independent union.

During the last three decades, the U.S. Congress hasn't exactly centered its attention on the plight of workers in

Jamestown—much less on that of workers in Tijuana. But in the fast track battle, these workers' voices were—at least temporarily—heard loud and clear. It was union members who delivered over a hundred thousand postcards to their representatives. It was union members who made hundreds of visits to congressional district offices and placed over ten thousand phone calls to Congress. It was union members who held dozens of rallies and teach-ins on trade. The anti-fast track coalition included environmentalists, consumer groups, and human rights organizations, all of which played crucial roles. But it was labor that did the heavy lifting. Defeating fast track was arguably the AFL-CIO's greatest public policy triumph in a generation.

It's worth exploring this triumph closely. Fast track renewal, like NAFTA before it, was opposed by a solid majority of U.S. citizens. Why did public opinion prevail this time when it did not in 1993? As we will see, this was partly a matter of luck; the Clinton admini-stration made several crucial blunders that helped spell fast track's doom. But luck was hardly the entire story: the fast track battle reflected a new level of willpower

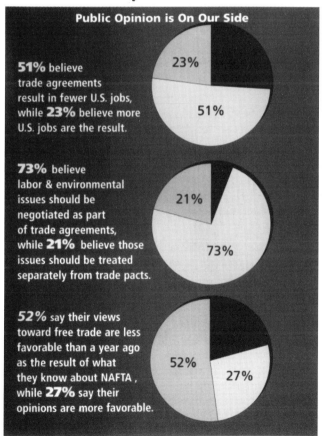

Public Opinion & Trade

Public Opinion is On Our Side

51% believe trade agreements result in fewer U.S. jobs, while **23%** believe more U.S. jobs are the result.

23% / 51%

73% believe labor & environmental issues should be negotiated as part of trade agreements, while **21%** believe those issues should be treated separately from trade pacts.

21% / 73%

52% say their views toward free trade are less favorable than a year ago as the result of what they know about NAFTA, while **27%** say their opinions are more favorable.

52% / 27%

According to a recent poll by the Bank of Boston

and skill in the labor movement's institutions. Union members throughout the country were outraged and anxious at the prospect of an expanded NAFTA, and their anger and fear found effective expression in the labor movement's lobbying and grass-roots activism.

But the fast track campaign, for all its success, also revealed two severe challenges that still are critical for the labor movement. The first is a crisis of communication. Although coverage of labor has improved in recent years, in the case of fasttrack the mainstream press often seriously distorted labor's positions and labor's tactics. The second challenge concerns the shape of future trade agreements. The 1997 fast-track legislation was easy to oppose—it was sculpted by conservative Republicans and embodied a worst case scenario. But before long, the Clinton administration or its successor is likely to put forward a more moderate bill, perhaps with tepid, NAFTA-style "side agreements" on labor and the environment, perhaps even with provisions that appear truly progressive. How will labor reply then? Throughout the 1997 fast track battle, union spokespeople consistently acknowledged the inevitability and desirability of global economic integration; the crucial point, they said, is that integration requires appropriate safeguards for workers, consumers, and the environment. But it's not clear that labor leaders—much less the rank-and-file—have a unified or well-developed sense of what these safeguards might look like. Someday (perhaps quite soon), Congress will take up a more palatable trade proposal, and labor will need to be prepared to respond.

How the War Was Won

In early 1997, the prospects for defeating fast track looked rather grim. The conventional wisdom was that the NAFTA battle had been, as two political scientists wrote in 1996, evidence of "the low and declining electoral power of organized labor." The economy was far stronger in 1997 than it had been in 1993, with unemployment at twenty-five-year lows—and it was commonly believed that this prosperity would mute public anxiety about trade issues. And labor itself was divided about how to proceed. At the February 1997 meeting of the AFL-CIO's Executive Council, a few voices expressed worry about appearing to "betray" President Clinton just months after labor had been a crucial part of his re-election machinery. More seriously, there were extended arguments about whether to trust and support any labor-friendly provisions that the administration might include in fast track legislation.

As it turned out, this last question was moot: the bill contained no labor-friendly provisions whatsoever. Throughout the spring, U.S. Trade Representative Charlene Barshefsky worked the halls of Congress trying to cobble together a politically feasible compromise on the question of labor and environmental standards. But the Republicans, whose chief negotiator was House Trade Subcommittee chair Bill Archer of Texas, insisted that trade agreements must not address such issues. In August, the Clinton administration finally agreed to Republican provisions—more restrictive than any that had appeared in earlier fast-track legislation—that forbade U.S. trade negotiators from taking up questions of labor rights, consumer safety, and environmental standards, except in matters "distinctly and directly related to trade." The administration apparently calculated that Republican support had to be locked in first, and that, as in 1993, just enough Democrats could be bullied and bribed at the last minute to push the bill through.

The Archer language meant that the battle would be clean and stark: Congress would be considering one of the least democratic imaginable models of economic integration. As John Sweeney put it in testimony before Congress, "To replicate the failed trade policies of the past, to write more rules to protect corporate interests at the expense of everyone else, is simply unacceptable. . . . The proposal put forward by Chairman Archer. . . would be a big step backwards from the language included in the inadequate 1988 and 1991 fast-track legislation, which listed 'worker rights' among the negotiating objectives, but did not limit their scope." This threat lent a new edge to labor's efforts during the summer, as the AFL-CIO and its major affiliates began to marshal their forces. By August, the Federation had set up an elaborate and detailed "stop fast track" web site; established a toll-free telephone number to allow union members to call Congress; and created a national fax distribution network, through which the field mobilization staff sent weekly updates and talking points.

By the time Congress returned from its summer recess, the pieces were in place. Several affiliates—especially the Teamsters, the Steelworkers, and UNITE—had strong and independent mobilizations. And far more effectively than in 1993, the AFL-CIO provided a general clearinghouse for ideas and resources. Thea Lee, the Federation's Assistant Director for Public Policy notes, "The field mobilization department was in contact every day with the affiliates, and with our local and state reps. Almost every day we would have a national conference call, in which people in the field would raise concerns. And all of this was fueled by the energy of rank-and-file members, who constantly brought forward new ideas."

These tactical innovations extended into labor's inside-the- Beltway operations. The Steelworkers' efforts, for example, were coordinated by Legislative Director Bill Klinefelter, a veteran of the National Wildlife Federation. "For many years, it worked for the Steelworkers to lobby on an institutional basis, as major players in the economy," says Klinefelter. "But after the 1994 elections they realized that that era is dead. We're not part of the Establishment, and no one in Washington wants us to be. We had to remind ourselves how to do legislative business as an outsider, like an environmentalist group."

In that spirit, the Steelworkers established a national "rapid response" program. "We've identified serious rank-and-file activists in all of our locals," Klinefelter says. "We fax bulletins to them, they go to the shop floor with messages that bear on our workers' lives, and the response is incredible. In the fast track fight, our members sent over 160,000 handwritten letters to their congressional representatives. Not petitions, not prepackaged postcards, but handwritten letters. This made a huge impression on congressional staff."

The Steelworkers also established a Washington internship program, in which rank-and-file members live and work in D.C. for six to ten weeks. These interns apprentice under the legislative staff, attending coalition meetings and lobbying sessions on Capitol Hill. "We had a dozen interns during the fast track fight, and they made an enormous difference," says Klinefelter. "We're developing the union's next generation of leaders. And a few of them have expressed interest in running for elected office—someday I hope to be lobbying these people."

One of those dozen interns, Patrick Saltkill, now serves on the Steelworkers' staff, doing legislative work and field mobilization in Tennessee. "Those weeks in Washington were one of the most tremendous experiences of my life," he says. "There was electricity throughout the campaign. People got up before dawn and worked until almost midnight. Back in 1993, before the NAFTA vote, we'd sort of gotten slack. We took certain [Democratic] votes for granted, and we let the top brass of the union do all the work. This time, it was a serious rank-and-file fight, from the beginning until the end."

By late September, when the AFL-CIO held its convention in Pittsburgh, the campaign was in full gear. The Teamsters had distributed hundreds of copies of a "stop fast track" videotape. UNITE had published 40,000 copies of a pocket-sized anti-fast-track booklet. And the AFL-CIO's Political Department was preparing to broadcast television and radio advertisements in the districts of two dozen undecided members of Congress. All of these efforts—the Teamsters video, the UNITE booklet, the AFL-CIO advertisements—heavily emphasized environmental, consumer safety, and human rights themes. This choice was, to be sure, partly a matter of political calculation: polling data revealed broader public anxiety about tainted raspberries than about labor rights. But it also reflected the honest convictions of labor activists. Far more than in 1993, unions acted as an effective coalition partner with the broad range of trade activist groups. Labor staffers participated in weekly strategy meetings of the Citizens' Trade Campaign, the umbrella under which all of these groups came together. (The less palatable members of this coalition—the narrow nationalists who fly Pat Buchanan and Ross Perot's flags— were much less prominent in the fast track fight than they had been in the NAFTA wars. But this heartening development was completely ignored in most press accounts of fast track's defeat.) At the Pittsburgh convention, Sweeney rallied labor for the coming battle: "The battle over fast track is important to every union in this room," he told delegates. "Craft, industrial, service, and public unions alike—because trade agreements without worker rights and human rights and environmental standards undermine the wages and jobs of us all just as they damage the communities where we live and work."

During October, congressional district offices were bombarded with messages from union members. The Steelworkers distributed new fax machines to many of their locals, whose lines were dedicated to sending messages from members. The Pennsylvania state AFL-CIO set up its own toll-free line to the congressional switchboard. Six hundred Steelworkers traveled to Washington by bus to meet with congressional staffs. And several unions introduced the tactic of bringing cell phones onto the shop floor, so that workers could call Congress in a coordinated fashion during breaks.

The anti-fast-track mobilization reached its highest pitch during the third week of October, when Sweeney and House Minority Leader Richard Gephardt addressed a series of rallies in major cities. The close relationship between labor and its congressional allies extended throughout the battle. As early as March, labor staff members had been participating in meetings convened by fast track's principal congressional opponents: Gephardt, David Bonior, Bernie Sanders, Dennis Kucinich, and Marcy Kaptur. (Another crucial ally was California Democrat Estaban Torres, the chair of the Congressional Hispanic Caucus. Torres had supported NAFTA, but subsequently charged that the Clinton administration betrayed several of the promises it made in 1993. They had taken almost no action to clean up the Rio Grande basin's severe environmental contamination, and had not moved forward with an Inter-American Development Bank.)

In early November, as the congressional leadership tried to bring the bill toward a vote, the anti-fast track coalition began a round-the-clock lobbying vigil. "We had excellent systems in place for keeping tabs on the vote counts," says Klinefelter. "And in the home stretch, as the administration began to offer pork-barrel bribes to undecided members, we were usually able to learn about those deals and embarrass the members out of accepting them." Just before what turned out to be the final weekend, John Sweeney and almost every president of the AFL-CIO affiliated unions arrived in Washington to lobby members of Congress personally. "The fast-track effort was the best work I've ever seen the labor movement do," says Klinefelter. "From top to bottom, everyone worked very hard. When you think that workers' voices were heard—that we were able to stymie something that the President of the United States wanted, that the business lobby wanted, that the Republican congressional leadership wanted . . . it was a huge victory for democracy."

Fast Track in the Media

For democratic victories to stick, however, they need to be discussed and remembered in intelligent ways. In the wake of fast track's collapse, the public conversation about trade policy and unions' political power moved in deeply unintelligent directions.

If you first learned about fast track by reading newspaper editorials on the morning of November 11, you were told that labor won the battle by sending its lobbyists to bully and to blackmail members of Congress; you were not told about the hundreds of thousands of labor activists who appealed to their representatives' good judgment. You were told that labor and other selfish narrow interests had scuttled a trade policy that was in the nation's best interest; you were not told that in 1994, narrow corporate interests "selfishly" squashed an earlier fast-track initiative, because they found it too labor-friendly. You were told that the AFL-CIO was cruelly indifferent to the suffering of the working poor in developing nations; you were not told that U.S. unions and the Chilean trade union federation had worked together to draft an acceptable framework for the extension of NAFTA to Chile.

"Our message was very clear throughout: we wanted a *different kind* of trade agreement," says Thea Lee. "But most reporters weren't prepared to hear that message. They have a script that calls for backward-looking, protectionist trade unionists. They don't even do us the courtesy of calling up to make sure their accounts are accurate."

In particular, the ex post facto editorials on fast track tended to caricature the labor and environmental provisions labor sought. They sometimes asserted that fast track opponents were demanding that developing nations' minimum wage levels be immediately raised to U.S. levels. In fact, the call was for something far more modest: provisions, to be included in the core language of trade agreements, that would require signatory nations to enforce their own labor and environmental laws effectively and consistently.

Predictably, the mainstream press devoted hundreds of column inches to the story's horse-race elements. Did the defeat signal a waning of Gore's presidential prospects and the rise of Gephardt? Was Clinton already a lame duck, only ten months into his second term? And just as predictably, most press accounts did a poor job of exploring the conflict's historical contexts. Not a single morning-after article—not even the lengthy postmortems in the *New York Times* and the *Washington Post*—mentioned the administration's unsuccessful efforts to revive fast track in 1994 and 1995. In those instances, the efforts were scuttled even before legislation was crafted—but not because of opposition from labor. Instead, the Republicans, under pressure from the U.S. Chamber of Commerce and other business lobbies, strangled the proposals in their cribs, because then-U.S. Trade Representative Mickey Kantor had introduced labor and environmental provisions. The morning-after editorials almost unanimously mentioned labor's "arm twisting and horse trading" and denounced unions for corrupting the integrity of the Democratic Party. But only one major newspaper, *USA Today*, deigned to mention that the Republican leaders of the Ways and Means Committee had turned

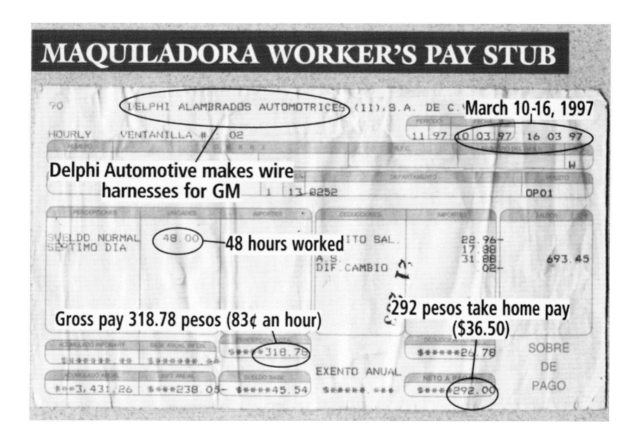

over an entire conference area in the Capitol building available to corporate lobbyists as a "war room" during the battle's home stretch.

In the days after fast track's defeat, Gephardt, Bonior, and other Democratic leaders often tried to redirect the "dinosaur" label onto fast track's corporate supporters. "This is a defeat of an old trade policy that was insisted upon by Newt Gingrich and the Republican majority," Gephardt told CNN. And David Bonior, appearing on public television the night of November 10, stressed that "What we saw this week. . . was that we are ready to move the trade issue to another level, to include labor standards, environmental standards, and food safety standards. That is the future."

But the nation's editorialists wrote as if the anti-fast-track coalition was disingenuous about these. For example the *Arizona Republic* wrote: "Labor's congressional allies demand more environmental and worker protections. . . But it is a sham, for they will vote no in any event." And the *Atlanta Journal-Constitution* started: "If [members of Congress] genuinely thought any new agreements should include measures to protect the environment or laborers in other countries, they could simply vow to vote against agreements that didn't contain such features. But that would be too easy. The real purpose of blocking fast track is to make sure there won't be any new trade pacts coming to Congress in the future." (This argument, of course, ignores a central feature of the fast track battle: the Archer provision, which effectively would have prevented any measures to protect labor or the environment.)

Time and again, the nation's editorialists ignored the plain meaning of fast track opponents' words. In nearly every public pronouncement on the issue, Richard Gephardt declared that global economic integration is inevitable and desirable, and that the question was under what ground rules it will take place. But, stupifyingly, the day after fast track's collapse the editors of Gephardt's hometown newspaper, the *St. Louis Post-Dispatch*, denounced him as if he had never said any such thing: "Mr. Gephardt should think twice about trying to ride a protectionist horse to victory in a presidential race. In the long run, it's a loser. The global economy is a reality." A more sophisticated, but still seriously muddled, account appeared in the *New Republic*. In an essay entitled "The Nationalist Revolt," Peter Beinart described fast track's collapse as a product of "the growing power of nationalism" in post-Cold War America. This analysis notes that of the approximately fifty House Republicans who declared their opposition to fast track, many were freshmen and sophomores, and some of them spoke in the hypernationalist idiom of Pat Buchanan. And these Republicans did, of course, play a pivotal role in the scuttling of fast track. But Beinart's argument is too quick to paint the entire anti-fast-track coalition with the narrow-nationalist brush. Like many commentators, he makes much of the strange-bedfellows alliance of the Sierra Club, Greenpeace, the AFL-CIO, and followers of Ross Perot and Pat Buchanan. (An analogous "working group" also developed among left- and right-wing Capitol Hill staffers and lobbyists.) But is this coalition fundamentally "nationalist," as Beinart claims, just because a few of its components are? Those fifty Republican defectors in the House were crucial, but the center of gravity in the fast track fight was with the close allies of Richard Gephardt, whose rhetoric was consistently internationalist. If the coalition "has not broadened beyond [issues of] trade and sovereignty," as Beinart notes, then, it should be clear by now that the Citizens Trade Campaign is strictly a tactical alliance. Pat Buchanan is hardly going to embrace a labor movement whose leadership argues—as John Sweeney did in 1997—that "the question is not. . . whether we are internationalists, but what values our internationalism serves."

Will the worldwide labor movement have the vision, and the political strength, to fight for a worthy internationalism? "We now have a sort of standoff in Washington," says Thea Lee. "The administration has the business community screaming in one ear and progressives in the other. We just have to work to make sure that when the stalemate breaks, it breaks in a progressive direction." In the fast track fight, the U.S. labor movement demonstrated that it has the passion and the tactical savvy to shatter the elite's policy consensus. The next step will be to apply that passion to building a new trade framework—a framework that serves the democratic interests of workers in Tijuana and in Jamestown.

LABOR'S CAPITAL STRATEGIES

david moberg

For many years after World War II, the goals of unions seemed fairly straightforward: organize workers, bargain with employers to get contracts, call strikes if necessary. In politics, unions backed "friends of labor," then lobbied for legislation. Unions had cut a wider swath, of course, forming close alliances with communities, building labor banks or cooperatives, using tactics like secondary boycotts or even sabotage, and at times supporting parties and movements that posed radical critiques of capitalism.

Yet the passage of restrictive labor laws, the silencing of labor radicals, and even the relative success of unionism all helped to focus labor's ambitions more narrowly in the postwar decades. As corporate attacks ratcheted upwards in the 1970s, labor fell into steady decline, irreversible within the cramped confines of existing unionism.

Gradually labor leaders realized that they needed to once again broaden their conception of union strategies.

Since the election of John Sweeney in 1995, work at the AFL-CIO on novel pathways to power has been concentrated in the new Department of Corporate Affairs. Elaborating on strategies developed within individual unions, Ron Blackwell, Director of Corporate affairs and a former top strategist of UNITE (Union of Needletrades,

the Worker and the Ceo
Accidentally Exchange Paychecks

Industrial & Textile Employees), wants to strengthen traditional collective bargaining, using comprehensive campaigns that attack companies on many fronts—targeting weak points in a company's finances, regulatory reviews, or public image, for example. But he also wants the labor movement to work more both "below" and "above" collective bargaining. "Below" collective bargaining are issues of workplace design or new technologies, which unions can no longer leave under management's exclusive purview. "Above" collective bargaining are issues such as government monetary policies, financial markets, corporate governance, capital investment strategies, or mergers and divestitures, all of which profoundly shape workers' fate even though unions have rarely made their voices heard in these high realms of economic decision-making. Historically many union leaders have resisted involvement in management affairs, and the few who have tried have typically been rebuffed (as the auto companies, for example, rejected Walter Reuther's challenge to open their books to union scrutiny). But in recent years, unions have made ever more forays into the domain of high finance. The AFL-CIO Corporate Affairs department is trying to consolidate that trend with its new Office of Investment, designed to aid and encourage unions' use of their pension fund influence, and with the Center for Working Capital, an independent center for research on how capital markets affect workers and strategies for pension fund managers.

Even before the change at the AFL-CIO, which accelerated work already begun under Sweeney's predecessors, a core group of unions had engaged corporations on many fronts that are normally protected from labor's influence—over issues of corporate control, worker ownership, managerial perks, investment rules, and the behavior of investment managers—attacking directors and managers of poorly performing corporations. Although for at least two decades executives faced critiques by church-based pension funds (on human rights, apartheid, and the environment, for example) and from big public pension funds (over poor performance), union pension funds—associated with the Teamsters, Service Employees, Carpenters, UNITE, and others—have emerged as innovative, aggressive leaders among the swelling ranks of activist investors. And they're winning growing percentages—often majorities—of proxy votes, performing on average better than other investors.

Sometimes with little more than a symbolic bloc of stocks, unions have trekked to shareholder meetings protesting labor-related issues about organizing and contracts that embarrass executives but that have little chance of winning a stockholder vote. In the spring of 1998, for example, the United Farm Workers asked the trendy organic grocer, Whole Foods, why it refused to support rights for strawberry workers. The Oil, Chemical and Atomic Workers likewise brought community and environmental allies to the annual meeting of Crown Petroleum to demand an end to a lockout of Houston refinery workers that had hurt workers and the neighboring community.

More often, union resolutions are only indirectly linked to traditional union goals. In 1998, there were roughly one hundred cases where unions tried to hold managers accountable for their actions. Pension representatives asked directors of scandal-plagued—and strongly anti-union—Columbia/HCA hospitals to guard more vigilantly against fraud. Pension representatives demanded that toymaker Mattel guarantee that its suppliers respect basic labor rights. Pension fund resolutions also questioned executive compensation at U. S. Surgical and the soft money political contributions of companies like ARCO. Though some proposals were ruled inappropriate by the Securities and Exchange Commission or were dropped by union pension funds, often after a private talk with managers, unions continued to rack up respectable vote totals at annual meetings. Yet even failures can be successes. "The real virtue of the shareholder resolution process is that it gets your foot in the door," argues Cornish F. Hitchcock, attorney for The LongView Collective Investment Fund, which was established by the Amalgamated Bank, owned by UNITE. "It's not like writing a letter to the investor relations department. The company can't blow you off as easily."

Yes, unions frequently do make proposals that can win support from a majority of shareholders, especially the big public employee pension funds, and that threaten the power and perks of top executives. Typically these actions focus on arcane issues of corporate governance—eliminating "poison pills" that protect managers from potential takeovers, forcing companies to elect all their directors at the same time (making it easier to change corporate policy), or expanding the number of independent directors.

For example, this year Marriott International needed shareholder approval of its acquisition of Sodexho, a French food services firm. The company tried to include new corporate rules in the vote. Those rules would have further entrenched management and given the rabidly anti-union Marriott family a special class of stock so that they could retain control while cashing in much of their holdings. The Hotel Employees and Restaurant Employees Union (HERE) launched a counter-solicitation of shareholders attacking the rules and won enough support from big shareholders to force Marriott to separate the merger and the rules changes, some of which were then dropped.

These actions often catch executives by surprise. They expect annual meetings and the resolutions at them to be quiet affairs, largely deferential to managers, part of a cozy relationship between managers and owners. Most people—including corporate executives—still don't think of workers as providers of capital, even though management theoretician Peter Drucker proclaimed the arrival of "pension fund socialism" more than twenty years ago. But through their pension funds, employees of all types provide about $5.2 trillion in capital to American business and own more than one-fourth of all corporate stock. Unions play a role in pensions worth about $2.8 trillion, most of it (nearly $2 trillion) through public employee funds in which unions have varying degrees of influence. Unions bargain for but have little influence over about $550 billion in single employer funds controlled by corporations, but they split control evenly with management over $330 billion in assets of multi-employer funds—the so-called "union" funds that have recently become more active. Unions also have broad control over the smaller assets of funds for union staff.

Nobody knows the potential of these funds. It is clear, however, that unions have begun to tap this latent power, even though there are huge impediments to using these trillions for traditional labor goals. For example, control of multi-employer pension funds is shared with management and highly fragmented among trustees of the 2,100 plans. Trustees who manage the funds also are cowed by legal mandates to use the funds solely for the economic best interests of participants. Professional asset managers, who typically invest the funds and vote the proxies, interpret the trustees' fiduciary responsibility narrowly—the best short-run returns—even though trustees legally can take a longer-run perspective or pursue other social benefits for investments with comparable risk and return. However, these asset managers often turn workers' collective wealth against them through their investment decisions and by openly supporting downsizing, capital

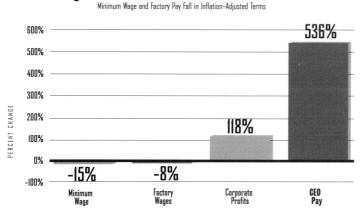

CEO Pay Soars 536% Since 1980
Minimum Wage and Factory Pay Fall in Inflation-Adjusted Terms

flight, anti-union managers, and anti-government political crusades. And even when unions take more control and initiative, they encounter strict legal and political limits; most immediate labor interests are off limits as shareholder business and unions must win over other, often unsympathetic investors to rack up meaningful vote totals.

Unions don't question the mandate to pursue the best interests of pension plan participants; the specter of long-ago Teamster pension mismanagement still looms darkly, even though the history of corporate run funds is littered with financial failures and raids on workers' assets. Unions are arguing that the best interests of workers, even as pension beneficiaries, are served by a more stable, egalitarian economy and by corporations that, in AFL-CIO Secretary-Treasurer Richard Trumka's words, "rest on partnerships among the various constituencies that come together to produce a successful business."

In a broad way, unions hope to orient corporations towards a variety of long-term strategies that are less hostile to workers. "We're interested in our employers being successful, but we care a lot about how they compete," explains Blackwell. "They can compete on the high road where it benefits not just the chief executive officers and shareholders but also workers and their families and the communities where the company operates. Most companies follow the low road where they compete by attacking employees." Blackwell argues that companies need patient capital, which recognizes that investment in research and in workers—the high road—will pay off in higher returns in the long run. In that scenario, the interests of active workers and participants in union pension funds converge despite the inherent conflict over dividing a company's earnings between workers and capital.

Yet the conflict between worker and owner may not be so easy to resolve, even when the two roles are played by the same person. "It's hard to argue that there's a fix that would make that conflict of interest go away," argues Margaret Blair, a Brookings Institution scholar of corporate governance. "It's pretty fundamental. It's not just between capital and labor or owners and workers. A corporation involves investment by many stakeholders, including customers and creditors. In the end, there's tension between things that make the pie bigger and those that just divide the pie." Unions hope to lay out strategies that expand the pie but in a way that at the least maintain, if not enlarge, workers' share.

When union shareholders propose, for example, that all directors are elected at the same time, so that they will be more accountable to shareholders, they often win support because many institutional shareholders see these "good government" proposals as ways to increase their power. Yet labor, more fundamentally, sees such proposals as small first steps in a campaign to radically reform and to democratize the American corporation. In the long run, changing the character and governance of corporations could have tremendous impact on workers' lives. In the debate over the role of markets and governments, Blackwell insists, there has been too little attention paid to powerful corporations, both to how they are controlled and to how they formulate strategies: "We want to change the discussion from a sterile debate on the omnicompetent market and incompetent government to focus on corporations and strategies that buttress or undermine living standards of the American people."

Labor has an interest in more than this grand strategy, however. Unions often have urgent and legitimate reasons for using their pension power to attack managers of companies like Gannett, Union Pacific, or Columbia/HCA, which have broken strikes or fought organizing drives. Even shareholder proposals unrelated to those grievances open a new front in labor battles and remind companies that their owners include workers who dislike their hostile policies. Sometimes shareholder proposals open doors to private discussions of labor issues with top executives. To avoid legal complications, unions routinely deny that they are trying to pressure management on labor issues, and management routinely insists that unions are only interested in shareholder proposals as extensions of "corporate campaigns."

The truth is more complex. Unions take corporate reform seriously, but they also seek tactical gains in some cases—to send a message to a company or to executives everywhere. At K-mart, for example, the Teamsters and UNITE, often joined by a public employee fund, have battled management of the faltering company for four years. At first they won majority opposition to a poorly conceived ersatz spinoff of some subsidiaries, precipitating the ouster of the company's CEO. Then they ran an alternative candidate for director, forcing the company to drop its vulnerable candidate. (Teamsters have aggressively focused on derelict individual directors and, starting in 1997, have issued lists of America's "least valuable directors.") In 1995 and 1996, unions won advisory votes in favor of annual elections of directors, which management ignored.

Beyond their interest in corporate performance and management accountability, both the Teamsters and UNITE also resented K-mart's aggressive fights against their organizing campaigns and hoped that management might conclude that there was a price for its hostility. The shareholder campaign "had a major impact, no question" in forcing K-mart to recognize UNITE at a distribution center in North Carolina, argued Bruce Raynor, now Secretary-Treasurer of UNITE. "It added a new dimension. . . . We interfered in the corporation's running itself."

Similarly, the Service Employees Union (SEIU) has used many shareholder tactics at Columbia/HCA, the once high-flying hospital chain that saw its stock value plummet, as it faced a major investigation of Medicare fraud and widespread accusations of malpractice. SEIU has promoted shareholder resolutions, such as a winning vote in 1997 to eliminate a poison pill. The next year it joined in a New York State public employee pension lawsuit against directors for their responsibility in the fall of Columbia stock. The union also distributed information about Columbia's financial and managerial problems to Wall Street asset managers. Most significantly, SEIU persuaded two individuals with solid credentials in finance and health care to run in 1998 as alternatives to the company-backed slate. Worried that it might lose the vote, Columbia named three independent directors and, in an unusual move, promised to have them meet with the Council of Institutional Investors. It would not be surprising if some institutional investors suggested to Columbia's new independent directors that the company would do better to stop fighting unionization and start treating its workers more like valued partners.

Managers fume about such pressure, but a study by two law professors, Randall Thomas and Kenneth Martin, indicates that other shareholders don't care what union motives might lie behind a proposal. They're often grateful that an independent, critical voice expresses what they may be reluctant to say. In any case, if the value of a corporation over the long haul depends on treating workers well, as research the Labor Department conducted during Robert Reich's tenure indicates, then unions should air labor relations problems among shareholders. "The argument is made that if there's an entrenched management not listening to workers, then they're not listening to anybody," says Ken Bertsch, director of corporate governance at the non-profit Investor Responsibility Research Center. "That's a legitimate tie."

Shareholder resolutions may be weak, but managers are very touchy about losing control over their communications with shareholders and are fighting hard to restrict such proposals, especially by unions. In 1997, the Securities Exchange Commission proposed new rules that would have made it more difficult for shareholders to introduce resolutions. But a united campaign by labor, public employee funds, and religious and social investors at least temporarily blocked the worst changes.

Shareholder proposals are only a small indicator of how labor is trying to exercise its potential clout representing workers as owners. The Office of Investment, under veteran pension activist William Patterson, educates union trustees and the pension industry about labor's rights and responsibilities. Its Executive PayWatch website educates union members about why their boss is paid too much. It has also produced new guidelines for proxy voting to try to get union pension funds to follow suit. About 30 percent of pension funds now turn their votes over to services that follow AFL-CIO guidelines. Such decisions can make a difference: while its parent, Institutional

Shareholder Services, supported waste giant Laidlaw's unfriendly takeover bid for Safety-Kleen, an industrial recycling company, Proxy Voter Services followed labor guidelines and voted labor pension shares against the takeover (which nevertheless won approval).

Labor hopes to persuade asset managers to adopt a worker-friendly, long-term investment strategy for all of their clients but especially for union pension funds. "Those asset managers that show clear anti-worker bias will be weeded out," warns Steelworkers Secretary-Treasurer Leo Gerard. In 1997, the Steelworkers and other unions turned United Asset Management from being an open advocate of Wheeling-Pittsburgh's strike-breaking strategy into a proponent of reaching a settlement by reminding the firm of its dependence on union accounts. Then in a fight with Oregon Steel, the Steelworkers pressured investment firms and organized withdrawal of union and pension funds from Wells Fargo Bank, the company's main line of credit. In both cases, the union argued, company actions not only hurt workers but also sharply reduced the firm's market value. Similarly, when some firms like State Street Research began advocating privatization of Social Security, the AFL-CIO pointedly suggested that companies dependent on workers' savings shouldn't undermine their interests. Jack Marco, a leading pension fund consultant, says that "the sensitivity of investment managers [to labor's perspective] has grown a hundredfold in the last five years."

Beyond educating union pension trustees, labor is trying to boost its influence at public employee pensions and to bargain for more influence over corporate funds through worker director or policy guidelines. Some unions are shifting workers from small corporate plans into multi-employer plans where labor has more control. The AFL-CIO also is likely to encourage or even to establish investment funds with a pro-labor policy where individuals can invest IRA or defined contribution pension plan money. UNITE's Amalgamated Bank is expanding as a bank. It also established the previously mentioned LongView Collective Investment Fund, a stock index fund that is a leading shareholder activist.

Union pension fund activists typically argue that it makes more sense to be an active investor trying to influence companies rather than to dump stock of "bad" companies. But there are still undeveloped possibilities for "economically targeted investments" with social goals. Over the past two decades, for example, unions have invested several billion dollars in funds that finance construction by union workers. One new fund, partly backed by union pensions, played a key role in financing revival of Newport News Shipbuilding with a contract for environmentally secure double-hulled ships. Pension money could help labor develop new models of community development. For example, Steelworkers and the Steel Valley Authority, a longtime proponent of worker ownership, are exploring a regional investment fund—drawing on the experience of Canadian labor solidarity investment funds with over $3 billion in assets.

Union members on several public pension boards, starting with CalPERS, the huge California fund, have helped establish "responsible contractor policies" for their real estate investments. So when a Denver building maintenance contractor was actively fighting an organizing drive, the Service Employees contacted CalPERS, which had its management company replace the anti-union firm with a unionized contractor. SEIU continues to recruit other pensions, including church funds and a big Dutch public employee fund, to win responsible contractor policies for entire building management firms, not simply single buildings.

Unions, at times using their pension clout, have tried to protect workers' interests in battles over restructuring of companies. Union pension funds played a key role in protecting Chrysler management's cash cushion for a future downturn against a takeover bid by investor Kirk Kerkorian, who wanted to distribute the money to shareholders. As management slashed and burned its way through Sunbeam and Hathaway, UNITE was able to find a friendly buyer or help "restructured" workers buy their own plants to save jobs. Using wage concessions as investment, workers at airlines from United to Northwest have gained ownership and influence over corporate strategies. Two fledgling funds, initiated with only limited union pension money, plan to offer financing-from equity to loans—to help worker buyouts.

Though there is little opposition to labor's new investment strategies, especially as a pressure tactic, there is skepticism about the ambitious strategy of corporate reform and a belief in some quarters that pension power has been vastly overstated. Research also suggests that the governance reforms unions push do not by themselves clearly improve corporate performance, though there usually are positive results from owners actively prodding management. There isn't even conclusive proof that labor's alternative strategy pays off, but since all investment—even by the professional managers—is a gamble, the money might as well be bet on a worker-friendly "high road." As political humorist Jim Hightower notes, "the problem with the low road is that it only goes downhill."

It's also not clear that the interests of individuals as workers and as owners perfectly converge. Even if the "high road" strategy enlarges the pie, there's still the question of how it's divided between labor and capital. Carpenters union pension activist Ed Durkin worries whether emerging labor strategies on corporate governance simply feed into prevailing views that the sole object of corporations is to enhance shareholder value. If so, does that simply pressure managers to extract more from workers to enrich shareholders? Obviously labor must make corporations more democratic for workers as well as shareholders. Such potential tensions are not fatal objections: unions are accustomed to balancing conflicting interests among workers. At best worker interests are going to be only partly represented at the corporate level. Even now union-nominated members of boards of directors often end up identifying as much or more with other directors than with workers. The corporate reform strategy does not lessen the need for unions to play their traditional role. Nor does it replace the need for broad mobilization of the public against corporate power and government-mandated reform of corporate charters. If reform of corporate control and capital markets is rooted in the labor movement's traditional critique of business, it can strengthen labor's hand. Likewise, a stronger labor movement is essential not only for the future of labor pension funds, as AFL-CIO president John Sweeney, has argued, but also for labor's effort to craft an alternative view of corporations.

Labor traditionalists, who think managers should manage and unions should bargain, file grievances, and strike, may worry about the divided loyalties and conflicted consciousness of workers who also think as investors. Traditionally unions have wanted workers to be able to rely on guaranteed social security rather than the vagaries of capital markets. It still makes sense to expand and to protect Social Security, but private pensions already exist, and unions need to maximize their value for workers. Also, many workers, simply as a result of popular culture, think about the world both as workers and as business people or investors, but they have only a worker-unfriendly view of how corporate strategies succeed. Unions can play a role in defining strategies that start with the view that workers create the company's value. If a strong alternative view of how to do business successfully is presented, it will influence the thinking of workers, citizens, politicians, and maybe even managers and investors. To that end, William Patterson wants to develop a new culture of management of investments that "can achieve optimum return in ways consistent with the interests of workers."

Union pension power may be able to push capital a little ways towards that goal, but in the long run, corporate reform will have to be a political fight, with support from both labor's rank-and-file and the general public. Pension fund strategies can also penalize individual companies for their hostile practices towards workers, but corporate reform must be imposed across the board, and that will require legislation. In the meantime, labor can win some gains by flexing the muscle of its trillions of dollars in assets and, equally important, can educate workers and their allies about the pressing need for reform and democratization of corporate power.

ON THE FRONT LINES

The Labor Movement Around the Country

noel beasley

Everything I never wanted to know about strikes I learned in Kentucky in the late 1970s. For seven and a half months 400 workers struck two plants where tiles for flooring were shaped and baked with clay from the quarries that pock the banks of the Ohio River. Only seven workers crossed the picket line during the entire strike; we blocked highways, went to jail, and shut the factories down through three seasons of the year. My job as staff strike director was to keep up morale, to distribute benefits, and to figure out how to win.

Unfortunately we thought if we just choked the tile plants long enough we could force the company to cough up a better contract. The workers were strong and militant; the two little river towns where they lived backed us to the hilt. But the twin factories ten miles apart were just pins on the map of a major multinational corporation that cared a lot more about its tough track record at the bargaining table than it did about the families of the tobacco farmers and moonlight fishermen who made the tiles. In the eighth month the company brought in a new attorney with a union busting reputation who jammed the negotiations, hired replacement workers, and broke the strike. No one in Lewisport and Cloverport, Kentucky had ever heard of such a thing. This was two years before PATCO walked and the declaration of war against strikers' rights was issued from the Oval Office. The workers united had been horribly defeated.

Total loss is sensual: it's the taste of gun barrel dragged across your tongue; the smell of smoldering wires in a burnt-down barn; the sound of a card table collapsing on concrete; the feel of broken glass on bare feet; the sight of your own face in the mirror twenty years later as you confront another major company trying to bust your union. The stakes are even higher this time: there are over two thousand members in four different locations of a major catalogue sales company; you hear again the echoes of the shouts of the workers at the final gymnasium rally before the picket shacks were torn down and the signs were dropped like the last flags on the field.

There were only two ways, really, for union leaders assigned to field positions to respond to the tough lessons of the 1980s. Once you realized that 90 percent of all strikes were lost before you started them, once you recognized that most workers would take concessions before they'd let their factories close, once you knew that any company could break every law in the book in an organizing campaign and the Labor Board at best would charge a few chump change fines, once you understood why the international activities of the AFL-CIO were so generously paid for by the State Department, you either worked on your golf game and patiently, in a tired voice, lectured workers to not expect too much or you dug in, built a base, created alliances, signed on for the duration and swore that the only constant factor would be the fight for change. Change the rules, change the players, and ultimately change the terrain. Instead of endlessly protecting the small, self-confining defensive corner, help lead the charge back onto the

battleground. And we did. The new AFL-CIO is the accomplishment of thousands of union activists who pushed and shoved and argued against stagnation, who shook off the status quo.

What do we do differently now? Almost everything. We have researchers who know every intimate detail of a corporation's physique, who steer us to the weaknesses we can exploit in what we've come to call "comprehensive campaigns." In the big fight with the mail order house, the union prepared for over a year for a war to be fought on the ground in the shops, on and under the seas of the company's internal structures and in the high altitudes of Wall Street. In stark contrast to how we fought in the tile plant strike of the seventies, we knew and understood all the early warning signs of a deteriorating relationship with management and ran workshops and schools to train a hundred shop floor activists in the agit-prop techniques of mass grievances, breakroom demonstrations, and informational picketing. We sent out warning shots to the CEO and CFO by politely intervening in the annual shareholders' meeting and by mailing letters of concern to the key portfolio managers who together controlled a majority of the stock. As we came closer to the edge of the contract expiration, we stockpiled unfair labor practices with the National Labor Relations Board, in case we had to hit the streets. In the closing days, the company removed its hostile chief negotiator and sought peace. An honorable settlement was reached and disaster for both sides avoided.

"It's all about power. There can be no justice without power. We have to focus on rebuilding our POWER." It's the electric voice of Bob King, the director of Region 1A of the United Auto Workers, representing eighty thousand members in Detroit. King is one of the leaders who feels the difference between then and now. He points to the contrasts in the way the Federation recently has fought two big trade battles: NAFTA and fast track. "We could never have stopped fast track under Kirkland and Donahue. They didn't understand activism, mobilizing the rank and file, building community coalitions; Kirkland could never have created the *presence* that the new leadership built with street actions. Before we were passive, now we're direct and we're loud." King has activated not only his current members but linked them with thousands of militant retirees to create a fighting force in Michigan that cuts across the generations, maintaining the firm foundation of a great historical legacy while responding to new conditions.

Monica Russo is the manager of UNITE's Florida operations and the director of an organizing project based in Miami, Florida that is aggressively and effectively organizing health care workers. She senses the new momentum brought in with the change in leadership and finds a boost in morale for those who have spent years in the arduous struggles to add new members. "We would organize, we did organize, whether there was this new leadership or not, but now we're not swimming against the current . . . it just feels more like a movement now. Projects such as ours, that are experiments in new ways to organize immigrant workers, are being funded; that wouldn't have happened before. Unions are being encouraged to pool resources and be innovative; there's *space* now to debate and test out approaches; but we're going to have to deliver some results too."

Both King and Russo applaud the restructuring of the old central bodies and state federations. New appointees with deep understandings of campaign strategies have spread a fresh image of the labor movement with billboards, TV and radio ads, and more demonstrations in two years than in the previous twenty. Organizers can for the first time in decades depend upon strong support from community and state-wide networks of labor activists officially encouraged and indeed mandated by the AFL-CIO to mobilize for political action and the expansion of the membership. As Russo says, "It just feels *better* knowing that the Federation is more progressive, there's a sense of hope; the rank-and-file feel like they're players and it's invigorating."

David Foster is the director of one of the largest regions of the United Steelworkers, one of the unions deeply and consciously involved in internal changes that directly drove and often reflected the intensity of the dramatic transitions in the Federation. He points to a significant shift in tactics and strategies of collective bargaining, especially in the area of practical international trade unionism. "In the Bridgestone-Firestone fight, we fought a global industry with global trade unionism. Steelworker members visited twenty-nine other countries during the campaign; in Brazil and Argentina there were support strikes; world conferences were held that led to coordinated demonstrations in dozens of countries. We had never seen anything of this scope before." Foster notes that the Federation in the past would never have facilitated this kind of activity and feels that even now we must escalate our commitment to build our capacity to fight in the global marketplace.

My father gave me good advice years ago when he warned, "Don't break your arm trying to pat yourself on the back." In discussions with King, Russo, Foster, and many others who have reason to feel exhilarated by the new "space" (to use Russo's phrase) that we have fought to open up, there are also many cautionary notes and many concerns. We've all been at this too long to take much for granted. Most of us know enough to celebrate with one hand on the champagne glass and the other on the holster. Now that the confetti has been swept up and we continue on with the next phase of the battle to rebuild workers' power, here are some issues that must be faced on the front lines and some examples of how we're doing it:

ORGANIZING

When I joined the staff of ACTWU (one of UNITE's predecessor unions) in 1977, the organizers in my region were a dispirited quartet of veteran failures who hung around the office waiting for a phone call from a "hot shop." On those rare occasions when a desperate worker rang, leaflets and union cards would be passed out at the plant gate and the company would begin a relentless assault that most often annihilated the drive. It has taken us decades to break this mold.

In the midwest region, we set out four years ago to win recognition rights at an Indianapolis plant where workers assemble auto seat belts. We began by asking questions and looking for answers: what final assembly plants we do supply; what is the structure of the company (we discovered a fully unionized Scandinavian parent corporation); what is the composition of the workforce; how will existing contracts in this auto parts sector compare? Most important, we brought together a team of shop leaders from similar plants to augment the staff and to provide a base of credibility as we approached the workers in house calls and shift meetings. Unlike our campaigns in the seventies, we had the full resources of the entire union available to us. Key organizers were brought in from other regions and videos were produced that get us in front of the workers and entire families in their living rooms in a manner in which a crumpled-up, tossed away leaflet never could.

Smelling victory, we planned a strategy for the first contract campaign weeks before the National Labor Relations Board election. More volunteer organizers from the shops were brought in as the company's campaign heated up. An elaborate chess game went on night and day, across three shifts, and into weekend overtime. Workers were trained to confront their supervisors and managers in captive audience meetings, where union staff weren't permitted a presence. We were "on the doors," housecalling around the clock. We swept the election two to one. Using the momentum from the victory, we kept our core organizers in place while we hammered out a first contract within three months of victory. As the stewards, officers and other volunteer organizers returned to their shops, they carried the stories of the battle, which embodied was the union's mandate for change.

Thus we try to counter the tension and resentment that develops if locals are isolated from the organizing activities. The push to restructure the unions for massive organizing of the unorganized is necessary. But we must be careful that our public relations initiatives don't outweigh the substance of our accomplishments. As David Foster points out, the work is tough and the ongoing structural resistance at the local and regional levels can be intense. The frenetic style of organizing work that we pioneered in the 1990s,

Dave states, "can bust the psyches of the best organizers." Rebuilding has to be coupled with a foundation of support within the membership. A strategic commitment to do more than to win elections and to guarantee the construction of strong locals will flow from the active involvement of shop leaders in the campaigns.

Political Action

Two years before Minnesota Senator Paul Wellstone made his run for re-election, UNITE knew he was in trouble. The right had targeted him as vulnerable and had pumped millions into preparations to defeat him, but more importantly his progressive positions on issues such as a woman's right to choose, environmental preservation, and the right to bear arms could be manipulated to disfigure him as the enemy of our own members, putting at risk one of working America's best senators. No senator was a stronger supporter of a working families' economic agenda than Paul Wellstone, yet his social votes offered the right wing the perfect opening to try to create a wedge with union members. We hired professional pollsters to conduct focus groups and surveys

in our members' homes. We poured over the right's literature and puzzled out how to clarify the label "Senator Welfare" so that we could turn his record from a minus to a plus. We held classes and workshops for activists, training and retraining ourselves to talk about the politics of guns, abortion, and water rights in ways that stressed the unifying issue of workers' rights. We refused to tolerate the partitioning of workers' vision of the world. Wellstone's campaign victory was more than a revalidation of a champion of social justice. It also became a crucible for a style of political work that put us back in the lunchrooms and at the plant gates where we should have been all along.

At last some leaders are decisively jabbing the Democratic Party. Initiatives like the Labor Party and the New Party are welcomed by Federation leaders; local and regional structures are affiliating with independent forces among the unemployed and homeless. But we are still far from having a mass political movement that is aware of itself and not dependent on personalities and slick slogans.

Education

Three years ago the Midwest region of UNITE made a commitment to create a new kind of school for our activists. Recognizing that you can pass through every formal level of education that this country offers and not know a damned thing about history, economics, and practical planning, we also knew our leaders worked complicated shifts, often had several jobs and enormous personal responsibilities, and that we couldn't depend on half-hour classes or one-day workshops on the grievance procedure to rebuild the movement. We allocated significant human and economic resources to insure that the schools focused on small groups in tranquil, isolated locations that offered a tone of reflection. The hand-picked participants were nominated by the staff and veteran shop leaders for their potential as volunteer organizers or steadfast fighters at their worksites and in their communities.

In the most successful model, fifteen or twenty emerging leaders came together for three or four days. Together we watched and discussed videos (*At the River I Stand*, *The Killing Floor*, *Not in Our Town*), reviewed our history with veteran leaders who continue to redefine the idea of "retirement," and always prepared and executed an action. A few months ago in Bedford, Indiana, at a Laborers" Union training center, such a group met at the height of the Teamster/UPS battle. We argued politics, struggled with the intricacies of global economics, played volleyball, did support actions on the UPS picket line—and leafleted the local post offices as part of UNITE's "Stop Sweatshops" campaign. The young activists quickly sensed their place in history, and those of us privileged to be with them got recharged. Late at night, over a couple of beers and some chips, some of the loneliness of these long distance runners melts away and the lasting comradeships are formed.

We're scrambling everywhere to figure out how to capture enough time to get workers together and to illuminate the neon darkness of the TV room. This is no joke in an era when workers have nothing in common but the workplace. The old neighborhoods are shuttered, the mills are ghostlands of the industrial revolution. The driving radius around a factory now is fifty to eighty miles, as any organizer who ever put a blitz together can tell you. Leadership schools, retreats that teach how to advance, must be moved to the top of the list of priorities. Crash courses that lead the way to a life-long thirst for knowledge must counter the conversion of public schools into metaphorical prisons for youth that lead to the literal prisons of death-for-life terms now privatized into a "growth industry" that shames the soul of the republic.

International Solidarity

Like charity, solidarity begins at home. Here's a recent example. In 1985, we organized a small factory of a hundred workers making plastic trays and dining utensils. The plant is twenty miles north of Milwaukee, Wisconsin, bordered by a tiny town and acres of pasture land. The workforce then was totally white, drawn from the dispersed farm communities. By the mid-1990s, over four hundred workers were pounding out the plastic, 90 percent of them Mexican and Central American. At the height of reorganizing the shop under these new conditions, with bilingual staff struggling against a contract expiration, an INS raid wiped out over three hundred of our members. Three years later, we were rebuilding again with a mix of African-American, Asian, and Latino workers. Union meetings were conducted in four languages, amid a half-dozen cultures. Welcome to the global workforce.

In this context, UNITE's and the new AFL-CIO's carefully-honed positions on trade, immigrant rights, and cross-border organizing became concrete and immediate. Always at organizational risk because of difficult working conditions and high turnover, we pulled the leadership in the shop and through them the entire membership into unity with anti-sweatshop demonstrations at post offices in all of their communities. These actions stress our shared responsibility to fight for the rights of workers everywhere, as the cornerstone of equal treatment in the factory.

The new Federation is making great strides in converting what was a nest of cold war careerists into an alliance of international activists who see the direct link between the maquiladoras lining the Rio Grande and the decline in wages in Milwaukee, between the oppression in Indonesia and the crushing of an organizing campaign in a shop hidden in an Indiana cornfield.

Declare Victory And Retreat?

But some of us are starting to get scared. The direct attacks launched against key leaders and the most militant unions may be retaliation and revenge for our street heat, our union summers, our comprehensive campaigns where we attack in the sacred temples of the boardroom and the shareholders' meeting. We lack depth. Anyone who saw the collapse of progressive politics in Chicago after the death of just one (albeit great) man, Harold Washington, cannot rest easy in the current situation. There are forces both inside and outside our movement who would like to drag us back to the days of compliance and complicity. As Russo says, "The good old boy network is alive and well and we'd better not go to sleep." We need to spend less time on rah-rah self-congratulatory public relations and more time laying the only foundation that can assure the longevity of our movement for continuous, progressive change: the non-stop recruitment, training, nourishment, and retention of strong, independent workplace leaders.

I owe the tile makers of Kentucky a lifelong debt. Now when I see a fight brewing with a company, I start planning months and sometimes, years ahead for a struggle with multiple weapons that begins and ends with a strong base of support on the shop floor. But now we also have corporate research teams, comprehensive campaign strategists, and lead organizers who know how to hit from every angle with precisely timed blows and plenty of surprises. Some of us still don't know how to play golf, but we know a lot more about how to win at the one thing that counts: the fight for social justice.

West of Wall Street and far from Foggy Bottom, the terms and conditions of the battle for a redefined and restructured trade union movement are being drafted, critiqued, re-written, and resubmitted every day. Aided and abetted by a new AFL-CIO that we have envisioned and shaped, the practical struggle to train more leaders and arm them with the knowledge and skill to rapidly recruit and replicate their ranks will continue to accelerate. Fasten your safety belt.

AN INTERVIEW WITH
JOHN SWEENEY

juan gonzalez

JUAN GONZALEZ When you came into office, you talked about increased organizing. How do you emphasize organizing within your overall vision of rebuilding the
AFL-CIO?

JOHN SWEENEY We're involved in a real monumental task of rebuilding. Rich
Trumka, Linda Chavez-Thompson, and I were elected on a platform of rebuilding.
We've seen a lot of change, but this is not a short term project and we're not going
to truly see overall continuous results in reversing the trend in the short term. We
know that, but what we are doing is investing in the long term, by training a crew
of organizers and asking national unions and their locals to commit more
resources to organizing.

We're seeing a lot of change take place. At the national level, we're seeing unions change their own structure and resources to put more money into organizing. We're also seeing them use the pool of organizers that we're training. The most impressive example is the building and construction trades, where these unions have come together to pool their resources—several million dollars—into organizing in Las Vegas. The trades have never organized together. This is the first time. Hopefully, it will be a model for future campaigns in other cities. They're also using our pool of organizers and they're asking us to coordinate with them .

The AFL-CIO doesn't do organizing. It's the affiliates that do organizing—but, the unions are looking to us to play a stronger role.

What we're seeing at the national level is a change in attitude, like the Asbestos Workers recently, who—at a national convention—voted to create an organizing fund where three dollars per member per month of their dues would go to organizing. That's very impressive. And there are many stories like that. A lot of this has filtered down to the local level. In New York City, you are seeing a lot of this work: the Machinists organizing limousine drivers, 1199 getting together with SEIU to organize health care workers. Brian McLaughlin, head of the New York City Central Labor Council, is coordinating the local effort like we are trying to coordinate nationally, by forming a coordinating committee, and there are multi-union campaigns with more than one union involved. These are all indications of what I think is going to be a master plan to rejuvenate and reactivate the labor movement.

JG When you came into office most of the journalists who covered labor and the political pundits had declared the labor movement dead. Now, all of a sudden, that tune has changed. Certainly in Congress, it has. What's been the essential thing that you've done to change the perception of the labor movement?

JS I really think that while our heavy focus is on organizing and reversing the decline of our membership, it is so important that we build a stronger voice for workers, a stronger political voice, a stronger legislative voice. And, I think that what we're doing in that arena is going to help us with our organizing as well.

In the '96 election, there was a lot of talk about the amount of money that was spent, but the impressive part is not the amount of money that was spent. The impressive part is that all the unions came together in solidarity and approved an assessment, which was approved by individual unions under their own constitutions.

That money essentially went to TV issue education. Our primary focus is educating and mobilizing our membership. We used TV, which is the best opportunity to get to people on issues that are important to them: Social Security, education,

Medicare, and the environment. We learned a lot from focus groups—that our members don't want to be told who to vote for, they want to be educated on the issues; they want to make up their own mind; and, they want to hold politicians accountable.

I think that's a lot of what we saw in '96. And that's what our critics are so outspoken about. They don't want to see an active, vibrant labor movement speaking out on these issues. They don't want to see workers coming together.

The money we spent is probably one-tenth of what the corporations spent. We're not going to be able to match them with money, but we are going to be able to match them with our members' activity. We're seeing hundreds of rank-and-file activists getting more active in every congressional district in the country.

JG Are you going to target specific congressional districts this year?

JS We are going to learn from examples that we used in last campaign. We're going to have a more active strategy because we're going to redouble our efforts. We saw over the debate on fast track trade authority that there are some moderate Republicans who do want to stand up for workers and working family issues and I'm sure that some of them will be endorsed in their districts. This is not about political parties. It's about candidates who are accountable to workers and their families on issues that are necessary and important.

JG The Corporate Campaign Office that you established—which is attempting to develop strategy to deal with union pension funds and the battle between labor and management in the boardroom—what is happening with that and how important do you think it is to changing the conditions of labor in the country?

JS It is so important that we have created this Corporate Affairs Department and that we focus on the issues of labor-management questions, collective bargaining questions, and developing economic policy. Everything is up in this current economic period which is successful—stock market's up, profits are up, productivity's up, CEO compensation is sky high, and yet, with the exception of some modest gains and raises, wages have not kept up with the standard of living.

It wasn't always like this—we had a better labor-management relationship in the 1950s and 1960s. There was a spirit of government, business, and labor working together in the interest of working families. We have to restore that kind of philosophy.

People really misunderstand how workers feel. We opposed NAFTA because we thought our trade policy ought to include labor standards, environmental protection, and human rights protection. We believe that NAFTA has been a bad deal. While there has been some modest gains in jobs—low wage jobs with no benefits, things are no better in Mexico.

JG You were just in Mexico—

JS All one has to do is see the new factories in the maquiladoras and within fifty yards, shanty towns, polluted streams, people living in the worst poverty—this is not a decent way to live and this is not a successful trade agreement.

JG What's going to be the effect on American workers of the Asian crisis and the restructuring required by the IMF?

JS We are very concerned about how the Asian crisis is going to affect jobs in our own country. We have implored the IMF as well as our own government to make sure that there is consideration about imports being dumped in the U.S. at lower price levels than American products to such an extent that products would create substantial unemployment in our own country. This is because devaluation in those countries is making labor cheaper.

We're also concerned about what's happening to workers in other countries, especially Asia, and we believe that international human rights agreements need to be implemented. We're concerned that workers are being asked to take the pain of all this to a far greater extent than the capitalists with the workers' depressed wages and high unemployment in their own regions. We want to propose that workers be involved in these discussions—especially where there is a democratic trade union movement, like in Korea, where the workers are at the table negotiating.

In the past, the austerity has been placed on the workers, and not on the speculators, the capitalists, and the financial institutions. They should share in the pain. They reap all the profits of the good economy and now they want to attach the pain on the citizens of those countries. We're especially concerned about countries where the leadership is corrupt—like Indonesia—where labor leaders are imprisoned for speaking out. We expect and hope that our government will bring pressure on the IMF to address these issues.

JG Do you think that the AFL-CIO should put out some kind of guidelines on the relationship between unity and democracy in the labor movement?

JS I think that basically most unions have a very democratic process under their constitution and by-laws. There are wide differences because of the history of unions, culture, jurisdiction, and so on. Some are more progressive than others. They usually reflect the attitude and philosophy of their members. There are unions that have been organized more recently than others, some have a higher proportion of males over females, low wage workers over high wage workers. There are all kinds of differences that reflect the kinds of procedures they have.

But I think that our members are the same as the public at large. There are changes in attitude that you see in people all across the country in terms of their political activity. People don't want to be dictated to. You're seeing a lot of variance in priorities in different regions of the country. Our members are like the communities they live in to a great extent, with feelings pro and con about issues like gun control and abortion.

But I really think our members are very anxious to be very involved and to be more outspoken. They like the programs we've developed like Union Cities. They are also responding to the disputes of others; we see a lot of solidarity around a particular strike or lay-off. We have to capitalize on that because there is a lot of strength in that solidarity.

And, it goes beyond our own borders. This is what we're trying to develop with the Mexican labor unions around issues important to workers on both sides of the border. The Bridgestone-Firestone Steelworkers' strike is an example of international solidarity. That strike was really won—and this is in the words of the Steelworkers—was really won by the solidarity shown around the world, including by the Japanese labor federation and other federations in other parts of the world who came together against this employer to achieve a decent contract for the U.S. workers.

JG You have certain targets like the Nevada hotel workers' campaign, strawberry workers, nursing home workers—have there been any successes yet in these campaigns where you've decided to concentrate the resources of the national movement?

JS Oh, I think that there are indications of success in all of these situations. The building trades coming together in Nevada—they've organized thousands of workers in the last year. They are nowhere near where they would like to be, but organizing is long-term—I keep saying this. If you can rebuild the culture of organizing and get unions working together, hopefully they're going to be very strong there in five to six years. Other unions like the culinary union and SEIU in hospitals are all a part of the organizing mode in Las Vegas.

We're trying to translate that to other cities as well. Seattle has a tremendous amount of organizing going on all across the labor movement. The UPS strike was a real shot in the arm for the labor movement—solidarity and a good contract; even within the Teamsters, both sides came together for the success of that strike.

The strawberry workers' campaign is a very important campaign. It represents the best of what the labor movement could and should be doing in terms of workers who are living and working in the worst conditions. The labor movement is coming together to help a union that doesn't have a lot of money and doesn't have the staff and resources that other unions have. They are going to be successful. It's going to take time.

JG There are a lot of immigrant workers involved in these organizing campaigns. What do you see as the role of immigrant workers in terms of the revitalization of the labor movement?

JS The American labor movement was built on immigrants. I myself am the son of Irish immigrants. I'm very concerned and interested in the labor movement having the best policies regarding immigrant workers. I stressed to the Mexican unions how important it was for us to be working on the issue of Mexican nationals together. I think and feel strongly that we as a labor movement have to develop legislative initiatives and policy to help immigrant workers. That's the challenge before us.

JG You mentioned the importance of the UPS strike and the Teamsters, but that was of course followed up by the problems that occurred within the Teamsters. I know it's hard to talk about anything that's involved with legal questions, but in the recent meetings of the AFL-CIO Executive Council, have there been any discussions about policies that would prevent the kinds of fundraising problems that developed around the Teamsters' election and around the presidential election?

JS On internal political questions, we have had discussions. We've cooperated with every investigation we've been asked to cooperate with. Until we know completely what happened, it's premature to change whatever policies have been impacted. We have no reason to believe that there's any policy or program that contributes to what all these investigations have been about. We have been strong advocates of campaign finance reform.

JG The Organizing Institute has recruited a lot of young, college-age, idealistic folks that have come into the labor movement for the first time. What about attention to the young rank-and-file workers—is that going on as well or could that use more improvement?

JS There is always room for improvement, but I'm really optimistic about the development of young rank-and-file candidates for organizing positions. I think that the more organizing opportunities and the more rank-and-file activity that we develop the more candidates we will have for organizing positions. The most ideal candidates for organizing are from the rank-and-file. In some cases, it's a matter of economics in terms of how much volunteer time and sacrifice a rank-and-file worker can allow in terms of addressing his or her own family needs. I also do hope that as a result of our teach-ins on university campuses—and our union summer program—together with the development of volunteer organizer programs in specific campaigns—in the long run we will have more rank-and-file organizers.

JG You set a goal of 3 percent union increase across the board. Last year, you were able to stem the decline of membership, but to be able to reach that goal, you have got to have incredible organizing drives. What is going to be done differently? What's going to be the key to having this qualitative increase?

JS I think that the overall programs we're doing—organizing and building a stronger political voice for workers—are also contributing to a different image about the labor movement, improving the image of the labor movement. When a union makes up its mind to dedicate more resources to organizing—whatever the increase is, from year to year—to eventually get to the goal of 30 percent spent on organizing—you are going to see a stronger and stronger labor movement.

We have also begun an intensive effort to build support from allies and from entire communities for the right of workers to organize. Joining a union today, for too many workers, is an act of tremendous courage. In almost every private sector union election, employers use legal and illegal tactics to create an atmosphere of extreme intimidation. But when workers see that they are supported by their congregations, community leaders and other people they respect, it helps them overcome their fear and act on their hopes. We're providing tools to organizing campaigns and to central labor councils to help them make it happen. One of the most exciting developments we're seeing is the support that's building among religious leaders for union organizing.

We also have to have much more organizing. We have begun to see organizing drives that are bigger and more successful. Nineteen thousand passenger service agents at United Airlines voted for representation with the Machinists union. Ten thousand reservations agents at US Airways won representation with CWA. And we've had other big wins in the past year. But you're right. To reach our goal of 3 percent growth for every union every year, we need far more big organizing drives.

So in addition to building more support for organizing, recruiting and training more organizers, and winning more support from allies and communities for the right of workers to organize, we're also helping unions analyze entire industries and develop organizing strategies that can help workers build real power for the long-term.

Editor's Note: This interview was conducted in February, 1998.

FIGHTING FOR SOCIAL JUSTICE

A Teach-In with the New Labor Movement

at UCLA Feb. 20-21, 1997

Join labor, university and community activists to help build the movement to improve the lives of workers and our communities.

Speakers Include:

John Sweeney
Richard Trumka
Linda Chavez-Thompson
Dolores Huerta
Karen Nussbaum
Maria Elena Durazo
Harold Meyerson
Harley Shaiken
Mike Davis

...and many more!

Conference:

- Feb. 20, 7pm-10pm
  Moore Hall 100
- Feb. 21, 9am-5pm
  Ackerman
  Grand Ballroom

Admission Free

For more info,
call UCLA Labor Center
at (310) 794-0385

Endorsers Include: AFL-CIO Western Region• CA State Federation of Labor• AFSCME Local 3235• AFT Local 1990•AGENDA• ACLU• APALA• Asian American Studies Dept.• Asian Pacific American Legal Center•CSEA 728• Democratic Socialists of America•Federation of Retired Union Members• H.E.R.E. Local 11• IATSE Local 33• Int'l Labor and Working Class History• Korean Immigrant Workers Assoc.• Labor Community Strategy Center• CA Faculty Association• CSU Dominguez Hills Labor Studies• Liberty Hill Foundation• L.A. Building Trades Council• L.A. County Federation of Labor AFL-CIO• LA Trade Tech Labor Center• LA Manufacturing Action Project• Nat'l Assoc. of Letter Carriers• Nat'l Lawyers Guild-OCAW Int'l 675•Orange County Central Labor Council, AFL-CIO• SAGE/UAW• San Diego-Imperial Counties Labor Council• Search to Involve Pilipino Americans• SEIU Local 347, 399 & 660•Southern CA-Nevada Regional Council of Carpenters•Strategic Actions for a Just Economy•Tourism Industry Development Council•U.E.Int'l•UAW Region 5•U.F.C.W. Local 324&770•United Teachers of LA•UPTE/CWA Local 2•UCLA Undergrad Student Gov't• Working Peoples Law Center•UCLA Center for the Study of Women•UCLA Urban Planning•UCLA Concerned Faculty•

MARC BALDWIN is assistant director of the Department of Public Policy at the AFL-CIO.

NOEL BEASLEY is a vice president of UNITE and the manager of the Midwest Regional Joint Board for the union.

RICHARD BENSINGER was the AFL-CIO organizing director from 1995 through 1998.

KELLY CANDAELE is a trustee of Los Angeles County Community College and writes frequently for the *Los Angeles Times* Opinion Section.

AMY B. DEAN is executive officer of the South Bay AFL-CIO Labor Council and chairperson of the AFL-CIO's National Advisory committee on the Future of Central Labor Councils.

HECTOR FIGUEROA is assistant research director of SEIU and active in the Puerto Rican civil rights movement.

GEOFFREY D. GARIN is the president of Peter D. Hart Research Associates. He polls regularly for the AFL-CIO and many unions, and is a leading Democratic pollster.

DAVID GLENN is associate editor of *Dissent* magazine.

JUAN GONZALEZ is a columnist for the *Daily News* in New York City and co-host for *Democracy Now*, a national news magazine on Pacifica radio.

DAVID KUSNET was chief speechwriter for President Clinton during the 1992 general election campaign and the first two years of the administration. A former staffer for AFSCME, he is a visiting fellow at the Economic Policy Institute and a consultant to labor organizations.

HAROLD MEYERSON, executive editor of the *LA Weekly* and a member of *Dissent*'s editorial board, has also written about labor and politics for the *New Yorker*, the *New Republic*, the *Nation*, the *Los Angeles Times*, the *American Prospect*, and other publications.

DAVID MOBERG is senior editor of *In These Times* and a veteran labor journalist.

GUY MOLYNEUX is vice president of Peter D. Hart Research Associates, and has written about labor and politics for the *Atlantic, Dissent, Rolling Stone,* and frequently writes for the Opinion Section of the *Los Angeles Times.*

JO-ANN MORT is director of communications for UNITE (Union of Needletrades, Industrial and Textile Employees), and writes frequently about unions for *Dissent,* where she is a member of the editorial board, the *Guardian's* economics page, and other publications. She is also a senior editor of *Working USA.*

KAREN NUSSBAUM is the first director of the AFL-CIO's Women's Department, was a founder of 9 to 5, and is a former director of the Women's Bureau of the Department of Labor, serving under Secretary Reich.

STEVE ROSENTHAL is the political director of the AFL-CIO.

BARBARA SHAILOR is director of the International Affairs Department of the AFL-CIO.

RAND WILSON was communications coordinator of the International Brotherhood of Teamsters during the UPS strike.

MATT WITT was communications director of the IBT during the 1997 UPS strike.

Here is a list of union and union-related contacts. There are many resources to be found on the world-wide web for trade unionists, too numerous to list, but the addresses listed here are a good start.

AFL-CIO
815 16th Street, NW
Washington, D.C. 20036
Webpage: www.aflcio.org
This page includes links to affiliate unions, AFL-CIO departments, special political, legislative, and organizing campaigns, and other useful union resources.

AFL-CIO
Working Women's Department
815 16th Street, NW
Washington, D.C. 20036
Phone: 1-888-971-9797

AFL-CIO
Organizing Institute
815 16th St, NW
Washington, DC 20036
Phone: 202-639-6200

Fax: 202-639-6264
Email: organizers@aol.com
Find out how to organize a union or how to become an organizer.

AFL-CIO
Union Summer
Phone: 1-800-952-2550
Email: unionsmr@aol.com

LabourStart
www.labourstart.org
The only webpage that links the international trade union movement. Site includes daily updates of union happenings around the world, links to union websites, and resource information.

Scholars, Artists, and Writers for Social Justice (SAWSJ)
c/o Labor Relations and Research Center
University of Massachusetts Amherst
125 Draper Hall, Box 32020
Amherst, MA 01003
Phone: 413-545-3541
Webpage: www.sage.edu/html/SAWSJ
Email: sawsj@lrrc.umass.edu
This group is an outgrowth of the pro-union campus teach-ins.

Economic Policy Institute
1660 L Street, NW
Suite 1200
Washington, DC 20036
Phone: 202-775-8810
Email: epi@epinet.org
A good source for economic research and analysis of interest to working families.

IMAGE CAPTIONS AND CREDITS

p. i, ii, iii, and xiv Art by Paul Davis, courtesy of UNITE.

p. vii Photo courtesy of SEIU.

p. 5 4,600 union members rally to support fifteen musicians at the 5th Avenue Theater in Seattle, Washington who struck for better pay. The members of the American Federation of musicians local 76-493 won the strike due to a massive show of union solidarity. Photo courtesy of AFL-CIO.

p. 9 Student union summer activist organizing to increase the minimum wage. Photo © Daz Lamparas.

p. 10 AFL-CIO top officers take part in the 1995 anti-sweatshop rally in New York City on the day after they are elected to head the union federation. Left to Right: Secretary-Treasurer Richard Trunka, Executive Vice-President Linda Chavez-Thompson, and President John Sweeney. Photo courtesy of UNITE.

p. 15 Workers protesting to achieve a first contract in Greensboro, NC. Photo courtesy of UNITE.

p. 20 New York City Teachers' Union (AFT) members demonstrate for full funding of city education budget including infrastructure improvements. Photo © Earl Dotter.

p. 27 See page vii.

p. 28 AFSCME organizer in Maryland. Photo courtesy of AFL-CIO.

p. 29 SEIU Justice for Janitors campaign in Washington, DC. Photo courtesy of SEIU.

p. 30 Workers mobilize in pro-union drive in Arkadelphia, Arkansas. Photo courtesy of UNITE.

p. 31 SEIU Justice for Janitors campaign in Washington, DC. Photo courtesy of SEIU.

p. 32 Worker signing a union card. Photo courtesy of UNITE.

p. 35 Students from Union Summer join with union members at rally for worker health and safety. Photo courtesy of AFL-CIO.

p. 38 Sticker from the Las Vegas Building Trades Organizing Project.

p. 42 For the last two years, the TV game show Wheel of Fortune has featured union-made prizes during the week of Labor Day. Photo courtesy of AFL-CIO.

p. 45 Still from the 1997 AFL-CIO pro-union TV campaign featuring nurse Arthereane Brown, who tells the TV audience: "It should always be that doctors and nurses who run the hospital. But in some places it's more driven by dollars and cents."

p. 46 The final issue of The AFL-CIO News (October 14, 1996) announces the federation's new publication, America @ Work, a monthly magazine which debuted that same month.

p. 50 British singer/songwriter Billy Bragg performing at an anti-sweatshop rally in NYC. Photo courtesy of UNITE.

p. 51 Bragg as the headline act at a pro-union concert held in Pittsburgh with Toshi Reagon and Tish Hinajosa—the first concert sponsored by the AFL-CIO to specifically reach out to young people.

p. 58 Photo © Robert Gumpert.

p. 61 Photo © Earl Dotter.

p. 69 Photo © Earl Dotter.

p. 86 United Farmworker member in California. Photo courtesy of UNITE.

p. 88 See p. vii.

p. 92 Unite members and students demonstrate outside a GAP store. Photo courtesy of UNITE.

p. 97 United Farmworker member in California. Photo courtesy of UNITE.

p. 105 Sample of a 1996 AFL-CIO leaflet emphasizing the candidates' stand on the issues.

p. 112 Photo © Earl Dotter.

p. 113 See page 46.

p. 133 National Council of Senior Citizens, an organization of union retirees, has been very active around health care issues. Photo © Bill Burke/ Page One, courtesy SEIU.

p. 149 Zenith is the largest employer in Reynosa. Photo © Sharon Steward, courtesy of UNITE.

p. 152 Photo © Richard Gerharter/ Impact Visuals, courtesy of AFL-CIO.

p. 156 Photo © Earl Dotter.

p. 159   Source: Bureau of Labor Statistics, Employment and Earnings, January 1998.

p. 162   Xerox worker Gay Gritto, Webster, NY. Photo © Gary Schoichet.

pps. 183 (detail) & 184   UNITE members and their families during the 1997 Labor Day Parade in New York City. Photo © Gary Schoichet, courtesy UNITE.

. 189   Photo courtesy of UNITE.

p. 190   Photo courtesy of UNITE.

p. 193   Photo courtesy of UNITE.

p. 197   Artwork courtesy of AFL-CIO.

p. 201   Artwork courtesy of AFL-CIO.

p. 202   Cartoon by Nicole Hollander highlights wage inequities in U. S. economy which has activated many union members to fight for wage increases after decades of freezes and givebacks

p. 209   The AFL-CIO Executive Pay Watch website features information on CEO pay.

p. 214   Photo © Earl Dotter.

p. 215   Debbie Allen, a UNITE member in Tennessee, protests against a 6-day work schedule that disrupted her time with her family. Photo courtesy of UNITE.

p. 219   Sterling Heights police attack strikers at the entrance to North Printing Plant in an attempt to escort scabs into work during the Detroit newspaper strike. Photo courtesy of AFL-CIO.

p. 223   AFL-CIO president John Sweeney.

p. 230   Leaflet for a teach-in sponsored jointly by the AFL-CIO and the UCLA labor center.